Praise for *From Vision to Exit*

"An **excellent primer** ... I commend this book to both those who are already running an established business, and those who are minded to start one and become their own boss. It is written in a practical style, **full of useful tips** and pertinent questions. It is a manual that can be used very much as **a reference source**, to be dipped into when needed."

— Luke Johnson, chairman of Risk Capital Partners, former chairman of Channel 4 Television

"*From Vision to Exit* is **a must-read book** for any aspiring entrepreneur."

— James Caan, founder and CEO of Hamilton Bradshaw, former investor on *Dragons' Den*

"I am often asked for advice about starting a business and I was thinking of writing it all down. Guy has saved me the effort. **I will just hand out a copy of this book.**"

— Nick Jenkins, founder of Moonpig.com

"An excellent work. A story of vision, passion and the journey through growth and exit. Immensely helpful and practical. **This book's got it all.**"

— Wilfred Emmanuel-Jones, The Black Farmer

D0308326

"If you want to run your own business, **you need to read this book**. I thoroughly recommend it!"

— Rowan Gormley, founder of Naked Wines

"I wish I'd read this book before I started my entrepreneurial journey — I might have made it to the beach already."

— James Lohan, founder and CEO of Mr & Mrs Smith

"As someone who has chaired nearly 500 roundtable discussions with Britain's most successful entrepreneurs, I know it's not easy to assimilate best practice into a book. Guy has managed to combine current insights and anecdotes with great, practicable tips. **This is the book I wish I'd written**: Guy's saved me the trouble. This should be essential reading for any aspiring, high-growth entrepreneurs."

— Duncan Cheatle, founder of leading entrepreneurs club The Supper Club and the Prelude Group

"A definitive handbook and guide. Everything you'll ever need to know about building and selling a business."

— Kevin Stopps, managing director of Smith & Williamson

"I only wish this book had been around for me to read before setting off on my entrepreneurial journey. A very thorough and informative book that covers every aspect of going it alone."

— Kanya King, founder and CEO of MOBO Awards

"Guy Rigby's new book is full of practical advice and **covers everything an entrepreneur would need** to run their business successfully. Highly recommended!"

"A must-read tome for any aspiring entrepreneur. **Guy unpacks entrepreneurship** in an enjoyable, fascinating manner."

"A top class explicit guide about **how to navigate the rollercoaster ride** of succeeding as an entrepreneur."

"This book is **a business masterpiece** and its principles will be sustained through the generations. I would **recommend it to anyone** seeking to be highly successful in business. Not only has the author provided a comprehensive guide to creating business growth, he has also given us invaluable insights into the experiences of many of the world's most successful entrepreneurs."

"This is a MUST read for fellow entrepreneurs on the journey. Full of pragmatic experiences of how to accelerate growth in your business. Reading this **will seriously enhance your profitability** and your wealth."

— Sir Eric Peacock, chairman of Baydonhill FX, entrepreneur
and serial non-executive director

"**This book will be invaluable** to any entrepreneur in a start up or existing business. It gives **instantly useful, practical insights** on every important element of making a business successful and is firmly rooted in the deep experience of Guy and fellow entrepreneurs. It will prove of benefit to many a business."

— Alex Cheatle, CEO of Ten Group

"Guy has managed to combine **years of practical experience**, an extensive knowledge of the financial world and pragmatic advice into one easy-to-read volume."

— Neal Gandhi, serial entrepreneur and investor

"To a hungry entrepreneur, this book is an invitation to **a lip-smacking smorgasbord** upon which to feast. Easily digestible, never dry, stuffed with sage anecdotes and wit, it can be devoured in one full-fat sitting, or you can pick and mix from the menu, depending on your appetite. The tasty top tips at the end of each chapter should become the staple diet of anyone wanting to run a healthy, growing business. It deserves a Michelin star. **Bravo.**"

— Tristram Mayhew, founder and Chief Gorilla, Go Ape!

**FROM
VISION
TO EXIT**

FROM VISION TO EXIT

The Entrepreneur's Guide to Building and Selling a Business

By Guy Rigby

HARRIMAN HOUSE LTD

3A Penns Road
Petersfield
Hampshire
GU32 2EW
GREAT BRITAIN

Tel: +44 (0)1730 233870
Email: enquiries@harriman-house.com
Website: www.harriman-house.com

First published in Great Britain in 2011

Published by Harriman House Ltd

The right of Guy Rigby to be identified as the Author has been asserted in accordance with the Copyright, Design and Patents Act 1988.

ISBN: 978–0857–191–47–2

British Library Cataloguing in Publication Data
A CIP catalogue record for this book can be obtained from the British Library.

Set in Minion and Francois One.

Printed and bound in Great Britain by Marston Book Services Ltd, Oxfordshire

 Harriman House

CONTENTS

ABOUT THE AUTHOR

Guy Rigby is a chartered accountant and an entrepreneur. He is a natural and driven enthusiast who built and sold his own accountancy firm, as well as pursuing other commercial interests. He has been a director and part-owner of a number of different ventures, including businesses in the IT, property, defence, manufacturing and retail sectors. In an unusually varied career, he has been the senior partner of two accountancy firms, a finance director, a sales and marketing director and an advisor and mentor to many entrepreneurial businesses and their owners.

Guy now leads the entrepreneurial services group at Smith & Williamson, the diversified financial services group. His day-to-day activities include advising entrepreneurs and their businesses and coordinating Smith & Williamson's activities in this vibrant and exciting market.

ACKNOWLEDGEMENTS

The idea for this book was born on a pavement near Tower Bridge in the City of London. "Why not write a book? It's easy!" said Neal Gandhi, entrepreneur, author and founder of Quickstart Global.

So thank you Neal! It's been a fascinating, challenging and soul-searching journey, during which the entrepreneur's mantra – 'never, ever give up' – has been tested to its limits.

But with the support of friends and colleagues, clients past and present, contacts, publishers and family, we made it.

My thanks go to Cheryl Rickman for her help in researching and developing content. Cheryl, your involvement has been invaluable.

To my friends and colleagues at Smith & Williamson for their enthusiasm, support and wise counsel. It's good to work with professionals who care.

To the many contributors who have given their time and helped illustrate key concepts with excellent and thought-provoking quotes. Your insights are inspirational to me and, hopefully, others.

To my publishing team at Harriman House. Myles, Chris, Suzanne and Louise, it has been a pleasure working with you to bring this book to fruition.

And finally, to my wife Nicky and our family, Oliver, Katie, Lucy, Camilla, Simon and Freddie. Thank you for allowing me this latest indulgence. You light up my life and this book is dedicated to you all.

FOREWORD
By Luke Johnson

"An excellent primer for any entrepreneur ... offers the most tremendous value"

This book is an excellent primer for any entrepreneur. It covers an extraordinary range of topics, from writing business plans and pitching to investors to how to achieve international sales. Guy Rigby is the ideal author for such a guide: he has been a business owner and advisor to companies for decades, and brings vast hands-on experience to the task. He is also a qualified accountant, which means the chapter on financial matters has special rigour.

I commend this book to both those who are already running an established business, and those who are minded to start one and become their own boss. It is written in a practical style, full of useful tips and pertinent questions. It is a manual that can be used very much as a reference source, to be dipped into when needed. Guy includes countless relevant examples and quotes from well-known entrepreneurs, ranging from Julie Meyer to James Caan to Richard Branson. They all provide good advice.

I have always believed a sound business book like *From Vision to Exit* offers readers the most tremendous value, compared to very expensive experts who typically charge hundreds of pounds an hour to provide essentially the same information.

Anyone managing a company or founding an enterprise needs all the knowledge they can get. Guy's words help fill the gap. An entrepreneur's journey is not an easy one, but I believe that for most the sacrifices are worthwhile – not simply for the financial rewards, but also the creative ones. Moreover, Britain needs as many entrepreneurs as possible right now, to help revive the economy and create new jobs, so tackling the misery of unemployment.

So good luck to every reader – I am sure you will find some valuable nuggets in these pages.

Luke Johnson
2011

Luke Johnson is the chairman of Risk Capital Partners and the former chairman of Channel 4 Television. Luke also writes a weekly column for the Financial Times *and wrote for the* Sunday Telegraph *for eight years.*

His new book, Start It Up: Why Running Your Own Business is Easier Than You Think, *was published by Penguin in 2011.*

INTRODUCTION

G reat ideas are two a penny, but great businesses are rare. Growing a great business involves intuition, skill and stamina, with significant challenges to be tackled along the way.

Businesses that achieve scale and long-term success share distinct characteristics: vision, strong leadership, an enthusiastic and effective management team, great products or services and a clear value proposition. These businesses typically challenge the status quo, finding a better or different way to achieve their goals and overcome their competition.

Some entrepreneurs have an innate ability to manage this process, but others have to fight harder for their success. Having worked as a mentor and advisor to entrepreneurs for over 25 years, I've seen success and failure, joy and despair. I've witnessed good-luck stories and horror stories. At the end of the day, with only the very occasional exception, there are clear reasons why businesses succeed or fail.

Just as great ideas don't amount to much if they are poorly planned or executed, businesses don't succeed if their strategy is flawed, or if their business model is unsustainable. An idea is nothing without effective treatment. Strategies must be achievable and adaptable. The potential in a great idea, market or team can only be realised if an assortment of variables function harmoniously and efficiently together.

These experiences have driven me to write this book. It's not just a book for start-ups, although much of its content is relevant to them. Its main purpose is to help established businesses – those that have already overcome the initial obstacles of foundation. It recognises that if you want to build a great business, there are a host of things you'll need to control and do better than anyone else.

Successful entrepreneurs understand that there's no need to embark on a long and uncertain voyage of discovery; plenty of people have been there before. The trick is how to shorten the learning curve, how to divide the business into its core elements and functions and how to maximise the opportunities in each area. In almost every case, there will be a better, more efficient or more profitable way. So here's my motto – *if it isn't broken, break it!*

This book recognises that business is challenging and that for the majority of entrepreneurs the odds are stacked against them. Alarming failure rates (over 50% of early-stage businesses fail within five years) may be discouraging, yet it is small and medium-sized enterprises (SMEs) that power the global economy. They employ more people than any other type of organisation, and the high-growth businesses amongst them create the majority of new jobs.

"What turns pain into growth is how you make decisions, how you manage, how you balance management and how you cope with stress," explains the author of *My Digital Footprint*, Tony Fish. It is these areas, among others, that I have attempted to cover in this book.

There's a huge amount to be encouraged about. Many SMEs are dynamic, innovative and insightful. These businesses, together with their owners, are flexible enough to adapt to market shifts and can react with speed to whatever opportunities or threats are levelled at them.

But in an increasingly competitive marketplace, they can also face strong headwinds. To stay ahead of their competition, they must communicate a clear vision, develop their markets, build their brands, achieve targets, improve processes and secure and maintain their supply chains. And they must do all this without running out of cash.

Fortunately, an instinctive desire to learn from the experiences of others is a key success driver. All the more reason, therefore, for a truly definitive, practical and comprehensive guide covering almost every business area to help SMEs navigate the minefield of growth.

In the process of writing this book, I've quizzed leaders in their field and consulted with successful and inspirational entrepreneurs. The upshot, I hope, is an authoritative and definitive 'how-to' guide which delivers a road map for growth, a framework for improvement and a blueprint for business success.

Guy Rigby
2011

CHAPTER 1

Strategy: Part One — Vision, Strategy and Tactics

"Luck is when preparedness meets opportunity."

– Earl Nightingale

Having a great strategy will not necessarily lead to business success, but a poor one will almost certainly prevent it. Strategy goes to the heart of a business, determining direction and the actions you take on a day-to-day basis. Get strategy right and your business will probably fly. Get it wrong and, even if you survive, you will forever be pushing water uphill.

Notably, the word 'strategy' is of military origin, derived from the Greek word *strategos*, which roughly translates as leader or general. It refers to a plan of action to achieve a particular goal, acting as a guide and dictating both direction and scope. In business, strategy embodies our vision of where we are heading and how we will get there, aligning our intentions with our expectations and values.

As David G. Thompson, author of *Blueprint to a Billion*, says, "the journey to achieving exponential growth – across, up, and down economic cycles – is rarely a smooth one." For this reason, it is essential to have a well-defined and carefully considered strategy. It needs to be capable of guiding you through the ever-changing business landscape towards the goals you want to achieve.

Strategy is shaped by our knowledge, experience, relationships, resources and competencies and our assessment of the best way to leverage these; it is shaped too by our vision and values. Strategy is always emergent, responsive to market conditions and customer needs and altered by fresh opportunities and threats.

Once you've determined the overall strategy for your business, you'll need to consider your sub-strategies. For example, there is operational strategy (how you organise your business in terms of processes, resources and people), product strategy (how you will source and deliver your products or services), marketing strategy (how you will raise awareness and stimulate demand) and financial strategy (how you will structure and finance the business). In short, strategy has an important part to play in every area of your business.

So how do business leaders create successful, workable and achievable strategies for their businesses?

For me, there are three key stages:

1. **Vision:** The vivid mental image and perception of your end game. Knowing where you're heading and being able to see the destination in your mind's eye.

2. **Strategy:** The direction you'll follow to pursue your goals and achieve your vision over time.

3. **Tactics:** The actions you'll take daily to assure the delivery of your strategy.

Envisioning a worthwhile future has long been a key motivator for successful business leaders. They use it to develop their strategies and tactics to bring their vision to fruition.

Amazon is a great example of this. Despite investors thinking he was crazy, on realising in 1994 that web usage was growing exponentially, Jeff Bezos's view of the future of e-commerce was clear. His founding dream and vision was to become the best retailer on the internet and "build a book store with universal selection"; a store without walls that he hoped would become "Earth's most customer-centric company".

His belief in this vision was so strong that he resigned from his highly paid job to establish Amazon.com and sell books over the internet. The site subsequently became the largest retailer on the internet and a point of reference for all online retailers. Amazon has seen an astounding rate of growth, with well over 100 million customers worldwide buying everything from books and music to clothes and DVDs. This is because Jeff Bezos didn't just dream his vision – he also created a strategy and deployed tactics to implement it.

The strategy was twofold, offering both an improved choice and experience and, crucially, cheaper prices. Recognising that the fundamental problem with a traditional book store was the size-imposed limit on how broad a selection of books it could stock, his strategy involved creating a store without walls on the web, boasting a universal and almost unlimited choice. (Whilst high street book shops could, like Amazon, order any book requested by a customer, they could not display them all.) This was combined with an interactive online environment, providing a speed and sophistication of service that superseded anything a traditional book store could offer.

His specific tactics included building an unrivalled payment platform, offering purchasing recommendations based on consumer-buying habits (and the buying habits of consumers with similar tastes) and, ultimately, focusing on the customer experience above all else.

So what's *your* vision? What's *your* strategy? And what are *your* tactics?

Thankfully, there are many tools and guides to help you devise an achievable and workable strategy and many tactics that will bring your strategy to life. We'll explore some of these later in this chapter, but the first thing you'll need is vision.

Vision

Developing a strategy and then working out how to reach your goals isn't easy. However, it's far more achievable if you have a clear vision of the future. The tactics you use along the way may involve experimentation and change, but vision is a constant. So it's important to begin with the end in mind.

Henry Ford turned his dream of the future, producing a "car for the masses", into fact. Bill Gates visualised "a computer on every desk and in every home". Boeing's Bill Allen dreamt of a jet-powered passenger aircraft. The business world is littered with entrepreneurs who based their strategies around their own long-term visions. Great leaders visualise and strategise. They consider the ideal and the real side-by-side, simultaneously mapping out idealistic and realistic eventualities in order to build successful, sustainable enterprises.

Strategy

If your vision is clear, it's time to consider the strategies you will develop to achieve your goals. You'll need to get all of the pieces on the table to complete the jigsaw, so here are some of the places to start:

- research and gather knowledge about your market

- open dialogue to gain insight and understanding

- assess and analyse your current business position.

Research and gather knowledge about the market

Most successful entrepreneurs build businesses based on their passion or experience. They already know a huge amount about their market or have had direct experience of working in it over many years, noting the inefficiencies and opportunities. They create businesses in areas they understand. And that remains their focus. How many times have you heard of entrepreneurs 'going round again' whilst remaining in the same industry?

Robert Wright, an entrepreneur and alumnus of Cranfield Business School, started his career as a pilot with British Airways. He then founded and sold two airline businesses – Connectair to International Leisure Group and CityFlyer to British Airways. Following these successes, he became a director and founding shareholder of Wizz Air, a low-cost Eastern European airline. He has stuck to his métier, pursuing opportunities in an area which he understands and in which he has been working all his life.

So experience helps – but new opportunities emerge and it's not impossible to break into new markets. To do so, however, you will need a strong blend of insight, data and knowledge.

"Knowing what products and services are being offered, how they've developed over time, what the current issues are in the marketplace … having this detailed knowledge enables you to see the opportunities for materially high growth," says Sir Eric Peacock, an experienced chairman who has bought and sold many businesses, including Babygro Plc.

Kodak is an example of a company that spent a huge amount of time and effort studying the behaviour and needs of consumers as it launched its digital strategy. It discovered that women in particular enjoyed taking digital photos, but moving those images onto their computers was an area of frustration for many. This unmet requirement created a huge opportunity and they set about improving their offerings to entirely remove this frustration. They created printer docks and other products with one strategic focus: to make it easier for consumers to share digital photos. They identified the issues and opportunities in the marketplace that would maximise the success of their digital strategy. (We'll look in more detail at Kodak's shifting strategy in Chapter 3.)

Open dialogue to gain insight and understanding

Talking to customers and suppliers is crucial. It's important to fully understand what they want and need, what they are doing now and what their plans are for the future.

Such a dialogue is something which Piers Daniell, IT expert and director of independent telecommunications carrier company Fluidata, views as critical for his company.

Part of his strategy has focused on customer engagement, not only to demonstrate his own products and services, but also to learn about his customers' businesses and the issues they face on an individual basis. His future depends on their future. "From our perspective, we can't grow if they're not growing," he says.

Through this dialogue with his customers, Piers discovered that they were asking for products that Fluidata didn't offer. So he decided to become a supplier to his suppliers and competitors – a bold move but one that has afforded him worthwhile growth. He did this by entering into a joint venture with his supplier in order to offer a wholesale product to his competitors.

"This means we're in the fortunate situation where we grow irrespective of what our principal customers do. If we lose business to a competitor we will hopefully still win overall, because we will often get that custom or revenue back through our supply chain." Intuitive and unusual, to say the least, and not a direction he would have thought of without developing a strong feedback strategy.

Talking to customers will often reveal their challenges and lead to potential growth opportunities. By addressing market sectors that are under-served and identifying these unmet needs, you can create a winning strategy for growth.

Consider how your customers' needs are not being met by identifying their pain and their frustrations. Is there a need for more flexibility in their contracts? Do they want more products or services of a certain type? Do they need a better quality of after-sales service? Is there some part of their business that they should be outsourcing? Are they over-dependent on certain key suppliers?

If so, can you satisfy any of these needs? Can you fix the pain by doing something better, faster or cheaper? Or can you add value around the relationship as a whole, enabling you to increase your own share of the available business and grow?

By talking to customers (and in Piers's case, his competitors) and doing whatever you can to see things from their point of view, you can redefine markets, uncovering unique or improved value propositions to gain real competitive advantage – the critical success factor in any sustainable strategy.

"Too many people think we can't talk to our competitors because they might get an advantage over us. But actually, when you look at the size of a market and what your business contributes to that market, there's still tremendous growth there for everybody."

This is echoed by Penny Power of Ecademy in her book on social networking – *Know me, Like me, Follow me*. She argues that, with modern communication tools where everybody can find out about everything, it is no longer appropriate to be "closed, selective and controlling". Instead she believes in communication that is "open, random and supportive", gaining the respect and trust of the community. It's the way the world is going.

Severin Schwan, CEO of leading pharmaceutical and healthcare innovator Roche, has used collaboration strategies and dialogue to help him take steps towards changing the face of healthcare into "personalised medicine" that is customised to individual needs.

His vision is being fulfilled through a strategy of knowledge acquisition using research and dialogue. By its very nature, as one of the world's greatest knowledge-based healthcare companies, Roche does its homework well. It tests and trials; it researches, analyses and diagnoses. The ethos of digging deep to gather knowledge is echoed in its future planning. Schwan's insight came from a combination of research, talking to people on the frontline and his own in-built knowledge of the company and industry. "I'm not interested in PowerPoint presentations," declares Schwan, "but prefer to go to the source.

You can learn a lot from people in a true dialogue." And Roche is the only place Schwan has worked since his first day as a trainee finance officer.

With the knowledge gathered and digested, Schwan created a strategy to bring his vision to fruition. He would achieve it through collaboration between researchers from pharmaceuticals and diagnostics teams, through targeted acquisitions of diagnostic testing companies and by boosting his R&D spending. He opened dialogue with everyone in the chain and created a clear plan which outlined the actions he needed to take.

Consequently, Roche became the world's most profitable drug-maker. Its results since Schwan took the helm speak for themselves – evidence that his vision and strategy are working.

Leading with your team

But dialogue in the wider market is only part of the solution. What about your own team? It's all very well leading from the front but it's better when the troops are up alongside you. Getting too far ahead can bring isolation and danger, as well as apathy and disillusionment in the team.

We'll talk about the importance of strong management in Chapter 9, but it's worth mentioning the difference between leadership and management here. Whilst leadership is about doing the right things, management is about doing things right. It follows that strategy is more aligned with leadership, but how can this be developed in an inclusive and beneficial way?

When it achieves scale, every successful business will have a strong leadership team. These are typically board directors who meet regularly to discuss the business's activities and performance. In growing businesses, structures may be less formal but there will normally be key staff that the business relies on for its well-being and success.

In my view, strategy should always be developed in conjunction with your senior team. Not only will this avoid isolation but it will also add insight (there is no monopoly on good ideas!), gain buy-in and, ultimately, spread a wider understanding and purpose across the business. It will also serve to reality-check your plans in a way that you would be unable to do on your own. It's therefore essential to allocate sufficient time at management meetings to discuss and debate the big picture.

And what about your employees?

How do you get them on board? Do they understand where the business is going and how they can help? Have you given them a roadmap to show them the way?

To translate your strategy into organisational action you will need to communicate it well. Successful implementation will therefore come down to your leadership style and the effectiveness of your management team. Remember that this need not be difficult. With a good strategy and a committed management team, the energy and enthusiasm should be infectious!

There will, of course, be challenges. Communication channels must always be open, with strong alignment across functions, departments, business units and geographical locations. But when your team is excited about your business's future, you are well on the way to success.

So where do you start?

Assess and analyse your current business position

Always begin at the beginning. By examining the wider environment in which your business operates, by considering your strengths and weaknesses, as well as your opportunities and threats, you will be far better positioned to create a sustainable, long-term strategy.

So consider what's working in your business and what's not. Be objective and consider what you need to change to improve the business and its prospects. Remember that if you keep turning the same handle, you'll get the same result.

Ask yourself some difficult questions. For example, here are just a few around sales:

- Is your product or service fit for purpose?
- How could it be improved?
- Is your pricing competitive?
- Is there a demonstrable need and sufficient demand?
- Is it scaleable?

- How do you stand out from the crowd?

- Do you have loyal and reliable customers?

- Are you making an acceptable margin?

If you can't answer these questions satisfactorily, don't just put them at the bottom of the pile. Get your senior team together and consider what needs to change. Even if you can answer them satisfactorily, banish complacency and look at what can be improved.

Being a perfectionist can pay off. Clive Woodward, manager of England's successful World Cup winning rugby team, famously said that when his team won a match, they would go back to the classroom, work out what they did well and how they could improve on it. If they lost, they went to the pub!

By assessing and analysing your current position, key themes and opportunities should become apparent. What is your competitive advantage? Are global markets and exports important to you? Do you have sufficient resources? Do you have the competencies and capabilities to grow a great business? Ask yourself what's missing. The questions will differ from business to business. But examining them in detail will enable you to fill the gaps.

Tactics

Successful businesses don't just have a strategy, they have a strong and executable plan. They recognise that even the most well-developed strategy will achieve nothing without effective execution. Without action, vision remains in the imagination – an empty promise. It is therefore critical to establish your tactics, i.e. how you will implement your strategy.

"Too many people focus on what or why rather than how they intend to achieve something in terms of the actions they need to take to make something happen," says James Caan, a successful entrepreneur and CEO of private equity firm Hamilton Bradshaw.

So what specific tactics should you deploy?

Your business may already be hugely successful, in which case it may simply be a question of turning the same handle (but remember Clive Woodward's philosophy) or you may still be wondering how you will achieve that success. If the latter, and you haven't got your vision and strategy worked out, you should go back to the drawing board. But if you have, then it's simply a question of tactics.

Let's assume you have an established consultancy business that has been operating for many years. You have a good track record, capable management and a supportive staff. So far, so good.

However, you know that the business could do better and you are frustrated by the gap between its actual and potential performance. You recently had an enlightening discussion with the CEO, now retired, of one of your client companies. He highlighted a need for advice in an area that you hadn't even considered – a variation on your service but still within the core competency of your business.

You realise that using your expertise in this new way could revitalise your performance and enable you to significantly grow your market share. Suddenly everything has changed. The enthusiasm returns and you set about how you can deliver this new and exciting opportunity.

So what do you do? You build a tactical plan to develop and market the new service, whilst maintaining your existing business and keeping an eye on any dangers this may present. In simplistic terms, it might look something like this:

- raise the opportunity with your senior team to obtain their insights and views

- consider the demands on your resources – particularly management time and cash

- commission research amongst your clients to assess potential demand

- consider commerciality and scalability

- design the new service according to feedback received

- test the service on a friendly or existing client

- tweak and finalise the service and pricing

- explain and promote the new service to your internal team

- train your staff to sell and deliver the service

- use marketing and PR to raise awareness of the service

- consider viral and online strategies

- market the service to both existing and new clients

- monitor performance and profitability.

Looking at it like this, it's completely obvious that each step requires specific actions and that these can be planned and considered in advance. It's not complicated, but many businesses will take a different and far less organised approach. This will often end in failure and may even threaten the long-term viability of the business.

In this example, the business was able to discover a new and exciting opportunity. In most cases, however, it will be evolution not revolution, so your tactics may simply be to do more than you are already doing, and to do it better.

Perhaps your future will be determined by recruiting more people? Perhaps by a change in your business model? Maybe you need to consider your use of technology, perhaps by creating some kind of information engine that will bring more people to you? Perhaps you need to strengthen your sales team? Or perhaps you need to revisit your marketing activities to build your brand and reputation? At the end of the day, it's just a question of identifying what you need to do and how you are going to do it.

As you progress, you'll need to specify targets, identify your critical success factors and consider the key performance indicators you will monitor along the way. I hate mnemonics, but some people use SMART (objectives that are Specific, Measurable, Achievable, Relevant and Time-bound) to check that their thinking is on course.

Ian Marchant, CEO of Scottish and Southern Energy (SSE), has a clear vision of the future – to revolutionise power generation, moving the industry towards clean and green renewable energy supplies. What's more, he identified the alternative and renewable energy trend long before it was in vogue. He used this vision and his own expert knowledge of the market (he started with Southern Electric in 1992) to strategically map out the business's future. Ian knew what his objectives were but, more importantly, he knew exactly what he needed to do to implement his growth strategy. He has focused on the 'what' in order to realise his vision, tactically buying wind farms, power stations and gas-storage facilities.

At the time of writing, his action-oriented tactics have saved his company £10m per annum in waste reduction and led to SSE becoming the largest company in Scotland.

Back to strategy

As we have discovered, a flawed or inferior strategy will usually mean pushing water uphill and potential business failure. So it's got to work and it's got to be commercially viable.

Validating your strategy is therefore an essential part of any plan of action, ensuring commerciality and, ultimately, proving the market demand. While validation may lengthen the journey to market, it's a central part of the process.

According to Julie Meyer – online Dragon, co-founder of First Tuesday, Ariadne Capital and the Entrepreneur Country movement – there are five key phases to consider over the lifetime of a successful business:

1. Concept

2. Validation

3. Commercialisation

4. Scale

5. Exit

Your go-to-market strategy will focus on the first four of these. We'll cover the fifth stage in more detail in Chapter 19.

"Your strategy has to revolve around your unfair advantage," says Julie. "And that unfair advantage is not necessarily that you have better technology than somebody else, it's that you have a unique insight into the market, which you've proven; you've demonstrated the market demand."

So vision paves the way to strategy and strategy leads to tactics. The tactics determine what you do on a day-to-day basis to achieve the vision, so creating a virtuous circle to enable your business growth.

┌─ **Top tips** ─

- **Adopt a planning horizon** (perhaps three years).

- **Define your vision.** Describe in one or two sentences what you want the business to look like in three years' time.

- **Identify four or five factors that are critically important** to achieving your three-year aims (what does success really hinge on?).

- **Specify targets** for each factor to monitor your progress and confirm that you're on course.

- **Identify your tactics** for year one (important actions that will ensure your future success).

- **Consider things that could go wrong** and include tactics that will reduce or manage these risks.

- **Always involve your senior team** to yield additional insights and ideas.

- **Remember** that a well-developed strategy achieves nothing without **effective implementation**.

- Allocate time at management meetings to **ensure that the big picture is not forgotten**.

- **Be ready to change plans and priorities if circumstances dictate.**

- **Build a sense of direction and energy** by communicating the strategy clearly.

- **Celebrate success** frequently. It's important to enjoy the journey.

CHAPTER 2
Strategy: Part Two – Growth, Pace and Profit

> **"Time is the enemy of the poor business and the friend of the great business."**
>
> — Warren Buffett

It's the economy, stupid!

James Carville, Bill Clinton's political strategist in the 1992 US presidential election, coined the phrase "It's the economy, stupid!" in order to give the political campaign a central theme and focus. It ultimately helped to unseat George H. W. Bush by promoting the notion that he had not adequately addressed the financial challenges in an economy that had recently suffered a recession.

For entrepreneurs and SMEs, the health of the economy will often determine the focus of a business, as well as its appetite for risk and growth.

During recessions, the focus tends to shift towards short-term survival. Prudent practices become the order of the day and longer-term aspirations are often supplanted by cost-cutting and essential cash management. The challenge that follows any period of economic uncertainty is to refocus on the longer term.

In general, focusing on the short term is unlikely to generate long-term growth or value. Indeed, it can often lead to failure. Referring to the financial crisis that followed the Lehman Brothers collapse in 2008, Matthew Bishop,

American business editor of the *Economist* and co-author of *The Road from Ruin: How to Revive Capitalism and Put America Back on Top*, wrote: "It was the endemic short-termism of the business world that got it into the mess in the first place."

But what about profits?

I asked the business leaders I interviewed for this book about the need to focus on long-term strategies over short-term profits, and received a number of emphatic responses.

Focusing on the longer term

"If the aim is to build up value in the business so the business has an asset value which is independent of the owner, then [focusing on the longer-term] is often the view you have to take," says David Molian, director of the Business Growth and Development Programme at Cranfield School of Management. And it's certainly an opinion echoed by many successful entrepreneurs.

Of course, your more immediate goals, as well as your cash flow requirements, will determine what you focus on in the short term. If, for example, your goal is to sell the business sooner rather than later, you'll probably want to focus on profitability by maintaining performance and keeping the business as lean and efficient as possible. Alternatively, you may be focused on scaling the business, in which case you may be less profit-driven in the short-term, using any available cash flow to invest in your rapid expansion.

In reality, with some notable and often venture capital-backed exceptions, most businesses have to focus on both value growth and profitability simultaneously. But let's start by looking at some of these VC-backed businesses, the more well-known being consumer-facing businesses with disruptive technology and large followings, where cash outflows, sometimes in the tens of millions of pounds, precede revenue generation and profitability.

High risk, high reward

Some businesses that are focused on a long-term value creation strategy will happily endure losses in the early stages. These will typically be VC-backed businesses, where success or failure is ultimately determined by the quality of the proposition, the intellectual property rights (IPR) and the expertise and ability of the management team.

As Julie Meyer, online Dragon and co-founder of First Tuesday, observes: "When you're building something which doesn't exist and bringing something brand new to market, there's an investment and a cost of customer acquisition. So, while profit is hugely important, a lot of early stage companies have a J-Curve [initial losses followed by an uplift in performance, like the curvature of a 'J']. Why is that? Because they're investing in and betting on their insight."

Such companies and their investors have a patient attitude to profit, coupled with an unshakeable belief in their strategy and business model. They are certain they will profit in the future and they are prepared to risk financing their growth by using their own or external capital.

Take Moonpig.com, the online greeting card service. Founder Nick Jenkins adopted an incredibly patient attitude to growth which has reaped remarkable rewards. Having launched the website in 1999, it took six years to reach break-even. The business lost £2.5m before it made any money. But a little over a decade later, in 2010, turnover reached £31m with a pre-tax profit of £11.2m, with the company owning the vast majority of the UK's online card market. At the end of year one, revenues were a mere £90k while overheads reached £1m. The story shows that short-term losses can often be par for the course if your long-term strategy is to build a market-leading enterprise.

The good news is that Moonpig's cash flow is no longer a problem. No cards are printed until they've been paid for by the consumer, whilst stock "accounts for less than half a per cent of turnover" says Nick. The result is a cash-rich business – one which has benefited from a long-term strategy that didn't focus on short-term profitability.

Nick recognised that his business was growing organically and would eventually succeed. As early as 2002 he could see that if the business carried on growing at the rate it had been, it would break-even purely on organic growth. It was just a question of waiting and funding the losses until that happened.

"What's important is that I understood that it was going to work, because I spent a lot of my time measuring the data and working out what the lifetime value of the customer was," explains Nick. "I was able to model it forward.

That understanding gave me the confidence to realise that we were going to break even."

Once the company had started to make a profit in 2005 it was able to begin to reinvest its profits in growth. Part of that reinvestment of the profits was wisely spent on its catchy and highly successful TV advertising.

Along the way, Nick didn't just focus on data and customer analysis. He also devoted a lot of time to fine tuning the technological infrastructure. He needed to create a "complex automated system" that would record each stage that every card goes through, a system which has taken ten years to refine.

Plus, there's ample opportunity to continue growing, with the entire UK greetings card industry estimated to be worth approximately £1.5bn.

Moonpig is a huge entrepreneurial success story. It shows that, whilst profitability is extremely important, it can be elusive in the formative years of a business. In addition, it seems that too much focus on profit in this kind of early-stage business might cause lasting damage and act as a barrier to future success.

What's the lesson? It can take both time and money to build a great business, so make sure you've got enough of both!

Freemium power

Some high-growth companies have not only made significant early losses, they've created brand new business models by giving stuff away for free. The Googles, YouTubes and Skypes of this world made significant initial losses, but look at them now.

From search to email (or should I say Gmail) Google's consumer-facing offerings are all free. By offering these free services they've attracted huge numbers of users. This strategy has enabled them to create an advertising business bringing in billions in revenues and profits.

"We are an advertising company," says Google's executive chairman (and former CEO) Eric Schmidt. "Today we say our strategy is search, ads and apps."

The Google strategy has inspired those who've followed, as online businesses have prioritised market share and user numbers above profits and even revenues. As such, data and 'eyeballs' have become a new currency.

As Jeremy Levine, an investment partner in Wikia, the for-profit sister site of Wikipedia says, "Content begets eyeballs, eyeballs beget business model." Indeed, the 'freemium' model can deliver big profits if a product has inherent value, low costs and a large reach.

Skype, for example, built a hugely successful business using the freemium model. Founder Niklas Zennstrom saw his alternative to the traditional telecoms operator business model as a great viral (and therefore rapid growth) strategy. By using their own bandwidth and P2P software, users didn't cost anything to serve. This meant that, unlike its traditional counterparts, Skype had no customer acquisition, marketing or distribution costs. Hundreds of millions of people have since downloaded Skype software, which enables users to make free calls, with just a minority of users paying for premium landline or mobile calls. Yet this strategy afforded its founders an incredibly attractive exit, when they sold the business to eBay in 2005 for US$2.6 billion! And it was subsequently built on by much-admired former CEO Josh Silverman from 2008 onwards, leading to a further sale to Microsoft for $8.5 billion in 2011.

Similarly, open source software business MySQL was sold to Sun Microsystems in 2008 for $800 million, proving that open source software could be the foundation of a profitable, growing business. By giving away free software to its supportive and evangelical community, MySQL was able to build a massive audience. It then charged enterprise customers for maintenance and support, creating a dual-licensing strategy and a sustainable business model in the process.

The perfect example of a pure venture capital play is Twitter, the free and increasingly popular social messaging utility. At the time of writing, this company, which has raised many tens of millions of dollars of venture capital, has no discernible business model. As Biz Stone, one of the co-founders, famously said, "We are not trying to be vague – we are still trying to figure that out." What Twitter does have is incredible reach. It would take a brave man to bet against the company's ultimate success, either on a stand-alone or an acquired basis, where other services might be cross-sold to its huge and growing audience.

Building a global business

Twitter is unusual, and most businesses seeking to build market share and inherent value before focusing on profit do have a clear strategy and plan.

Take AIM-listed company Monitise, originally funded by Morse plc under a corporate venturing agreement in 2003. You could say they're on a long road to profit, because they're helping to build an entire industry from scratch – global mobile banking. Notwithstanding this, they have got all the major banks and operators on board and secured substantial investment from VISA. As a result, they have already gained recognition as being a worldwide leader in a brand new industry, allowing customers everywhere to manage their money with text messages, apps and mobile sites – on almost any mobile device.

Apart from profitability, Monitise ticks a lot of boxes. They have a board and management team that is probably the envy of many larger FTSE companies. In fact their board reads like a veritable who's who of banking, telecoms and technology VIPs.

Even more admirable, Monitise founder and CEO Alastair Lukies is succeeding where mobile operators have previously failed. He has managed to persuade the majority of major UK banks and mobile operators to cooperate in order to build his mobile banking application – Monilink – which runs across all banks and mobile networks.

Monitise is leading a sector in which other much larger and profitable businesses have tried and failed to enter. It's also expanding globally and taking advantage of a market which is growing exponentially. (Juniper Research predicted that more than 41.4 billion financial transactions will be carried out on mobile phones by the end of 2011.) Monitise's product could even become the global standard.

"Monitise could have focused on short-term profits," says Ariadne Capital's Julie Meyer. "They could have tried to maximise revenues through licensing. But, had they done so, they would have missed the overall market opportunity to build a global mobile banking industry."

Alastair Lukies couldn't agree more. Building an enabling infrastructure while growing consumer uptake and market share are what drives his vision of Monitise being a £1–£3 billion business.

For Monitise – like Google, Skype and MySQL – it's been a numbers game rather than a profits game. Each strategy has been shaped by customer and partner needs alongside the long-term business vision. The point is that profitability has not yet been prioritised, whilst growth has.

This is the same strategy adopted by other high-growth businesses, including European online search pioneer Espotting, which was sold to FindWhat in 2003 for a reported £97 million.

"If you're trying to build up a global business then you're not going to be looking at the bottom line," says founder of Espotting, Seb Bishop. "You know that your business plan is going to be showing a loss over a four- or five-year period, because it's a long-term strategy. You're building a brand; you're building a customer base. Most of the big businesses you see today had a loss for the first few years. And that's the role of the venture capitalist [to fund those losses]."

If he'd decided instead to focus on profit, he might have had a healthy-looking balance sheet but wouldn't have been able to manage his expansion. "Do you choose not to expand into new territories in order to make a profit?" questions Seb. "The US company that comes to buy you isn't going to give you a greater multiple because you've added something extra to your bottom line. They're going to give you a greater valuation on the basis that you're saving them two or three years worth of work by delivering them all these different territories."

Seb's thought processes illustrate that, more often than not, core strategy should be all about the bigger picture, the long-term aim.

"Of course, it depends on the business," clarifies Seb. "If you're looking at opening a chain of restaurants, then profit matters over the short term. But if you're looking at building a business in order to sell it over the long term, then you're going to reinvest that money to ensure that you deliver whatever the acquirer is likely to value the most, be that traffic, staff, offices or geography. You need to figure out what is the most important thing to that organisation that they'll be willing to pay for. For us it was a geography game. We invested in people, we invested in technology and we invested in geography."

Since achieving his vision by selling to the US company FindWhat, the merged company – re-branded Miva – has won an award for fastest-growing IT company.

"It couldn't have been the fastest growing IT company if we were hell bent on making a profit," says Seb.

A marathon or a sprint?

While Espotting grew incredibly quickly (from start to sale in just three years), Moonpig and Monitise have taken a longer-term approach.

"We're seven and a half years into this company and I reckon we've got another seven and a half years to go," says Alastair Lukies of Monitise.

Nick Jenkins agrees that growing a market-leading company takes time and requires a long-term outlook. "You need to be aware of the long lead time it takes to build up the management resources to implement a strategy of expansion," says Nick. "One of the issues we had at Moonpig is that we could come up with ideas far quicker than we could expand our team and get them to the point where they're being productive."

Similarly it took Alastair Lukies 279 meetings and more than three years to prove his concept with one of the banks. Pursuing a long-term strategy requires a huge dose of persistence and belief too.

In terms of pace, the vast majority of entrepreneurs seem to believe that strong and steady growth is generally preferable to rapid, over-zealous (and potentially business threatening) growth.

"It's like running a race," says Alastair. "If you're setting yourself up for a sprint and the business is actually going to take a marathon, you're going to die. If you're a middle distance runner, which I think we are as a company, and you're set up to run a 10,000 metre race, then you're fine."

Prioritising profits – the traditional business model

When I asked Bobby Hashemi, co-founder of Coffee Republic and private equity investor at Risk Capital Partners LLP, whether, with the benefit of hindsight, there was anything he'd do differently, his answer confirmed the majority view regarding time frame. With, however, one critical caveat.

"One of the things I've learned is to pace the growth," Bobby admits. "From my own personal experience and if I could do it all over again, I'd grow at a more manageable pace. I would grow more surely, more slowly – and *focus on profits*." [emphasis added]

In contrast to the global, VC-backed businesses and entrepreneurs featured so far, Bobby believes that profitability should *always* be the priority. "The sooner a business reaches profitability, the more options are available to it," he says. He believes that many fast-growth businesses don't focus enough on achieving profitability from day one and, as such, they're always chasing finance. For Bobby, a business that is profitable has endless growth options, because it often doesn't need anyone else to help it grow.

"That's a huge learning curve that I went through in the early part of my career as an entrepreneur," admits Bobby. "Learning about putting the brakes on, going more slowly, not overpaying for assets, running a tight ship and making sure that the business pays for itself on a day-to-day basis."

Bobby recognises that there's a big difference between high-risk, VC-backed businesses and more traditional businesses, of which there are a far greater number.

"I think a lot of internet businesses learn the hard way that it isn't just about market share. The market share numbers, the value of the brand, all of those have to translate into profits and, without profits, there is no business."

It's not a surprising stance for someone who now works as a traditional private equity investor, investing only in businesses that are already profitable and with growth potential. Indeed, Bobby believes that, in principle, outside of the technology sector, traditional businesses should focus on profitability all of the time.

The benefits of investing early

"The end game for any business is to make profit," says James Caan. "There's an old saying that says 'turnover is vanity, profit is sanity'! Because, if you're not making more than you spend, you're going to be out of business pretty soon."

"However," adds James, "when you are growing your business, it is crucially important to reinvest profits into the company, especially during the early days where a company is trying to establish itself and is at its most vulnerable."

How you spend your profits makes all the difference. Reinvesting profits back into the business will strengthen its foundations and enable it to grow over the long term.

James continues: "We come across many entrepreneurial businesses at Hamilton Bradshaw and one of the most common features we see is that the owner-manager has taken out all the profits of the business each year as his or her personal earnings. This inevitably slows the growth of the business. Every year, the company is starting from the beginning again rather than with last year's profits to reinvest.

"Most people know how to run a business to make income, but we work with our companies to teach them how to generate *value* – a business that funds itself, reinvests in its assets and grows exponentially because the owners aren't using it as their personal piggy bank. Ultimately, by doing this you create a sustainable business of real value that has the potential to be sold."

So it may not be so much about whether you make a loss or a profit initially. What's key is how you invest any profit that you do make, or how you spend the money you raise or earn. After digging deep into the assumption that short-term profit focus can be detrimental, it's clear that how you invest in your long-term strategy is perhaps the more vital question.

It is possible to focus on profits and a long-term sustainable growth strategy but, in all but exceptional circumstances, that's only a realistic methodology if you pace your growth. Both profitability and cash flow are likely to suffer from an over-enthusiastic approach.

All of this talk about growth and profit begs another question. Management guru Peter Drucker famously said that, "profit should be a mere consequence and not the main goal of a business when growing." Drucker's point is that *excellence*, rather than profit, should be the primary aim of a business.

The pursuit of excellence

"Peter Drucker is absolutely right," says David Molian. "Because the primary focus should be on serving the customer and building a loyal customer base. Everything else in the business should be secondary to that. Clearly if you don't make a sustainable profit you will at some point go bust, but if your initial focus is on making money and serving the customer slips into being the secondary focus, the business is doomed to failure."

Liz Jackson MBE, founder and CEO of Great Guns Marketing, also sees profit as a secondary driver to her strategy – that of delivering excellent results for her clients.

"Although we're very interested in making money, it's never been our main driver," says Liz. "Our main driver is delivering excellence; building something that's worth building, delivering what we deliver in a really ethical way. It's about winning the best clients, delivering the best service, employing the best people and the result of that is wealth. But it's only the result, it's not the focus."

By focusing on quality and excellence and by delivering great products and services to customers above all else, Great Guns has grown profitably at a rate of 40–50% per annum – fast but not explosive growth.

"Clearly what Peter Drucker is trying to say is if you give customers what they want, get good marketing programmes, look after your people and get the right team, then you will have profits, and that's true," says Brad Rosser. "But you do need to set yourself goals and targets."

"I need my profit goals, I need my sales targets and then I'll go about doing the best job I can," adds Brad. "Profits and cash flow are how you keep score in business. Just as a tennis player might say they'll just go and play the best tennis they can and, if they do that, they'll win. The problem with that attitude is that they might play good tennis for one set and then lose the other two and that doesn't help. If you're playing great tennis but are still losing your matches, you're not going to be a successful tennis player. In business, you've got to be focused on the results as well as the actions."

So, in terms of strategy: while vision is fundamental, it's ultimately tactics and results that make a good business into a great business. And, while good customer service is crucial, so too are targets and measurement of those targets.

Top tips

- **Consider the health of the economy** and sector in which your business is operating.

- **Determine your own goals.** Are you grooming your business for a quick sale or are you in it for the long haul? Remember that time is the friend of the great business.

- **Identify your value drivers and formulate your strategy.** Consider what will generate the most value in your business.

- **Develop and prioritise your tactics** based on your findings, whatever they may be – e.g. bootstrapping and profits growth, customer acquisition, supply chain efficiency, internationalisation, innovation, brand building, process control, cost control, etc.

- **Track and forecast your data** to establish growth rates and break-even points. Be realistic in your assumptions.

- **Be persistent.** Everything takes longer than you think it will in business. Understand how long it may take you to build up your team and customer base in order to implement your strategy and fulfil your vision.

- **Set your own business metronome** at a sustainable and manageable pace along with realistic KPIs that drive the business forward.

- **Focus on delivering quality and excellence** in order to give yourself the best chance of success in both the long term and the short term.

- **Give your management team the tools and resources they need** to get the job done.

- **Keep your eye on the bottom line.** Don't let your growth strategy run away with you and, whatever else you do, don't run out of cash.

CHAPTER 3
Strategy: Part Three – Flexibility and Focus

"Even if you are on the right track, you'll get run over if you just sit there."

— Will Rogers

The need for flexibility

Great businesses are ultimately distinguished by their ability to create and retain a strategic competitive advantage.

And yet markets constantly change...

As Herbert Hoover, the 31st President of the United States, said: "About the time we can make the ends meet, somebody moves the ends."

So while strategies must be focused, they must also be flexible. Business leaders must therefore sharpen their senses and nurture their ability to recognise both threats and opportunities. They must be adept at managing change, shifting direction and focus and constantly evolving their strategies in line with market developments and demand.

"You should know in the longer term where you want to get to, but in the short and even the medium term, how you get there might change quite dramatically from what you had planned. That's just life really," observes David Molian.

Change is a constant and, whether your strategy is to expand, acquire, diversify, internationalise or downsize, it should not be set in stone. Strategy is emergent and there must be a perpetual quest for renewal.

But it's not just the requirement for a flexible strategy that is critical to success in today's ever-changing business environment; it's the understanding that, in order to grow and cope with the necessary changes, businesses must also mature as they grow.

"Too many businesses assume that the business they'll have in year five will look pretty much the same as the business they have in year one; there'll just be more people, larger premises, more computing power and so on. But actually the business can change quite fundamentally over that time," explains David Molian. "It'll go through phases of growth where the kind of leadership and management processes might be quite different. So it's not just a question of getting larger, it's a question of the business having to mature as well."

Business maturity can manifest itself in many ways. Key areas include the development of a skilled management team (often involving the removal or sidelining of the old one) and a focus away from owner dependency, matters which we will consider in more detail elsewhere in this book.

Maturity aside, a business needs to be alive to the requirements of its market and have the flexibility to adapt both strategy and management processes as the market dictates.

A diamond in the rough

A good example of a mature company who did exactly this is the world's leading diamond company, De Beers. Their famous slogan said that "A diamond is forever", yet they realised that their business strategy was not.

A number of issues forced De Beers to rethink the supply control strategy which had thus far enabled them to maintain high prices. Issues included the entrance of new competitors and fresh sources of diamond supply, coupled with consumer alarm over 'blood diamonds' – rogue governments and cartels financing war through their mining and sale. This last problem in particular resulted in a drop in diamond demand, which finally forced De Beers's hand.

Up until that point they had mined, bought and controlled 90% of the world's diamonds. The subsequent smaller slice of a smaller pie led them to shift their strategy from managing supply to driving (or re-energising) demand. They've done this by going direct to consumers with branded jewellery, creating a certification process in collaboration with governments and NGOs, and establishing ethical joint-venture diamond mining and sorting facilities.

Review, measure and track

The De Beers experience is a good example and shows that, in order to stay ahead of the game, continuous assessment of markets, resources, opportunities and threats is critical to business success. Most CEOs are alert to this. When quizzed about strategy in the sixth annual 2006 *PRWeek*/Burson-Marsteller CEO Survey, 64% of participants indicated they re-evaluate their long-term business goals on a quarterly basis or more frequently. I believe 100% of businesses should be doing this.

Re-evaluation is crucial, because, if a business is solely focused on turning the daily handle, it may fail to notice important changes in the market such as the development of new technology or the emergence of a new competitor. It's therefore vital to take time out to check that the business strategy remains sound and that its goals are still realistic. Outdated strategies can destroy businesses, as can those which are so rigid that they prevent the seizing of new opportunities as they arise. Small businesses, in particular, shouldn't become slaves to inflexible strategies – they need to be opportunistic.

The best way to stay abreast of opportunities and maintain overall flexibility is to integrate new opportunities into an existing strategy each time it is reviewed.

"It's important to create an organisation which is adaptable so that the strategy becomes a living part of the culture which is refreshed and reviewed at frequent intervals," says experienced chairman Sir Eric Peacock.

"Certainly within my businesses we're doing a reality check on the strategy every few months and a full strategic review at least every year," he explains. "That gives us the adaptability and flexibility to add opportunities, or to eliminate things that are clearly not going to work within the time frame or the cost that we've earlier assigned to that strategy."

So how do you plan strategically and maintain focus whilst also retaining flexibility?

With markets constantly on the move, it's important to regularly assess, track and review your strategic plans and activities. This will keep you alert to potential opportunities and threats. Wherever possible, you should involve your senior management team and staff, taking time out to work *on* the business rather than *in* the business.

Liz Jackson of Great Guns Marketing has a clear and highly targeted strategy called 'Going For Growth' which analyses and measures everything that they do and involves her wider team. However, having such a focused growth strategy doesn't imply an absence of innovation. "We're entrepreneurial, so it's flexible all of the time," says Liz.

One of the keys to maintaining equilibrium between focus and flexibility comes from building strong foundations and robust internal processes alongside a flexible and innovative 'front-end'. These foundations will act as an anchor, preventing fanciful change and securing the core of the business. At the same time, market-facing staff can respond to customers' demands and gather external intelligence.

Strong foundations

While continuous assessment encourages flexibility and an openness to change, it is far easier to shift strategic direction if your business has strong foundations.

"Building a business is very much like a pyramid," explains Alastair Lukies. "Too many people focus on the top of the pyramid, but they don't spend enough time on what is inevitably the dull but essential stuff, which is: *how do I build the bottom of the pyramid so robustly and so scalable that, if my strategy at the top changes, it's only a tweak at the bottom to make it happen?*"

Microsoft is an example of a company with strong foundations which, particularly in the 1990s, effectively rode successive waves of change. For many years it focused on its core area of business: operating systems and software, seemingly ignoring the growth of the internet. Their strategy was in fact to explicitly ignore the web, deeming it a potentially damaging distraction for their staff. Behind the scenes, however, the senior management teams were assessing online opportunities, carefully watching developments and, as they did so, creating a strong strategy that harnessed what they saw as their internet opportunity. They worked on the strategy in the background and certainly didn't want it to have any negative impact on their core business activities. They waited for the right time to trigger the new strategy and, once the opportunity reached a commercially viable level, they launched. Over the course of one weekend, they redeployed 400 of their staff onto the new strategy.

By acting fast and with a small number of their overall staff, they minimised any disruption in the company. The strategy was then clearly communicated to the rest of the business and the management were able to focus on their core competencies of managing development projects. The result was the creation of an industry standard web browser which was installed on all PCs as standard.

In taking this approach Microsoft only extended their services when they were absolutely ready, when the market had been thoroughly assessed, when their concepts had been validated and when they had adequately evaluated the commercial opportunity. They demonstrated flexibility and focus simultaneously.

The Microsoft example provides a number of valuable lessons about shifting elements of strategy while sustaining competitive advantage. If a new opportunity arises, you should review it carefully before actively setting out in pursuit. If the opportunity seems to be worthy of further consideration, assign an individual or team to look at the commercial opportunity and the likely impact on your business. If, and only if, there is a compelling fit, draw up your plans carefully and resource the new project properly. In other words, act decisively and don't skimp and save. If the project is going to put undue stress on your business (e.g. your management team or your cash flow), don't do it.

"It's tempting to say yes to everything," says Liz Jackson of Great Guns. "Indeed, some opportunities are tempting, but you soon realise they're not important enough, they're not going to add to the bottom line, while they *are* going to divert me away from core activities. As a result you have to say no to some opportunities."

It all comes down to understanding your business so well that you can easily assess the relevance of each opportunity and how it would add to or detract from your overall objectives and vision. If you get it wrong, and end up going off on a tangent, you may end up fighting on too many fronts.

With strong foundations, the business culture is aligned and the team is united; the processes are robust and the communication is effective. With strong foundations, it's going to be far easier when it comes to making strategic shifts.

Diversification

As we saw in Chapter 1, most entrepreneurs prefer to build their businesses around their passion or experience. After all, if you've got a good formula, why go outside your comfort zone?

Sometimes, however, entrepreneurs choose to pursue diversification, either through acquisition or by developing new products and services to sell into new or unfamiliar markets. This can be a high-risk strategy, as the entrepreneur is effectively launching a new business within, or alongside, his existing business. It can put stress on the foundations of the business, on its management team and on its finances.

Properly managed, however, diversification may be a perfectly sensible strategy and complement the existing business in any number of ways. Perhaps the new business will help develop new customers for the existing business? Perhaps the new business will give more control over the supply chain? Perhaps it will simply alter the cash flow profile of the business and ease its financing. There is a plethora of possibilities.

As David Molian cautions, the key is to not diversify too early: "Growing a business is primarily about overcoming the barriers to growth, one of which is expanding too quickly into areas that are outside the core expertise of the business. Most businesses that grow successfully tend to identify a niche in which they can excel, and develop their business fully within that niche before they start to move outside it."

Some companies find it easier to diversify than others. These tend to be larger businesses with strong brands and loyal consumer followings. Virgin and easyGroup, for example, prove that a strong brand can facilitate a company's ability to diversify. But if you do not have the brand power of Virgin or easyGroup, you need to consider the many risks involved. The biggest of these may be financial risk, but reputational risk may not be far behind.

However, diversification of one sort or another is sometimes a necessity rather than an option. Perhaps the market for your existing product or service is saturated, or competitor innovation has impacted demand. British Airways responded to easyJet by creating Go Fly (known simply as 'Go'). It ended up being merged into easyJet in 2002. Yellow Pages responded to internet search by developing Yell.com. Another good example of diversification through necessity is Eastman Kodak, known to many as Kodak, a multinational US corporation in the photography and printing fields. It's a story worth telling.

Kodak moments

Faced with its core business of print and film being disrupted by technological shifts in 2000, Eastman Kodak vowed to become a market leader in digital cameras. A change in strategy was implemented. The new approach focused on the production and sale of digital cameras and a move from paper to pixels. And, while Kodak's change in strategy did generate substantial market share alongside Sony (with $5.7 billion revenues in 2005), their strategy was flawed.

Firstly, they had reacted far too slowly to the digital revolution. Acting like the stereotypical large corporation with a lack of agility and a lack of urgency, they didn't give themselves enough time to dominate the market before a huge array of competitors joined in the race for market share.

Secondly, the 60% margins that the company had enjoyed from its core printing and film businesses simply weren't materialising within the new digital model.

With the old core business declining ever more rapidly, this meant that – despite their initially impressive digital camera sales – another strategic rethink was needed.

Having joined the company as COO in 2003 and led the initial move towards the digital sector, Antonio Perez realised that a strategic focus on product innovation simply wasn't enough, nor was the company's model of doing everything in-house (something which it had done for 120 years – comprising everything along the chain from manufacturing to retail).

His vision was no longer to lead the market in digital cameras and film, but to lead the field in digital image products and services overall by helping consumers to organise their digital photo libraries. The strategy aligned to that vision was to commercialise existing innovative technologies and make them more accessible, focus on new product and service innovation and create a cultural change within the company. His supporting tactics were to collaborate with other companies, restructure personnel, create in-house think tanks and create a whole host of products and services from online photo sharing and mobile phone sensors to retail kiosks and rapid scanning.

Another strategic shift involved the tactic of focusing on making strategic alliances work. Collaboration had been an area that hadn't paid off in the past, but Perez began to set up effective alliances with the likes of Motorola, Adobe, Microsoft and Amazon.

Rebels with a cause

After being promoted to CEO in May 2005, Perez began to take a more urgent approach in spearheading this transformation. He had already closed film factories and shed 27,000 jobs, whilst starting to invest in digital technologies. But the new digital initiatives and core business areas were performing at odds with one another, as the digital camera operations had been placed within the traditional part of the business in order to share resources. Perez realised the two areas of business should be split in order to give the digital business room to breathe, so he made that change.

Still, he realised he needed to do more. Firstly he summoned the leading executives for a 'no turning back' meeting where he told them they'd "have to burn the boats", and shift direction entirely in order to commercialise their technology and create new digital services. Having already recognised that product innovation alone was insufficient, he began to replace the company's executives with those who had digital experience. He also assembled a committee of sceptics called the R Group (the 'R' stood for 'Rebels'). It was their role to suggest improvements, discuss strategy and figure out what new digital services could be created. An inclusive feeling of importance led this sceptical group to work hard on their new role, creating winning ideas and spreading the word to others about the credibility of the changes.

Kodak's product innovation has seemingly paid off. They now boast everything from digital picture frames and photo gifts, such as photo books and custom cards, through to pocket cameras that take high definition videos and photos that can be uploaded to YouTube, Flickr, Facebook and Kodak Gallery (formerly Ofoto, acquired in 2001) with a built-in share button. In 2005 Perez predicted that "[i]n two to three years, this will be seen as one of the most successful transformations in the history of our country."

Four years later the results were significant. "We delivered," said Perez. "Our momentum is returning and our strategy is paying off."

Twice in short succession Kodak had to diversify to survive. After the second attempt, the company generated significant traction with its key digital businesses, achieved sustainable operational improvements, improved earnings substantially, and ended 2009 with more than $2 billion in cash on its balance sheet.

Nimble and agile – the beauty of the SME

Smaller businesses benefit from built-in flexibility and agility, so change can happen quickly in SMEs. The main disadvantages they face are typically a lack of resources, a lack of time and financial constraints.

Espotting needed to be small and nimble in order to change direction when required. When they decided to sell up and shift strategy they had to do so quickly. Not only did they have to act fast, they also had to think big.

Julie Meyer sums up her approach which focuses on three key factors that smaller businesses should adopt in order to create a winning yet flexible strategy: *think big, start small, move fast.*

"That's my mantra," she explains. "Because if you ever stop thinking big as an entrepreneur it's over; that's what you're meant to do as an entrepreneur and that's why you're running a high-growth business. But you can start small today compared to say ten years ago, when the cost of technology was higher and you had to raise more money and so forth.

"What's more, companies have to be able to fail fast, because failing fast is learning fast. Some things don't work and you have to be able to assess that in the market and know when to persist and when to change and adopt a different strategy. If something doesn't work, that's fine. The most important thing is that you learned something; what did you learn? Move forward."

As an SME it's easier to learn and move on. And as an SME it's easier to strike the right balance between focus and flexibility. So, when you've developed your strategy and uncovered your competitive advantage, it's time to make a plan. That's where we're heading in Chapter 4.

Top tips

- **Be aware of the need for flexibility** in your business.

- **Regularly review your strategy** and track your KPIs.

- **Build strong foundations and robust processes.** Shifting direction is easier from a stable and solid base.

- **Assess new opportunities and threats** based on their relevance to your long-term vision and strategy.

- **Focus primarily on your 'competitive advantage'** and on doing what you do well. Only diversify once the core of your business is sound.

- **Remember that diversification can be difficult and dangerous.** Be careful when you leave your comfort zone.

- **Act swiftly and decisively** and be prepared to fail and shift strategy.

- **Allocate sufficient resources to new activities and projects.** Don't take them on if you have to skimp and save.

- **Don't run out of cash!**

CHAPTER 4
Business Planning

"Business, more than any occupation, is a continual dealing with the future; it is a continual calculation, an instinctive exercise in foresight."

— Henry R. Luce

Foresight, not oversight

There's nothing quite like a plan, and every business has one. Whether it's in the mind of the entrepreneur, a hastily written to-do list or a more traditional document, it's the plan that dictates what happens in a business everyday.

For a start-up entrepreneur, with no need for funding, one might be tempted to think that writing a formal plan is a waste of time, an unwelcome diversion of energy that could better be directed at, well, just doing it! You might be right. In certain cases, the idea is so crystal clear, the business model so simple, the demand so high, the profits so huge, that 'just doing it' may be the order of the day.

Indeed, some entrepreneurs dismiss the need for a formal business plan, with some outstanding business leaders allegedly shunning them entirely.

"I spent many years at Virgin," says Bill Morrow, founder of Angels Den, "and there's no way that [Sir] Richard would write a plan. He couldn't have sat still; he just wanted to get on with it."

In Sir Richard's case, it is perhaps not beyond the realm of possibility that others helped him develop the more detailed plans around his insightful entrepreneurial vision. In his book *Screw It, Let's Do It*, he talks about always carrying a notepad to write down his thoughts and new ideas, using mentors and coaches to help him with his work, and surrounding himself with good people. His passion, he says, is for leading teams and sharing the rewards. It sounds like a great combination.

So, why would you bother with a formal business plan?

There are a number of reasons.

Lighting the way

"Passion and drive make an entrepreneur. The very last thing you want to do is to write a business plan," says Bill Morrow, "but it's an important process."

And it is. Over the years I have witnessed many examples of potentially great ideas falling by the wayside through the lack of a coherent plan or roadmap. I have seen businesses start up and spend significant sums, only to find that insufficient research had been carried out and their business model was fundamentally flawed.

So barring the odd 'no brainer', the general rule is that if you fail to plan, you plan to fail. Apart from anything else, this is because a properly executed business-planning process will make you consider a host of issues that might otherwise slip under the radar.

Contrary to some entrepreneurial thinking, planning need not dampen drive or hamper creativity or passion. Indeed, planning can be an illuminating and inspiring part of the business-building process, as research leads to new ideas and, occasionally, that elusive eureka moment!

Jane Khedair, author of *Successful Business Plans* and founder and MD of Business Plan Services, believes that business plans are a fundamental part of the management process: "It brings a management team round a table and gets them talking. It helps them understand where they've come from, assess where they're going and how they're going to get there. It enables them to identify opportunities and strengths, which can then be built upon."

Business planning is not only good for the management team. Once complete, the key elements of the plan can be communicated and shared with all of the staff in the business. This will help instil a sense of purpose and engender loyalty to the cause, perhaps even passion!

Another powerful reason for having a business plan is that it creates a stake in the ground and a roadmap which gives guidance and can be followed. If you choose to take an alternative route, which from time to time will be both inevitable and desirable, the business plan will be there to remind you that you are changing your approach. It will prompt you to evaluate and justify your actions. Without a plan, many businesses simply drift from one unfocused activity to another, not really understanding what they are doing and why.

Fortunately, a carefully researched roadmap can provide focus, prevent business drift and reduce risk. It will help entrepreneurs and their teams to prioritise, set and achieve their goals.

But what about flexibility? What if you need to change your plan?

Business plans should not be written and put in the bottom drawer. They are living documents that need reviewing and updating on a regular basis, enabling you to focus on the right priorities at the right time and moving each area and function of your business towards your chosen goals.

Clarity of purpose

Business plans come in many shapes and sizes. They can also be written for a number of different audiences or purposes. It's important to consider what you are trying to achieve.

A strategic plan may focus on high-level options and key priorities. A financing plan may focus on sales, profit and loss and cash flow. An operational plan may look at responsibilities, targets and milestones. In addition, plans may be for internal or external consumption. Whatever the need, it should be identified clearly at the outset, with the readers' requirements being adequately anticipated.

Irrespective of external requirements, sustaining competitive advantage and focusing on continuous improvement are the key drivers of long-term business success. Spending intelligently and having the available capital and knowledge to take advantage of opportunities as they arise are also critical success factors. A good internal business plan will help you tick all of these boxes by enabling you to:

- **benchmark** your performance by comparing actual results against those set out in the plan

- **improve** your performance through analysis and assessment of resources, processes, operations and competencies

- **set targets** and KPIs and assess how you will resource, measure and achieve them

- **estimate** the time and money you'll need to reach your objectives and how best to invest your capital

- **define and understand** the opportunities, risks and rewards and how you will leverage these to maximise your opportunities

- **have confidence** in your management and decision-making processes.

For the purposes of this chapter, we will focus on the full business plan, designed to cover every aspect of a company's activities, and often used by start-ups and growth businesses to help raise external finance.

Building your firepower

Before you start documenting your plan, you will need to carry out detailed research and amass your supporting evidence. Without knowledge and understanding, it is impossible to evaluate, benchmark, define or establish anything.

For example, if you are writing a business plan to raise equity finance, your plan will essentially be selling the opportunity; pitching valid reasons why an investor should invest, and providing a compelling rationale. If the investor has to ask too many questions, the implication is that the plan is deficient. The plan will therefore need both depth and detail.

"You need to have market data, competitor analysis and facts that back up your assumptions and financial projections," advises James Caan.

If you believe that your business has the potential to be a strong player or even a market leader in a particular area, you'll need to demonstrate not only how you intend to grab that market share, but why the totality of your proposition is good enough to achieve it. You will therefore need to research and provide factual data about your product or service and your customers and competitors, as well as about your business as a whole. Here are just a few of the questions you might need to address:

About you

- What is your strategy to get to the centre of the market and acquire market share?

- What experience do you and your management team have in the market? Are your track records good?

- Is your business properly constituted, effectively structured and ready to take external investment?

- Does your business have robust operational and administrative processes?

- Does your business have strong financial management?

- Does the past performance of your business, if any, give credence to your future plans and projections?

- Does your product or service have longevity and is your supply chain secure?

- Are your pricing and margins at satisfactory and sustainable levels?

- What's in it for those who buy your product or service? What particular benefits define your offering?

- Which particular pain are you relieving and for whom?

- Why are you better than your competitors?

- What factors give you your competitive advantage?

The market/customers

- Who are your customers? Are you B2B or B2C, or both?

- What is the profile of your perfect customer?

- Are you serving a niche market or a broader market? If niche, will there be sufficient demand?

- Is the market growing, declining or static? What are the recent and forecasted trends for the market?

- Where do customers go to buy products or services like yours?

- What do customers feel about existing offerings (yours and your competitors)?

- What is the level of demand for your offering and what is the potential for this to increase in the future?

- What is your unique selling proposition (USP)?

- What share of the market are you targeting? Why is it achievable?

- How accessible are your customers and how do/can you reach them?

- How often do they buy goods and services such as yours?

- Why do they buy?

Review the buying and spending habits of your target audience alongside their expectations around quality, price and service. Find out what their core wants and needs are. Are they predominantly impulse buyers and bargain hunters or are they driven by status when making purchasing decisions?

Competitors

- Who is succeeding in your market and why?

- What do they offer? And, more importantly, what *don't* they offer? Seek out underserved segments and gaps in the market that you might fill.

- Are any of your competitors obviously overcharging or under-delivering?

- What about levels of quality and service?

- How do your competitors communicate with your target market?

- Who are your competitors' biggest customers and partners? Can you break in?

- Who supplies them and distributes for them?

- How will you beat them and grow your market share?

Gathering this information needs to be thorough but there are plenty of tools to assist you in your data-gathering endeavours. Internet search is a good starting point, but there are a host other sources.

Try competitors' websites, Chamber of Commerce directories, trade association literature and press, public filings, online forums, marketing collateral, trade shows and your own network of contacts. Look for industry statistics, press features, news stories and bestselling product lists.

Consider looking at international markets to see what's happening elsewhere. Use Google Alerts and Google News Alerts to receive links to news pieces and websites containing your competitors' brand names and activities. Try traditional yellow pages and online directories and places you would advertise your own business to seek out and learn about your competition.

If you need more, consider accessing specialist market research reports from Euromonitor, Mintel, Keynote or the *Economist* Intelligence Unit to uncover your competitors' share of specific markets. Are they featured as a key player in those reports? Is their market share revealed in them or in other PR material?

Who writes the plan?

Ultimately, a combination of desktop research and primary research can be used to gather data.

And once you have completed your research in these and other areas, it's time to start thinking about writing your plan. This leads on to another question – who should actually write it? Should it be the entrepreneur and the management team or an external third-party expert? There are differing views on this.

Some believe that third parties should not write the plan because, no matter how much they consult with the entrepreneur or his or her team, they simply can't know the business inside out.

On the other side of the fence, those in the business of writing business plans believe that, as long as they consult adequately, they can gather enough information and insight to shape a successful plan and, more importantly, challenge or validate the assumptions made by the business.

My own view is that whilst the entrepreneur and his team need to be wholly immersed in the planning process, and ultimately need to own and live the plan, it is generally beneficial to get a third-party specialist on board. The only exception to this is where the business has its own proven capability in this area.

Jane Khedair, who writes other people's business plans for a living, agrees that "people should be involved in writing their own plan."

"We certainly work with our clients on a very interactive basis. Yes, we're doing a lot of the physical hard work but it's always with the client's input. It's important that their vision for the business is clearly understood by whoever is writing the document and clearly reflected and challenged in the output. The value we bring to the process is in adding a third-party perspective."

Content is king

One of the reasons that entrepreneurs don't relish the process of writing a business plan is because it can be a daunting task. However, it can be perfectly manageable if you focus on it section by section.

As Coffee Republic founder Bobby Hashemi says in *Anyone Can Do It*, "You can eat an elephant if you approach it one bite at a time."

In any case, you don't want to overdo it. Nobody wants to read a 100-page document, so they probably won't. A business plan needs to convince you, your team and/or your backers that your business is viable, your opportunity is exciting and your projections are realistic. No more, no less.

"It is possible to include too much information in a business plan, especially when it's for the bank," says James Nicholson-Smith, director at the FD Centre, a company that provides part-time finance directors to SMEs. "The point of a business plan is to provide core information about the business in a clear and concise way. It's quite possible that the reader will want to know more, but that's no bad thing. After all, the relationship manager [if the business plan is for a bank] is going to need something to justify his arrangement fee!"

So how long should a business plan be?

Advice on this varies widely.

Peter Jones, the telecoms entrepreneur, says that "a compelling business plan can be written in three pages". Meanwhile, Angels Den founder Bill Morrow says it depends on the sector – but that their business plan template is eight pages long. Jane Khedair suggests it should be no longer than 20 sides of A4 plus 6–12 pages of financials. Any longer than that, and it's less likely to be read.

Whatever the final outcome, a business plan shouldn't be a chore, either to read or write.

One reason to avoid spending months on crafting a business plan is due to the changing nature of the business environment in general. Business plans, like strategies, need to be responsive and flexible. There's little point investing a huge amount of time into a plan that becomes redundant or outdated before it's finished. The reality is, that even when it *is* finished, a business plan is always a work in progress. It should evolve and adapt with your business, responding to changes in market conditions.

With our detailed research undertaken, it's time to start writing our plan. Long or short, there is a relatively established methodology. You'll probably end up including some or all of the following sections ...

Executive summary

As its name implies, the executive summary gives a brief overview of everything that follows. It is akin to Peter Jones's three pager (or less), so it should be designed to stand on its own. It will deliver the main headlines and enable any reader to immediately understand the purpose of the plan as well as any financing sought. Apart from outlining this purpose, the content should include a brief company history and track record, a summary of the market, the opportunity and the competition, details of your key management team and some summarised financial information. If the plan's purpose is to seek equity investment, the exit strategy should also be discussed.

Be aware that many people decide whether or not to read the entire plan on the basis of the quality of the executive summary, so make sure it's compelling and clear.

Here's a tip – writing a draft version of the executive summary at the outset can be a great idea. Whilst you'll need to revisit it later on, 'beginning at the end' can provide some real clarity and focus.

The business: history/model/opportunity/future plans and goals

This section describes who you are, where you've come from, what you do and where you're heading. It will summarise the history, achievements and current position of the business, as well as its ownership structure. It will also outline the future opportunity. This opportunity, and how you will access it, will typically be the main focus of the overall plan.

Your business strategy and action plan

This explains your vision and strategy, as well as the tactics you will use to move the business forward. It will focus on the strength of the business (i.e. its strong foundations) and explain the opportunity that the management team wish to pursue. It will outline the benefits of pursuing the opportunity (e.g. developing a new product, accessing a new market, acquiring another business, commencing international operations) and consider the benefits and risks involved.

Your team and management structure

This section specifies the skills, credentials and experience that you, your team and your advisors have, as well as any recruitment, training and retention plans that you have or intend to put in place. The management team is considered by investors and lenders as the key factor in any business plan. They believe, quite rightly, that the ultimate success of the business will depend on the skill and experience of this team. Intended management changes and succession planning should also be covered here.

Your operations and administration

This outlines your premises and production facilities, your assets, and the IT and management systems that help with the smooth running of your business. It also defines the mechanisms, processes and reporting systems you have in place to track, control and improve your performance.

Your products and services

This describes your products and/or services, including your value proposition and USP – why customers buy from you and why you are (or will be) successful. It will also consider how products are sourced or manufactured, as well as the product or service life cycle.

The market

This contains market research detailing the market size and your existing/potential market share in specific sectors; it identifies key trends and drivers in your sector, including windows of opportunity and chances to increase your market share. It considers wider trends in the market and how these may affect your business in the future. It profiles your competition, their share of the market and your customers/target audience. Essentially, it compares your business to other existing and potential competing businesses, and defines your competitive 'unfair' advantage.

Your marketing plan

This includes the methods you'll use to reach, attract and retain your customers. It outlines your positioning in the market, how you are pricing and promoting your products and/or services, where and how you will drive future sales and how you will deliver excellence and after-sales customer service. It also outlines details of any strategic alliances or distribution partners.

SWOT analysis

This provides an analysis of your main strengths, weaknesses, opportunities and threats. It explains how you will reduce risk by tackling threats and overcoming weaknesses and what you are doing in order to seize opportunities and play to your strengths.

Financial statements and forecasts

This summarises historic and forecasted financial information, including integrated profit, cash flow and balance sheet forecasts for the next (say) 36 months. It considers any financial issues or changes arising either in the existing market or as a result of pursuing the new opportunity. It details banking and financing arrangements and sets out the required funding and how it will be used. Typically it allows for funding headroom – an unspecified amount to be added to the fund raising – to cover uncertainty and contingencies. The key here is to convince investors and/or lenders that you will not run out of cash.

Appendices

These provide CVs of key team members, organisation charts, product literature, key contracts and details of IP protection. They can also provide more detailed financial analysis, market research reports or other relevant information.

SWOT

'SWOT' analysis, mentioned a moment ago, has become a hot topic of late. It's divided opinion, with some discrediting the analysis and others deeming it as an imperative for inclusion in any plan.

SWOT is an abbreviation of 'Strengths, Weaknesses, Opportunities and Threats'. A SWOT analysis is a strategic planning method that is intended to identify the internal and external factors that are favourable or unfavourable to a particular business venture or project. The findings can be used to help decision-making and increase competitive advantage. Certainly, one of the principal merits of the SWOT analysis is its simplicity.

Strengths and weaknesses are internal factors. For example, strengths may consist of your specialist expertise in a certain area, a well-known and well-perceived brand, a patent on a particular product or a skilled and loyal workforce. Weaknesses, on the other hand, might include poor financial reporting systems, a lack of technical expertise or resources, reliance on a small number of customers or reliance on temporary (and less loyal) staff.

Opportunities and threats are external factors. So opportunities might include increased potential demand for your products due to technological advances or a key competitor going bust. Threats could include a new competitor entering the market, a potential disruption in your supply chain or perhaps currency volatility which might impact your margins.

According to the *Economist*, there is another analysis that should co-exist with SWOT: "A second four-letter acronym is sometimes brought into play here: USED. How can the Strengths be *Used*; the Weaknesses be *Stopped*, the

Opportunities be *Exploited*; and the Threats be *Defended* against?" [emphasis added]

SWOT's the problem?

SWOT analysis *does* have its critics.

"SWOT analysis can be very subjective," says the *Economist*. "Two people rarely come up with the same version of a SWOT analysis even when given the same information about the same business and its environment. Accordingly, SWOT analysis is best used as a guide and not a prescription. Adding and weighting criteria to each factor increases the validity of the analysis."

Depending on the economic cycle, strengths can occasionally turn into weaknesses and vice versa. For example, you may list having a skilled and loyal workforce as a particular strength. During boom times, this would certainly be the case. However, during times of recession, if staff cuts need to be made, this could be deemed a weakness. Perhaps you should have considered a balance between long-term employed staff and shorter-term contract staff?

Jane Khedair sees SWOT as more fundamentally flawed. In her view, the analysis is far too textbook. "I think the SWOT analysis is a very academic approach and not particularly relevant in modern day business planning," she says. She doesn't include SWOT in her business plans.

My take on SWOT is that it can serve a useful purpose. It is a simple technique that helps businesses to consider how they can improve their operations and maximise opportunities while also identifying and dealing with areas of weakness. In carrying out this analysis, entrepreneurs can quickly evaluate their own businesses and the wider market.

Presenting SWOT in a business plan

If you've done a SWOT analysis, consider how this should be reflected in your business plan, particularly in relation to your identified weaknesses and threats. Some believe that, if you are creating a selling document, you shouldn't expose factors that might undermine the possibility of a successful outcome. They believe that this kind of transparency can be unhelpful and prejudicial.

Many, including me, would disagree with this approach, saying that it's far better to disclose potential threats and weaknesses and how you will deal with them. Such openness should help to build trust with investors or lenders and avoid unpleasant surprises or confrontations later on.

In my experience, investors are particularly adverse to two things: wasting their money and wasting their time. They don't particularly relish the idea of going through a time-consuming and often expensive due diligence process, only to discover that key data or problems have been hidden from them or glossed over, or that they've been misled or misinformed.

This is a topic that we'll review in more detail in Chapter 5 on raising finance.

Show me the money

What about valuation? If you are raising equity should you include your valuation of the business in your plan? Jane Khedair rarely does so.

"This surprises most people," Jane admits, "but we would rarely put a valuation in a business plan. We'd work with a client to gain a clearer understanding of the valuation of the business, but without documenting that, because again that's spoon feeding an investor who might come in at quite a different valuation to the one that's been identified by the client company."

Business valuation is an uncertain science and this can be a sensible approach to take. Beauty is in the eye of the beholder, and whatever valuation you put in your document it's likely to do you a disservice. By attaching a number, high or low, you can bet your bottom dollar that an investor will negotiate you down. If you've already priced it too low, you will be shooting yourself in the foot. On the other hand, over-enthusiastic pricing, often accompanied by hockey-stick-like financial projections, will most likely see your potential investor disappear in a puff of smoke.

As an entrepreneur, Seb Bishop has some sage advice for investors: "If you speak to any entrepreneur, they usually put numbers down that give them the right valuation. It serves its purpose for raising capital. Do they necessarily believe those numbers? If they put their hand on their heart? Not all the time. They put the best numbers that give them the best valuation at the point when they're trying to raise the capital."

So beware using valuations in business plans. They will rarely benefit you or your potential investors. If an investor is interested in your business, and you are interested in having them as a partner, a fair valuation will emerge over time. Ultimately, this is likely to be a lower figure than you would like to accept and a higher figure than your investor wants to pay.

Know your numbers

Just as you need good data to evidence your opportunity and likely future success, you'll be expected to have a good understanding and a strong grip on your finances. Lenders and investors will only be prepared to offer you funding if they can see a clear way of getting it back!

The BBC's *Dragons' Den* has famously flagged up this issue by focusing on the frequent lack of financial knowledge demonstrated by those pitching for investment on the show. When asked a simple question – 'What was your turnover last year?', for instance – it's alarming how often entrepreneurs lack the knowledge of such rudimentary figures. This generates an immediate and standard response from the dragons – "I'm out."

It's therefore crucial to have robust and supportable financial information in your business plan, and also crucial that you understand it. It may be that another member of your team, perhaps your finance director or your external advisor, has assisted in the preparation of the information. But you should understand all of the key figures and how they have been derived.

It is amazing how easy it is to pick holes in financial figures. With modern spreadsheet techniques and templates, it's not difficult to fill in the forms. But it's often the assumptions or what has not been thought of that causes the problems.

I once had a client with a 'no brainer' (unwritten) plan to import a particular item of clothing that they were going to be able to source and deliver far more cheaply than any other visible competition. With a price point just below that of their competitors, they were sure to sell shed loads of their product at incredible margins. The profits would be obscene! After making trips overseas, negotiating supply agreements and considering sales plans, all involving weeks and weeks of work, we were finally asked to look at the numbers. It didn't take long to identify that the business had completely underestimated its freight charges and simply forgotten to allow for import duties. The impact of these two discoveries decimated the margin and made the business model marginal. Needless to say, the business never went ahead, giving credence to the old adage – 'If it looks too good to be true, it probably is!'

Another golden rule in business is that everything always takes longer and costs more than you think it will. Notwithstanding this, passionate entrepreneurs are prone to demonstrating astounding over-confidence about the likely levels of demand for their product. This can lead to the ultimate business sin – running out of cash.

So, when it comes to your financial forecasting, how optimistic should you be?

A question of balance

As we've already seen in previous chapters, business success is generally all about balance – balance between strategic flexibility and focus, balance between short-term and long-term objectives, balance between profitability and growth. Financial forecasting also comes down to achieving balance. This time, it's balance between optimism, pessimism and realism.

So how do you get your forecasts right? The very nature of the words 'forecast', 'projection' and 'assumption' create uncertainty, striking terror into the hearts of mere mortals! By definition, forecasts are predictions based on assumptions. Whilst they may be anchored by historic data, they can never be right and they can never be 100% relied upon.

Most investors know that long-term forecasts rarely come true and are usually over-optimistic. As Seb Bishop points out, future forecasts are often taken with a pinch of salt, especially when the numbers have been prepared to secure investment.

One of the measures an investor will look at in considering your business is your past performance and how this compared against your earlier forecasts. In the entrepreneurial world, investors find that past performance is often a good guide to the future. In addition, investors will look at your performance against your forecast during the time they are considering investing in your business or whilst carrying out their due diligence. This is not a good time to be missing your immediate forecasts, as your credibility will be severely undermined.

So how do you get the balance right – optimistic enough to capture the attention of lenders and investors but realistic enough to actually deliver on?

"What I've always done in the past is prepare three versions," says Julia Hoare, company secretary of ?What If!, the innovations company, who always recommends that entrepreneurs do the first draft of each of these versions before giving them to accountants to review or fine-tune. These three versions should be flexed to give a range of outcomes, namely: realistic, optimistic and pessimistic.

After building in the most expected outcome, based on the history of what has gone before, it's then a case of flexing your initial assessment and considering different scenarios and outcomes.

Modelling reality

Assumptions are all important. It's not just about monthly sales and margins. Flexed plans should allow for a range of possible scenarios. If, for example, your sales are US dollar-based, volatility in the sterling/US dollar exchange rate may significantly affect your profitability. Alternatively, debtor collection forecasts may be too optimistic, resulting in unwelcome cash flow pressures. Just as blue-sky potential should be considered in your financial forecasts, so should the more negative possibilities and outcomes.

"Identify some likely sensitivity factors," suggests the FD Centre business development director, James Nicholson-Smith. "For example, 10% fewer sales or 30-day shorter supplier credit terms. Then run alternative scenarios that will impact on the repayment of bank facilities. This shows the bank (or investor) a potential worst-case scenario."

Ultimately, while forecasts should aim to be as realistic as possible, they will change as the business grows, and become less reliable over time.

Justifying the numbers

Some people think a business plan is simply a set of numbers. Hopefully, the contents of this chapter have now dispelled that myth. It is often forgotten that the numbers are the product of the plan, and that the plan is in the narrative.

So says Jane Khedair: "It's easy to window dress the figures. Anybody can put together a financial model with a hockey-stick implication to it. It's the story behind the numbers which is more important. There needs to be validation of the business opportunity, which is reflected by the market size and how you're going to penetrate that market. The figures need to be able to withstand challenges based on the narrative in the document, but nobody is going to put a gun against your head and hold you to them anyway."

Fundamentally, you need to show that the opportunity you are seeking actually exists and that you have created a sensible plan to grasp it. This should be backed up by solid evidence which supports the assumptions in your plan.

"It's not how do you get your assumptions right?" says business author Tony Fish, "It's how do you justify your assumptions? That's way more important, because there is no right assumption."

Tony says that's why he runs Mash Up (events that debate the key issues affecting digital businesses). He finds that in giving people the same base data, everybody makes a series of different assumptions and comes out with different answers. "None of the answers are right or wrong," he adds.

In fact, Tony says he's "never to-date seen a business actually hit its plan." They either exceed or fall short of their expectations, but very rarely match them. Sitting on his shelf is the Vodafone business plan when it came out of Racal. "At perpetuity their plan said there'd be 187,000 handsets in the UK market," he laughs. In 2008, handset numbers in Great Britain exceeded 75 million. "No," he says, "I've never seen a plan hit."

So in general terms, it's best to go for balance in your business and in your projections. Balance is believable and balance is common sense. A well-thought-out and well-balanced business plan will help you achieve your goals.

"I think it's balance that makes business so interesting," says Bobby Hashemi. "On one hand as an entrepreneur and a leader you need to be optimistic, you need to believe in the business, in yourself, in the team and your future – despite the turbulence around you and the competition. At the same time, when it comes to the financials of the business, you need to be very prudent and avoid wishful thinking. Keeping those balances are what makes a successful business. A business that has optimism in its soul, is customer-centric, is focused on high growth in the future; yet at the same time behind the scenes is run conservatively and tightly."

Which brings us neatly on to the importance of sound financial management...

Top tips

- **Business planning is an important and valuable process.** Don't be tempted to ignore it.

- Your business plan, or key points from it, should be **shared with all of the staff in your business.** This will instil a sense of purpose and engender loyalty.

- Be aware of who you are writing your business plan for, and why, to **ensure that the content is relevant and fulfils its objectives**.

- **Dig deep into your business and its offerings**, as well as your market and competition.

- **Consider using SWOT analysis** to identify the key issues facing your business.

- **Turn disadvantage to advantage** – highlight your internal weaknesses and external business threats and explain how you will deal them.

- **Know your numbers.** Be diligent. Prepare at least three versions of your forecasts: realistic, optimistic and pessimistic.

- **Beware using valuations in business plans.** They are rarely of benefit.

- **Justify your assumptions and forecast outcomes** with a clear narrative, supported by relevant, factual data.

- **Keep business plans concise, clear and compelling.** Use appendices to provide detailed information.

CHAPTER 5
Practical Financial Management

"Cash flow is everything."

– Simon Woodroffe, Yo! Sushi

Keeping the financial score

Businesses don't go bust because of a lack of profitability. They go bust because they run out of cash!

Sadly, many entrepreneurial businesses fail in their start-up and development phases and even mature businesses succumb from time to time. There are many reasons for this. Some businesses simply have poor strategies. Some are overtaken by the advance of technology. Others have poor management, often particularly evident in the financial area where entrepreneurial businesses can be prone to minimising or cutting 'back office' costs to the bone. Beware! This kind of penny pinching can often be fatal.

So while entrepreneurs are often 100% focused on achieving their wider goals, someone needs to be responsible for keeping the financial score.

It's worth remembering that it's not just bad businesses that run out of cash. As we have already identified, many early stage entrepreneurial businesses are consumers of cash. And, perhaps counter intuitively, cash flow difficulties can just as easily arise from rising as opposed to falling sales. Believe it or not, falling sales can often drive more cash into a business.

So cash is king! This may be a cliché but only because it's true. In order to build sustainable businesses, entrepreneurs must live by this mantra. They must effectively manage their cash in order to build firm foundations and keep their organisations in good financial shape.

In order to do this effectively, it's not just the management of the incoming and outgoing cash that needs close attention. It's also the management and control of a raft of other financial data. Effective financial management should not just help a business to survive. It should help it to grow and prosper.

"Fundamentally, a business must be able to understand and monitor its financial dynamics," says Giles Murphy, head of assurance and business services at financial services group Smith & Williamson. "This requires up-to-date, relevant and accurate management information which can be compared against budgets and comparatives from previous years."

In this chapter, we'll consider the basics of practical financial management, how you can keep control, what you need to monitor on a regular basis and how you can keep your bank manager on side. We'll also look at some regularly used financial ratios and phrases.

While the generation and preservation of cash will always be the number one priority for all businesses, they also need to consider how to invest in the future. The entrepreneurial business therefore needs to establish a balance between investing in growth, managing costs and, for most established businesses, maintaining and improving profitability.

In order to achieve this in your business, you will need a clear understanding of your current and future finances, including:

- the basics – recording and tracking your results

- budgeting and forecasting

- management information and key performance indicators

- key financial ratios and phrases

- protecting your assets

- focusing on profit

- collecting your debts

- keeping the bank on side

- investing in the future.

So let's examine each of these…

The basics – recording and tracking your results

A business that doesn't understand its financial position is flying blind. To many, this may seem irresponsible, but it's amazing how often it occurs. Such a business generally has no basis on which to make decisions, no ability to commit future investment and no understanding of what activity or issue will eventually cause it to fail, apart from the inevitable absence of cash.

Sometimes this unhappy state of affairs results from an accounting breakdown, a people or systems failure of such magnitude that basic accounting information is either unavailable or completely unreliable. Sometimes it arises as a result of fraud and the deliberate manipulation of financial information. And sometimes, perhaps most frequently, it arises because of a lack of understanding of the critical importance of the finance function, resulting in under-resourcing or the employment of unqualified staff, or both.

If you feel threatened by any of these, or don't know enough about your finance function to know whether you feel threatened, it's time to take a look. Here are some of the basics:

Bookkeeping

Every business should keep what are often referred to as 'proper books of account'. Before computers, these were real books that were used to record your cash inflows and outflows, your fixed assets such as plant and equipment, your sales and customer balances (debtors), your purchases and supplier balances (creditors) and, if appropriate, your stock or work in progress. These would enable the regular preparation of management accounts, probably drawn up monthly and typically consisting of a profit and loss account, a balance sheet and a cash flow statement.

These days, technology has simplified the process, enabling the creation of electronic books and records. This has many advantages as well as the odd disadvantage.

I remember the day that I interviewed a lady for an accounts role, asking her to prepare a profit and loss account and balance sheet from a pre-prepared, simple set of transactions. For an experienced operator, this would have taken 15–20 minutes. So after an hour had gone by I thought I would look in on the interviewee. To my consternation, she looked rather puzzled and was staring at the untouched paperwork in a somewhat terrified way. When I asked her whether she had a problem, she said that the profit and loss accounts and balance sheets she prepared in her existing job were the result of keying F6 on her computer!

The moral of the story is clear. Beware of using or relying on unqualified accounts staff who do not understand the figures they are trying to prepare.

The profit and loss account

The profit and loss account does exactly what it says on the tin. It shows all of your revenue, be it from sales, commissions, fees, royalties, rents or interest and sets it against all of the costs and expenses incurred in generating that revenue, giving you a balance which is your profit or loss for the period.

In general, profitable businesses generate cash over time and loss-making businesses consume cash. Ultimately, businesses need to make profits, as opposed to losses, in order to survive.

The balance sheet

The balance sheet gives you a picture of your financial position on a given date of your choosing. Typically this will be at a month or year end, showing your assets and liabilities and the balance between them. In broad terms, if your assets exceed your liabilities, you have some net worth (or net assets) in the business. If your liabilities exceed your assets, you have net liabilities, a situation where you owe more to your creditors than the total of your assets. This can indicate insolvency, so it's important to be aware.

Assets

Assets are generally split into two main categories, as follows:

Fixed assets

These are capital assets that are used by the business to carry out its trade. They typically include tangible assets like freehold or leasehold property, plant and equipment, fixtures and fittings and motor vehicles. These assets are known as fixed assets because they have a permanent presence in the business and are generally not readily turned into cash.

Fixed assets can also include intangibles, such as designs, copyrights, trademarks, patents and goodwill. The accounting treatment of these is beyond the scope of this book but the value of these intangibles often far exceeds the value of the tangible assets mentioned above.

Current assets

These are assets that are or will turn into cash within a relatively short period. They include stock, work in progress, debtors and cash. Ultimately, it is these assets that will feed into your cash flow and enable you to pay your staff and your suppliers.

Liabilities

On the liability side, balance sheets tend to differentiate between short-term creditors (current liabilities) and long-term creditors (creditors due after more than one year or longer-term liabilities), as follows:

Current liabilities

These are liabilities that are due for payment within a shorter time frame, or where payment can be demanded at short notice, such as a bank overdraft. They include your suppliers' invoices and other liabilities, such as taxes on your payroll.

Current liabilities typically consist of the creditors that will be paid from the cash realised from your current assets (see above).

Long-term liabilities

Long-term liabilities are those which are not payable now, but which will have to be paid in due course, typically a year or more from the balance sheet date. Bank loans that are repayable over more than one year are often a feature here, along with other longer-term financing, if this exists.

From the above, it can be seen that the key balance sheet numbers that affect the day-to-day running of your business are your current assets and current liabilities. Together, these form the 'working capital' of your business and determine its continuing ability to trade.

We'll look at financial ratios later in this chapter. However, the relationship between current assets and current liabilities is regarded as a key determinant of solvency. If your current liabilities exceed your current assets, where will the cash come from to pay for them?

The cash flow

Cash flow documents are typically forward-looking forecasts. However, some businesses prepare historic cash flow statements, showing the source of funds generated and how they have been spent. These statements can be useful to explain the reasons for increases or decreases in cash balances in your business. For example, if your debtor balances increase, this tends to consume cash, unless creditor balances increase by a similar amount. From this, it can be seen that slower debtor collection and faster creditor payment can create a double whammy from a cash flow perspective.

Historic cash flow statements will also show your expenditure on fixed assets, details of repayments of loans, tax payments and other useful information, such as new equity or debt funding.

Budgeting and forecasting

Sales rise and fall, markets fluctuate. This constant change makes it difficult for a business to cater for all potential eventualities. However, the need for flexibility does not excuse a lack of forward planning – yet many entrepreneurs do not adequately prepare or take the time to understand when shortfalls are likely to appear. This often creates trading and cash flow difficulties.

"What we find in 90% of cases is that entrepreneurs will say, 'Oh no, I've run out of cash … I'd better go and talk to the bank or get some angel funding on board," says Bill Morrow, founder of Angels Den.

"Yet it can take months just to get bank loan documentation together, let alone secure other forms of finance."

We discussed financial forecasting as part of the business-planning process in Chapter 4. The reason for mentioning it again here is that it forms a fundamental part of your financial management process. Businesses should do all they can to plan for the ups and downs in their economic and cash flow cycle.

So, what's the difference between a budget and a forecast, and exactly what do they cover?

The answer to the first part is that there isn't much difference, except that a budget is normally fixed based on expectations at the outset, whereas a forecast is updated to reflect actual financial results and expectations as you go along.

This means that you can compare your actual performance against your original expectations and against your regularly updated forecast expectations. Over time, the forecast becomes reality and the budget becomes history. Generally speaking, the older a budget becomes, the less likely it is to reflect the actual performance of the business.

In terms of content, budgets and forecasts should both consist of integrated profit and loss, balance sheet and cash flow forecasts. The integration is crucial. It proves that the numbers are aligned and identifiable as they flow through from profit-and-loss account to balance sheet and cash flow.

Businesses tend to get better at budgeting and forecasting as they go along, particularly if they have good management accounting processes that deliver accurate financial information. The reason for this is twofold. First, an early stage business that is preparing a budget for the first time is highly unlikely to get it right. There is simply no history, so there's nothing to compare or contrast. In my experience, these budgets tend to overestimate income and underestimate expenditure, often by leaving out particular costs and expenses in their entirety, even though these are bound to arise. Second, the budgeting process simply improves with experience, even in an established business. Like other things in life, the more you practise, the better you get.

So here are some tips on preparing and using budgets and financial forecasts:

Budgeting and forecasting tips

- Use the budgeting process to test your accepted wisdom. Challenge your assumptions or get someone else to question them.

- Consider your track record of meeting budgets. If it's poor, work out what went wrong and avoid making the same mistakes again.

- Remember that profit and loss, balance sheet and cash flow budgets should be fully integrated and reconciled.

- Don't be over-enthusiastic with your sales or income forecasts. No matter how good the product or service, revenue generation or increases in sales can take longer than you think.

- Beware of potential omissions. Have you allowed for payroll and other taxes in your forecasts? What about staff bonuses? Are the legal fees set at an appropriate level or could these be exceeded? Have you allowed for potential currency fluctuations? And what about bad debts?

- Don't forget to allow for potential fixed-asset replacement, loan repayments, hire purchase, and interest costs.

- Round up rather than down when estimating costs, and down rather than up when estimating income.

- Make realistic assumptions around debtor and creditor days and stock movements.

- Build in a contingency and allow headroom to counter unexpected variances or problems.

- Ask yourself what if...? Consider how sensitive your projections might be to external factors. For example, what will happen to your cash requirement if sales growth is less than you expect? Will it go up or will it go down? (That's not a trick question – it could go either way!)

- When presenting the budget to banks or other stakeholders, rehearse well. Try presenting to colleagues or close advisors in the first instance and get them to ask the awkward questions – then have your answers prepared.

- Once prepared, you should regularly review your actual results against your budgets, and update your forecasts with your actual results and new expectations. Where necessary, take corrective action to protect your profits and cash flow.

Management information and key performance indicators (KPIs)

Most businesses prepare management accounts on a monthly (recommended) or less frequent basis. By the time these are delivered and reviewed, valuable time will have passed. This may mean that corrective action is delayed, adversely impacting on future profits and cash flow.

For this reason, many businesses develop systems to monitor their day-to-day progress, rather than waiting for historic information to be presented in their management accounts. These normally take the form of daily or weekly management reports which include financial information and other KPIs to help the management team understand what is happening in the business and to shorten the decision-making process.

The sort of financial information that may be given in these reports varies but will often include some of the following:

- details of daily or weekly sales or billings, often compared to last year, or to budget or forecast

- bank balances, including totals of daily or weekly receipts and payments

- debtor balances – the total owed to the business at the time

- creditor balances – the total owed by the business at the time

- a cash flow forecast – a short-term forecast showing the likely receipts and payments over the next week or month, as well as the resulting bank balance.

This list is by no means exhaustive. Some businesses will also wish to monitor movements in their stock or work in progress, updates on job-costing systems etc. What is clear, however, is that this type of financial snapshot can give management teams some up-to-date insight into what is happening in the business.

In addition to financial information, many businesses develop key performance indicators, also known as KPIs, to help them understand how well they are performing against their goals and objectives.

For example, an airline might measure the number of flights and passengers, the average payload per aircraft, the aircraft utilisation and the food and beverage revenues per passenger. A hotel business might measure room occupancy, food costs, sales per staff head, bookings and function enquiry conversion rates.

An internet business might monitor its search engine ranking, the number of unique visitors to its site, the time spent by visitors in different areas of the site, the server availability percentage, referrals from third party sites, buyer conversion rates and abandonment rates.

These are just a few examples and, clearly, the KPIs selected for each business will differ. At the end of the day, just about everything can be measured.

Key financial ratios and phrases

Ratios

One could fill a book with details of financial ratios, along with a glossary of terms used by accountants and finance professionals. That is not going to happen here. However, no self-respecting guide for entrepreneurs would be complete without a mention of some of the key ratios and phrases that are used by investors, advisors and even by entrepreneurs themselves to describe the performance and characteristics of their businesses.

Here are some of the main ratios:

Current ratio

This measures your current assets against your current liabilities and is a good indicator of solvency, in this case defined by a business's ability to pay its debts as they fall due. The ratio is expressed as the number of times current assets exceed current liabilities. A high ratio tends to indicate financial strength, whereas a number of less than one means that current liabilities exceed current assets, regarded as a generally unhealthy indicator.

Quick ratio (also known as acid test)

This ratio measures your current assets, excluding stock, against your current liabilities. Because of the exclusion of stock from the calculation, it broadly measures the relationship between your debtors, your creditors and your bank balance. In the absence of unusual circumstances, a number greater than one normally indicates financial strength.

Gearing ratio

This measures the long-term liabilities of the business, such as loan capital or other debt, against the shareholders' equity. The higher the ratio, the more dependent the business is on external debt and the more vulnerable it is considered to be.

Gross profit margin

The gross profit margin is commonly used and widely understood. By dividing gross profit by sales, the ratio provides the percentage of profit on sales, after deducting the direct costs of those sales, but before deducting other overheads. In money terms, gross profit is the amount available to pay the overheads. So if gross profit exceeds overheads, then an overall 'net' profit arises.

Net profit margin

The net profit margin is calculated by dividing the net profit by the sales. It shows the percentage of profit earned on sales after deducting all direct costs and overheads.

Return on capital employed

This represents the percentage profit earned on total shareholders' equity. For this purpose shareholders' total equity (i.e. including accumulated profits and reserves) is used, not just the basic share capital. The profit used in the calculation is normally net profit before tax or EBIT (earnings before interest and tax – see later).

Debtor days

This ratio is intended to show how many days' sales are outstanding at any one time. It can be calculated by measuring the debtors against the annual sales and then multiplying the percentage result by 365. Alternatively a 'count back' method can be used, whereby debtors are deducted from the most recent month's sales first, then the previous month and so on, until the debtors have been 'used up'. The number of months it takes to 'use' the debtors then gives a result, such as 2.5 months, or approximately 75 days.

Stock turnover

The stock turnover ratio indicates how many times the stock in the business is being turned over on an annual basis. It is calculated by dividing the cost of sales by the average stock balance. Note that it is the cost of sales figure that is used here, not the sales. This is because stock is generally valued at cost in financial statements.

Interest cover

This ratio is regularly used by banks to calculate the amount they are prepared to lend. It calculates the number of times that the interest on any loans to the business are 'covered' by the profits generated. It is calculated by dividing the profits before interest and tax by the net interest paid or payable. A figure of 2 or more will generally be required.

Price/earnings ratio (P/E ratio)

A measure of value calculated by dividing the price of a share by its earnings. The price/earnings ratio is generally used to compare the value of a business with that of other businesses by contrasting the P/E ratios. This is typically done with companies where the share price is known or quoted on a stock exchange.

These are just a few of the more important ratios. You should be aware of them because they are frequently discussed in meetings with investors and finance providers. Understanding these basic ratios will demonstrate your knowledge and expertise, giving you confidence and providing reassurance in any financial discussions that may take place.

Phrases

And so, on to phrases. There aren't that many you need to worry about, but here are some of the more frequently used ones that may come up from time to time:

- **Annual percentage rate (APR)** – A finance charge expressed as an annual rate.
- **Anti-dilution** – A technique used by investors to protect themselves against losses in the value of their investment in the event of an otherwise dilutive capital raising by a business.
- **Basis point (BP)** – One hundredth of one per cent or 0.01%. Used to express loan and interest rates.

- **BIMBO** – A 'buy-in management buy-out' involving the internal management team and supplemented by additional management brought in from outside.

- **Buy-out** – The purchase or takeover of an existing business.

- **Call option** – A right, but not an obligation, to buy at a predetermined price at some time in the future.

- **Cap** – A credit arrangement whereby the holder is protected against rises in interest rates above a certain level.

- **Collar** – A two-way credit agreement to protect borrowers and lenders from interest rate movements, involving both a cap and a floor. Because a collar protects both parties, it is possible to structure these arrangements on a zero-cost basis.

- **Covenant** – A promise to do or not to do. Typically used by lenders and investors to protect the value of their loans or investments, e.g. not to allow certain balance sheet items or ratios to fall below or exceed an agreed limit.

- **Debenture** – A financial instrument that creates or acknowledges a debt, usually carrying interest and generally secured by the assets of the borrower.

- **EBIT** – Earnings before interest and taxation. A measurement of profit and free cash flow, typically used in capital intensive businesses.

- **EBITDA** – Earnings before interest, taxation, depreciation and amortisation. This is a frequently used phrase and is used as a proxy for free cash flow in most businesses. Purchasers of businesses tend to use EBITDA, as opposed to net profit before tax, as the basis for an offer, applying a multiple to determine the actual offer price.

- **Equity** – The capital introduced by the owners of a business, typically taking the form of ordinary or common shares in a company.

- **Floor** – A credit arrangement under which the holder is protected against falls in interest rates below a certain level.

- **Generally accepted accounting principles (GAAP)** – Best practice principles in relation to accounting policies and disclosures in financial statements.

- **Go public** – To float on a stock exchange, creating public ownership of shares

- **HNWI** – high net worth individual.

- **IPO** – Initial public offering. Going public and offering shares to the public for the first time.

- **IRR** – Internal rate of return. A tool to help investors calculate returns on actual or prospective investments, indicating whether an investment has been successful or is worth pursuing.

- **JV** – Joint venture. A project where two or more parties join together with a view to generating profit.

- **LBO** – Leveraged buy-out. A buy-out that is financed by borrowings.

- **LIBOR** – London Interbank Offered Rate. The rate at which banks are willing to lend funds to each other in the London interbank market, often used as a benchmark for loans to businesses by lenders, who then add their own margin.

- **Liquidation preference** – A right to receive a preferred amount at the time of a liquidity event (e.g. an exit). Typically used by external investors to protect their investment returns.

- **Loan stock** – Unsecured debt provided by a lender to a borrower.

- **LTIP** – Long-term incentive plan. Performance arrangements, often involving the issue of shares or options, to focus and motivate senior management.

- **MBI** – Management buy-in. This is where an external management team, often purpose built, buys into a business. Seen as riskier than a management buy-out, where the management team already understands and operates the business.

- **MBO** – Management buy-out. The buy-out of a business by the existing management team, often from a founder or from a corporate that wishes to exit from a non-core business.

- **Mezzanine finance** – A type of loan finance that sits between equity and senior debt, carrying higher risks and rewards than senior debt and often involving an equity option or interest.

- **Multiple** – A method used to determine the price of a business e.g. 'The business was sold for a multiple of 5 x EBITDA.'

- **Net assets** – The excess of assets over liabilities in a business, equating to shareholders' equity.

- **Post-money value** – The value of a business immediately after an injection of capital occurs.

- **Preference shares** – Shares issued by a company that rank ahead of ordinary shareholders, generally receiving preferential rights in terms of dividends and repayment.

- **Pre-money value** – The value of a business immediately before an injection of capital occurs.

- **Put option** – A right, but not an obligation, to sell at a predetermined price at some time in the future.

- **Senior debt** – Debt, typically provided by a bank, that has priority over all other classes of debt or shares issued by a company.

- **Shareholders' equity** – This is the interest of the owners of the business, represented by its ordinary share capital and reserves.

- **Subordinated debt** – A debt that has lower priority than senior debt.

- **Sweat equity** – Equity that is given to shareholders in exchange for work rather than money.

Protecting your assets

"A strong balance sheet is the best security for the future, so seize every opportunity to shore it up," advises David Molian of Cranfield School of Management.

While revenues and profits are important, so are assets, particularly when it comes to strengthening and protecting your balance sheet. As part of this process, it's sensible to ensure that both your tangible and intangible fixed assets are properly controlled and efficiently exploited.

Here are some tips on how to achieve this:

Control and protect your assets

- Ensure that all of the assets you need to run the business efficiently are either under your ownership or that your access to them is appropriately contractually protected.

- Make sure your systems accurately record the existence of the assets and their related costs.

- Check that the assets are insured and review your insurance cover regularly.

- Ensure that you frequently assess your future capital expenditure needs.

Exploit your assets efficiently

- In the case of direct revenue-generating assets, don't invest unless it's on the back of a financial model which shows a return significantly above your cost of capital.

- Be aware of the advantages of leasing (as opposed to purchasing) new assets, and the potential for selling and leasing back existing assets.

- Measure your asset utilisation ratios regularly, if these are important in your business.

- Ensure you maximise the residual value of your assets once their primary utilisation period is over.

Manage your intangible assets

- Check that all the intellectual property or technology you need is under your ownership, or adequately protected by license agreements.

- Ensure that your intellectual property is appropriately registered and protected (e.g. patents, trademarks).

- Keep an eye on third parties who might attempt to use your IP in an unauthorised way.

- Check that any license agreements are periodically reviewed and their provisions enforced.

- Review your talent management processes and keep them up to scratch.

- Don't forget other non-IP intangibles and how you can protect them, e.g. the value of contracts and customer relationships.

Focusing on profit

Businesses need constant reinvention. In order to thrive, they must:

1. Earn more (increase prices, sell more, find more customers or persuade existing customers to buy more frequently or spend more when they make a purchase).

2. Spend proportionately less (reduce costs or increase efficiency).

3. Spend wisely (invest in areas that will impact step 1 profoundly).

In this section we'll consider how you can manage your costs to improve your profitability. Let's start by looking at fixed costs.

Fixed costs

Fixed costs are those that occur irrespective of levels of business activity, so it's essential to keep them under control.

"Keep your fixed costs as absolutely low as possible," advises Ariadne Capital's Julie Meyer. "That lean operating model helps you to live another day. If you can't cover your costs you're going to have a problem."

The alternative to fixed costs are variable costs, which are either controllable in the short term or which vary with the level of activity in your business. Staff and property costs are good examples of costs that can be fixed (i.e. a long property lease or a team of permanent staff) or variable (a short-term serviced office manned by temporary or even outsourced staff).

As businesses grow, the level of their fixed costs tends to increase, becoming the major part of the costs in the business. This is because bigger businesses demand more permanent resources than smaller businesses and, by definition, are less flexible. If you've got a hundred people and rooms full of equipment, an office or factory move can take some planning. On the other hand, if it's just you, a couple of colleagues and your laptops sitting in a serviced office, you can move in a heartbeat.

It follows that smaller businesses can have a higher proportion of variable costs than larger businesses, but both should constantly review this balance in order to maintain maximum flexibility in an increasingly uncertain economic world.

Irrespective of whether costs are fixed or variable, they all need controlling. Here are some of the areas you might focus on:

Supply chain

If you manufacture or supply goods, have you maximised your profit through your supply chain? A global economy creates massive cost-saving opportunities, although these can sometimes give rise to logistical and communication problems. A sensible balance is required, but you should spend time looking for stable, reliable suppliers that will value and complement your business.

If you supply services, the chances are that your people are your main cost. They are your supply chain and probably your most important asset. We'll look at people management, retention and reward in detail in Chapters 10 and 11, but it's worth noting here that people are motivated by more than money. Where possible, create a system which provides both fixed and incentive-based rewards, but don't forget to take account of the softer issues. Do staff enjoy working for your business? Are colleagues and the work environment supportive? Do they clearly understand their role and purpose? And what about culture – do you create loyalty and buy-in by involving them in decision making?

Overheads

Most businesses have an established overhead structure that is predictable and easily forecast – IT costs, insurance, utilities, consumables, marketing, professional fees and a host of other expenses. It is the one part of the business that is easy to understand. Yet it is often poorly managed.

The key question that needs to be asked is whether the business is receiving value for money for the overhead costs that it pays. This can be challenging to answer, because the focus of the business is largely on delivering its main product or service, or on its core supply chain. In addition, new suppliers and opportunities arise on a daily basis, making it difficult to keep up. It suffices to say that, as businesses grow, there are normally plenty of savings to be made.

Consider the following:

- When did you last review your insurance? Are the right risks being covered and are the levels of cover appropriate? When did you last get an alternative quote?

- Can you make savings on your energy costs by switching suppliers?

- Do you spend much on travel? If so, do you have a travel policy for your staff and have you benchmarked alternative suppliers?

- What about IT services? Do you manage these yourself? Would it be cheaper or more efficient to outsource this function? Have you considered the benefits of cloud computing?

- Could you do better on web hosting, broadband provision, telephone or mobile phone contracts?

- Are your property costs fixed? Do you have any leverage with your landlord? Remember that landlords need tenants rather than expensive voids.

- When did you last review your courier costs? Is there a better alternative?

- Do you outsource your cleaning requirements to a contractor? Is it worth considering other suppliers?

- How about stationery, printing and office supplies?

- How many membership subscriptions do you pay and how many newspapers and journals do you buy? Do you really need them all?

- Might it be cheaper or more efficient to outsource your HR function or your payroll preparation?

- Is your bank competitive? Could you get cheaper bank charges or lower interest margins elsewhere?

Whatever you do, don't ignore these and other similar areas. Make sure that you have proper purchasing procedures, agreed supplier terms and appropriate arrangements for authorisation.

"Firms often enter into unnecessary liabilities that only get identified once the invoice is due for payment," advises Giles Murphy of Smith & Williamson.

Expenses

We've all heard stories about the abuse of business expense accounts. Many of us will have witnessed some of this abuse in action.

"Abuse of expenses policies often starts at the top," says David Hewison, an employment tax specialist at Smith & Williamson. "Once it becomes common knowledge that the boss is claiming generous expenses, employees can rapidly fall into a similar pattern."

You heard it here first. But assuming that you're not the one claiming excessive or unnecessary expenses, make sure your staff don't either. You can achieve this by setting clear expenses policies and reviewing them from time to time to ensure that there is clarity over the exact types of expenses that are eligible for reclaim. This should include guidance on classes of travel, types of hotel, subsistence allowances while travelling on business and expenses for client entertaining.

There is also another expenses-related tactic to reduce costs which may sound counter-productive as it involves paying staff more rather than less. However, by giving staff a minor pay rise but specifying that this means that they don't claim expenses at all, this eliminates the need for expense claims completely. This may not be suitable for all staff but, if it is suitable for your business, you will not only save the cost of the expenses, you will save on administration costs as well.

Hidden costs

In addition to straightforward overhead costs, many businesses suffer from hidden costs which can be far more difficult to ascertain.

I once worked with a manufacturing company who had a very big, well-known customer. Somewhere around 35% of the production was sold to this single customer, who kept the company on its toes by complaining about almost every order, raising inappropriate credit notes for a range of spurious reasons and then, to add insult to injury, delaying their payments. Because they were such a significant customer, the company did everything in its power to keep them on side. In due course, however, the customer found that they could source the products more cheaply overseas. A disaster, you might think. How are you supposed to cope with the overnight loss of 35% of your turnover?

You can only imagine the management team's surprise when they found that, as a result of losing the contract, profits increased and working capital requirements (in this case the bank overdraft) reduced. Apart from that, the company was a happier place without constant needling from a difficult and, as it turned out, unprofitable customer.

Has your business got any hidden costs? Think laterally and have a look round some corners to find out!

Collecting your debts

Like your costs, the credit you give to your customers needs to be carefully controlled. Late or non-payment are primary causes of cash flow difficulties and business fatalities. Despite clear and agreed trading terms and conditions (which your business obviously has) customers regularly exceed their credit terms for a variety of reasons.

Sometimes this may be because your invoice has simply been received too late to be included in this week/month's payment run. Sometimes it's because there's a query on the invoice which is preventing normal processing by your customer. Other reasons may include a lack of available cash, although this will rarely be offered as the reason. You are more likely to be told that the cheque's in the post or that the accountant has broken his right arm.

One of the key options at your disposal is to say no. You can say no to taking on a new customer if you're not happy with their credit rating or reputation. You can say no to allowing them excessive credit and you can say no to the provision of goods and services when they are in breach of their obligations.

However, saying no is sometimes not as easy as it seems.

Espotting founder Seb Bishop says: "You can get so obsessed with top line revenue and the gross figure in terms of the amount of money that you're bringing in, that you take your eye off the bottom line and forget to chase people up. Bad debt can be the resulting problem. People are quick to count revenue but it isn't real revenue unless you are paid."

According to Julia Hoare of ?What If!, growing businesses often take their eye off the debt collection ball. "Often you'll find that a business that's successfully growing its client base and its volume of sales misses late payments."

In case of doubt, sound account opening and credit control procedures are fundamental to the running of a successful business. Here are some tips on how to manage this process:

- **Thoroughly check your customer's credit rating** and, if possible, reputation, before opening their account. Consider the possibility that they might be moving to you because their existing supplier has stopped deliveries or withdrawn credit.

- **Agree terms and conditions and credit limits**, along with any special arrangements that may apply.

- **Confirm that the work has been completed to a satisfactory level**, or that the goods have been delivered in accordance with the customer's wishes. This can be a frequent excuse of non-payers.

- **Send invoices as early as possible** to the right person, including clear instructions on how to pay. Make sure you include the right details/purchase order number on your invoice.

- **Consider providing incentives**, such as discounts or rewards, for early settlement.

- **Send statements and reminders** in advance of the due date.

- **Use your accounting system to monitor late payments** and pursue these rigorously.

- **Log and maintain contact with late or non-payers.** You'll need evidence of correspondence and calls should you end up in court.

- **Consider using a debt collection agency or taking legal action** if payment remains outstanding beyond its terms and despite your efforts to collect it.

Invoice discounting or factoring can be used to speed up the cash flows due to you by your debtors, but the money you receive can be clawed back if late payments or bad debts subsequently arise. These arrangements are used extensively and are available through commercial banks and others.

Because of the risk of default, many businesses rely on credit insurance to protect them from bad debts. This is an insurance policy that will pay out in accordance with agreed credit limits for defaulting customers. It is by no means a panacea and needs to be managed carefully to ensure that claims will be successful.

Withdrawal of credit insurance cover on a particular customer can create huge problems for that customer. It will typically force suppliers to demand faster payment or to withhold supplies.

"Credit insurers are a key stakeholder in a business, even if businesses don't realise it," says Steve Ellwood, a corporate finance director at Smith & Williamson. "Companies needing cover should keep an open dialogue with credit insurers. Not doing so can have a negative impact on the company's credit rating and cause significant problems if cover ends up being withdrawn. Credit insurers should be viewed as friends."

And what about creditors?

Just as your customers need to pay you, so you need to pay your suppliers.

The general rule is that you should stick to the agreed terms, using your good behaviour to extract benefits such as reduced prices or discounts.

However, just as your customers may take liberties with you, it's possible that you may require some flexibility from your own suppliers. If you have to do this, don't just ignore them, but actively engage with them to tell them when they can expect your payment.

It is widely accepted that stretching your creditors (i.e. paying them late or outside their terms) can be an essential part of managing your day-to-day cash flow, but it's always better to do this with their agreement.

Keeping the bank on side

A bank is an essential trading partner, so it's surprising how little attention is paid to the process of selection. When businesses start up, many just want 'a bank', often asking for a random introduction from a friend or an advisor, or using their own personal bank to put them in touch with their business-facing colleagues.

But banks are different and relationships tend to be long term, so it's worth considering the particular attributes you are looking for. They will all be happy to talk to you and you will find no shortage of interest (no pun intended).

Decide what you are looking for. Is it a close personal relationship with a manager that you can relate to or are you more interested in your bank's ability to manage your foreign currency transactions? Do you need a bank with branches or offices in particular locations? Do you need to borrow money or will your account be operating in credit? What about bank charges and interest rates? If you are borrowing, will you be seeking fully secured senior debt or less-easy-to-find cash flow funding? What about other services like invoice discounting?

These are just some of the questions you should consider before deciding on your all important banking partner. For established businesses that already have one, inertia may prevent change. But take time out to consider your needs for the longer term. If you are unhappy with the status quo, make a move. Always try to do this from a position of strength and not at a time when you are in dispute or struggling to meet existing banking commitments.

Whether your business is credit-dependent now or likely to be in the future, you should always aim to maintain a healthy relationship with your bank. You never know when you might need their help. So here are five key steps to building a strong and mutually beneficial relationship:

1. Be professional

Plan ahead for meetings. Presentations should be detailed, accurate and realistic, showing an appreciation of the risks and how these can be mitigated. Always adopt a professional approach to seeking or renewing your debt facilities. Make sure that you are offering adequate security.

2. Build trust

Banking relationships are built on trust. Keep in touch and keep your bank informed at all times, not just when you need their help. Focus on the positive, whilst being open and transparent and alerting them to potential threats.

3. Be practical

Take care not to breach your banking covenants. Deliver financial information and other documentation in a timely manner. Remember that perceptions are generally regarded as reality, so don't create bad ones. Be proactive with business updates. Voluntarily provide regular copies of business plans, financial projections and reports before you are asked.

4. Show quality

The quality of your financial information is paramount. Provide reliable information and supporting numbers which are comparable over different time periods. Bad or insufficient evidence of your financial position and prospects may lead to your bank assuming the worst. Avoid this at all costs.

5. Be prepared

Make sure you understand who and what you are dealing with. Banks are in business to take deposits and to lend to customers. But they are not venture capitalists. Like any other business, they will protect their balance sheets and adopt stringent lending criteria. Do not make silly requests that will undermine your relationship.

Investing in the future

In order to grow, businesses need to invest. Your vision will probably not be achieved without significant investment in infrastructure, innovation and people. Small businesses that are initially easy to run can rapidly develop into much more complex organisations, requiring stronger management and better facilities as well as more robust systems and processes.

Investment may be needed in many areas, including recruitment, training, and marketing, or in new technology or equipment.

"These are often the first costs to be cut in a downturn," says Giles Murphy. "However, it is at this point in the cycle that spending in these areas can bring the most benefit. An analysis of the effectiveness of this type of expenditure is therefore fundamental to the success of a business throughout the economic cycle."

Downturn or no downturn, investment has to be prioritised and funded, so it's essential to identify the key activities and areas that will help you achieve your goals.

It's important to understand that not every investment will create additional revenues or growth, but no investment should be made unless it increases your capability, moving you further towards the attainment of your vision.

For example, as the founder of your business, you may decide that you are better at innovation and dealing with customers than you are at management. You may, therefore, decide to employ a professional managing director or CEO to work alongside you and help you professionalise the business. Whilst this should increase the long-term capability of the business, it will not produce immediate revenues or profits. In fact, the opposite is likely to occur, at least in the short term, as you have to find the cash to pay recruitment fees, salary and expenses in the initial bedding down phase.

It follows that businesses need to invest in multiple ways but, conceptually, these can be reduced to two:

1. investment in the infrastructure of the business, enabling you to manage and protect the business as it grows

2. investment in the profit-generating activities of the business, enabling increased revenues and/or better operating margins.

Both of these types of investment will increase the capability of the business and help it achieve its goals.

However you decide to invest your hard-earned cash, you should examine the projected long- and short-term benefits, along with the likely risks and rewards. Cash is the most valuable commodity. As Doug Richard wrote in *Growing Business* magazine: "Extra money does not exist in business. A business never has money to waste. It just can't happen."

Hopefully, the message is clear. Keep proper financial records and use these to help you run your business. Plan ahead and don't run out of cash. And if you need to raise additional finance to help you achieve your goals, read on. The next chapter will help.

⌐ Top tips ⌐

- Make sure that you, or someone you trust, is keeping the financial score in your business. **Don't penny pinch on the management of your financial position.**

- **Keep proper 'books of account'**, electronically or otherwise, so that accurate financial data can be extracted easily and efficiently.

- **Prepare integrated budgets and forecasts** to predict your expectations for the business. Challenge your assumptions and beware of errors or omissions.

- **Prepare monthly management accounts** and review these against your budgets and forecasts. Investigate variances and consider whether corrective action is required.

- **Implement daily or weekly reporting** to keep management abreast of key financial developments and KPIs. Use this information as a management tool to help you run your business.

- **Monitor the key financial ratios** in your business and investigate any unexpected changes.

- **Control and protect your assets** and, where possible, build reserves to strengthen your balance sheet. Don't forget the importance of your intangible assets.

- **Keep direct and indirect costs under review at all times.** Actively manage the balance between fixed and variable costs in your business to maintain flexibility. Don't forget hidden costs, such as staff inefficiencies or difficult customer relationships.

- **Choose your customers carefully** and **keep your debtors under control** at all times. Your debtors deliver the cash that drives your business.

- **Select an appropriate bank** for your business and focus on building a strong and trusting relationship in both good times and bad. Always say what you will do and do what you say.

- **Prioritise areas for investment in your business.** Make investments that will increase the capability or profitability of the business, helping you towards the attainment of your vision.

CHAPTER 6
Raising Equity Finance

> **"Business is a combination of war and sport."**
>
> — André Maurois

Equity — who needs it?

It is often assumed that raising external, or third party, equity is a prerequisite to business success. In the majority of cases, this could not be further from the truth. Most businesses start with very limited funding. This is typically provided by the founder, or by family and friends on an informal basis. As these businesses develop, they bootstrap their growth, using their own profits and assets to finance their needs. As a result, they get to keep their potentially valuable equity in the hands of the founder or the family, along with the choices and freedom that brings.

Keeping it in the family is generally the preferred choice for most businesses. However, some find that cash constraints or growth opportunities make it either necessary or desirable to raise additional finance. If this cannot be found through borrowing or other non-equity sources, then raising external equity may be the only option.

Ownership determines outcomes

Don't be tempted to underestimate the impact that external equity can have on your business. Your investors are there to make a profit. They will generally have the right to a say in your company's management, including how much money you are allowed to earn and how you will spend their valuable resources. If you fail to live up to their expectations, you could even end up being fired!

So as a general rule, if you want to run your business for life and make your own choices, try to avoid taking third-party equity. This kind of investment typically demands an exit at some point in the future, with varying levels of interference along the way.

Built to sell

Building a business with a sale in mind is a relatively new phenomenon. In the not-too-distant past, businesses were generally seen as longer-term ventures, providing income and benefits to their owners and perhaps being handed down through the generations. Only a decreasing number of these businesses still exist. Instead, increased levels of corporate activity and a requirement for growth in a dynamic and fast-moving society have led to the development of a build-and-sell mentality. Here the focus of a business is typically on high growth or the development of valuable IP, followed by an early or medium-term exit. In these circumstances, a business may be well suited to a mixture of founder and external equity.

Timing is everything

When it comes to raising external equity, timing is vital. Where you are in your evolutionary process will be key to determining when you go looking for capital, as well as who you approach to raise it.

"The problem with a lot of entrepreneurs is that they leave fundraising until the last minute," says Espotting founder Seb Bishop.

Last minute planning will certainly not impress your potential investors, who will wish to approach their investment in a measured and structured way. In the unlikely event that an investor is prepared to accelerate his investment process to meet your challenging timetable, you are likely to end up paying the price in terms of the level of equity you have to offer or the value at which you offer it.

Taking a long-term, planned approach to raising finance is therefore essential. The smartest approach is to prepare and act well before the funding becomes a necessity.

"Raise money when you don't need it," advises digital Dragon and First Tuesday co-founder Julie Meyer. "You need to be out there raising money before you need it and building relationships with investors continually."

So let's look at how to go about raising external equity.

How to attract external equity

We'll look at sources of equity and non-equity finance in more detail in Chapter 7, but in order to attract external equity, whether from a business angel, an institutional investor or even a corporate investor, a number of boxes will need to be ticked. Here are ten of the key drivers:

First impressions

You only get one chance to make a first impression, so make sure you get it right. Many investors will decide not to proceed within the first 30 seconds of any discussion, or within a minute or two of picking up your business plan. Here's how you can make sure you give it your best shot:

- Understand who you are talking to by doing your detailed research in advance. Where it is available, review your target investor's criteria carefully to ensure that you and your business will fit. Don't try to put a square peg in a round hole.

- Dress sensibly, be on time, know your market and understand your shortcomings. Think about your approach, test it on your friends and practise it to perfection. Don't fall at the first fence.

- Explain clearly and concisely what you do and what you are trying to achieve. Build a picture of the future in your investor's mind. Avoid the use of hearsay and jargon. Stick to the facts and keep it simple.

- Be enthusiastic, but realistic. Don't make outrageous claims or forecasts. Investors may get close to believing the impossible, but miracles are definitely a stretch.

Vision and strategy

Your investor will want to understand your vision and your business strategy. We discussed this in detail in earlier chapters, but it also features here.

You will need to demonstrate your competitive advantage in your chosen area and explain why your particular approach will succeed. Have you got some IP that will disrupt the existing market? Have you got a newer, better, faster or cheaper business model? Or do you simply have a profitable existing business that requires funding for local or international expansion?

"VCs are not gamblers, they're astute business people," says Seb Bishop. "They like to invest in a proven model."

Investors have to be able to buy into the overall vision. This requires the communication of that vision in an articulate and appealing way.

"In my experience," says Julie Meyer, "the better the entrepreneur is at articulating the core vision and developing the brand early, the easier and better the financing has been."

Taking that 'elevator pitch' methodology to the extreme, investor Simon Dolan requested investment proposals through Twitter, saying that the discipline of pitching within the 140 character limit would help to "focus the mind".

Similarly, Bill Morrow's Angels Den has pioneered the practice of 'speed-funding'. "We have thousands of companies registered and some of them are brilliant. Yet they are unlikely to get funded via speed-funding because they cannot explain easily, quickly and concisely what it is that the company does," says Bill. "Some people say, 'Three minutes? That's far too short.' And yet three minutes is more than enough time to hang yourself."

Business plan

A well-thought-out and comprehensive business plan is an essential part of any investment proposition. Make sure yours includes detailed and plausible information on where you see the business in three to five years, along with the clearly identified critical success factors that you'll achieve along the way. Refer to Chapter 4 for more detailed guidance on business planning.

Management team

Your pitch should clearly demonstrate the capabilities and competencies of your team, giving assurance to your investor that you have the skills and experience to manage the business and maximise its potential. Be aware that the skills and experience required to run a smaller business may differ from those required by a larger business. If any skills are missing it may be worth bringing someone in or identifying a prospective candidate with a suitable skillset prior to seeking investment.

Brian Livingston, head of mergers and acquisitions at Smith & Williamson, spent 13 years at private equity house 3i. "When considering investing in a business, we used three criteria: management, management and management."

And, he adds, it's not about having the best product, but more about being in the best market with the best team behind that product: "In a perfect world you are looking for a good management team in a good sector that is cash-generative, with a well-thought-out business plan and an established market position. Or, as someone once said to me, 'You always want to back a digger but, ideally, they should be digging on top of a gold mine.' You could have a good team digging in a bad sector or a bad team digging in a good sector. The latter can do OK for a while, and a good team digging in a bad sector can do better than anybody else, but not very well. So what you really need is a good team in a good sector. It's that winning combination."

Investor James Caan's advice echoes the importance placed on the management team when evaluating investment opportunities. "Management quality is the single most important intangible that outweighs all others when assessing the future potential of any business," he says. "What the business will do in the future relies very much on how the management thinks, how they operate and how they make business decisions."

To evaluate the quality of the management, James looks at the team's growth aspirations and plans, its financial track record and how it has grown the business since it was founded. He also considers whether they've delivered on bringing business in and whether their overall understanding of the business "demonstrates how well the team is in control".

"A combination of functional, operational and well-rounded business expertise would command premium value," adds James, who also assesses the ability of a company "to attract, motivate, incentivise and retain talent at all levels".

"This is another key intangible that drives value," comments James. "If the management has set up a business that is attracting and retaining talent then the future value of the business is more assured."

For this reason, James, who backs people rather than their ideas, examines the incentive structure in a business to see how it's aligned with its growth aspirations. He also evaluates the operational infrastructure and mindset, seeking well structured training programmes and an underlying mentality of excellence as a driving force.

Trust and transparency

Investors don't like surprises – they demand honesty and transparency. The quickest way to lose a potential investor is to sacrifice trust by embellishing the truth. Integrity is the name of the game and no business is ever entirely problem-free.

"Nobody expects everything to be completely and utterly perfect," says Brad Rosser. "So treat investors with common sense; be honest about the entire business from day one. Anything other than the truth slows deals down or kills them entirely."

Honesty engenders trust and, as Julie Meyer and Anita Roddick have both said, "Trust is efficient."

In general, investment doesn't happen until 'due diligence' has been completed. Due diligence is a process of discovery normally carried out by professionals, designed to provide assurance to an investor in relation to the current state of affairs of the business, as well as its future prospects. If there are false claims or mis-statements, they are likely to be discovered at this due diligence stage. This will often result in the withdrawal of the prospective investor. Even if they escape detection through due diligence, the problems are likely to surface later on, damaging the relationship with your new investor and potentially undermining your future.

So don't bury bad news or focus only on the positives. Just tell it like it is. If there are problems in particular areas, highlight them and explain how you will address them. By doing this, you will gain the trust and support of your investor, who will probably offer his help.

Advisors

They say that you're only as good as the company you keep. Raising external equity can involve a bevy of advisors, including accountants and lawyers on both sides and, often, a number of other experts. It's important that you select experienced advisors who are both appropriate to the size of the transaction and who have seen it and done it before.

Brian Livingston comments: "It's a question of horses for courses. You don't appoint the largest accountancy firm to the smallest deal or vice versa, but you should always use someone who is known at the appropriate level in the market, and who the investor's advisors respect."

Getting the right advice when you take in new investment can be crucial to your future wealth. There will almost certainly be an agreement containing clauses designed to protect the investor and you will need to understand these and work with your advisor to negotiate the best possible outcome.

Many entrepreneurs are in too much of a hurry at this stage, with the challenge and buzz of raising the funding giving way to the less interesting aspects of completing investment agreements and other formalities. Don't be one of the many who only discover what they have signed up to after it's too late.

So choose your advisors carefully and let them have the difficult conversations. Listen to their advice and use them as your gladiator to help you achieve your goals.

Financial results and forecasts

It goes without saying that your business plan will include your historic financial statements as well as realistic assumptions and forecasts supporting your future trading activity. We have already covered this area in detail in Chapter 4 and will not revisit it here. We will, however, touch on your understanding of these statements and forecasts, which is fundamental to any successful presentation.

Chapter 5 will help you with some of the terminology and some of the ratios that you should be aware of. Be particularly prepared for questions around your working capital, the engine of your ongoing solvency, and consider the effectiveness of your KPIs and regular management information. Don't just leave an understanding of this crucial area to your finance director or your financial advisors. This will probably not be enough to reassure your investor of your financial acumen and your ability to manage and grow his investment.

So take time out with your finance director or your financial advisors. Make sure that you fully understand your numbers and the drivers affecting your cash flow and profitability. Become familiar with commonly used financial language and its meaning. Finally, be aware of key threats and sensitivities.

Funding requirement and purpose

Your financial forecasts will incorporate the funding you are seeking, although it may be difficult to forecast the precise financial impact. This is because the investment you receive may ultimately be structured so that only part of the funding is reflected as equity, with the balance being treated as preferred capital or as a loan. Until the eventual funding structure is known, it will be impossible to finalise your forecasts.

Notwithstanding this, your business plan should include a separate section setting out the amount you are seeking and the purpose for which it is sought. In this way, your investor will be able to identify precisely what it is that he is funding and will be able to weigh up the likely consequences of his investment.

It is often difficult to assess exactly how much funding you will need. Whilst you will obviously allow for contingencies, your investor will be keen to ensure that you are not cutting it too fine. Think long term, as he would far rather provide additional funding at the outset than find a shortfall emerging later on.

Valuation and pricing

There are a number of ways of valuing a business. These will vary depending upon the type of business, its profitability, its maturity and its future prospects. In a start-up, values are often extremely difficult to assess, whereas this can be easier in more mature businesses.

Work with your advisors to establish a sensible valuation for your business. Whether this is based on hope value, assets or earnings, don't be tempted to overvalue your ideas or achievements. With the odd high-profile exception, we are a long way from the heady dotcom days when investors were persuaded to part with large amounts of cash based on little more than an idea. Nothing will put an investor off more quickly than an excessive or insupportable valuation.

Remember that external equity can be expensive. The more you need, the more you will have to give away. So be realistic, cut your cloth and take in as little external funding as possible.

Exit

It's very easy for an investor to put money into your business. But how will he get it back? A vague idea that you would like to buy his shares back at some future date is unlikely to be attractive. Taking in external equity means that you often need to 'begin at the end' in terms of thinking about exit, having a clear strategy and plan.

Who are the likely buyers of your business? What will the business need to look like in order to be attractive to them? Will the sale be to a trade buyer or competitor or might the business be attractive to a financial investor, such as a private equity firm? If the current funding round is the first step on the road to a buy-and-build strategy, where will the next round of funding come from? Should you be considering an IPO for the business?

These are yet more issues to discuss with your advisors. Plans may change as the business grows, but be aware of the possibilities and put your initial stake in the ground.

Pitching dos and don'ts

Having examined the drivers, let's summarise some pitching dos and don'ts.

- **Do make a good first impression** before you open your mouth. Wear suitable clothes. Clean your teeth! "We've lost deals on the back of bad breath," says Bill Morrow.

- **Do create a good storyboard** – a strong proposition that the investor can visualise and believe in.

- **Do present with accuracy and confidence.** Understand your numbers, your audience and your markets in order to gain credibility.

- **Do be specific about your goals**, i.e. you need x amount in order to develop or promote your product, win contracts, scale up, acquire another business or pay off debt.

- **Do create a sense of exclusivity or scarcity.** "You have to create that sense that if they don't give you a better deal, a better price, or better terms, they're not going to get the deal," advises Julie Meyer.

- **Do focus on both emotional and analytical persuasion.** "Securing investment is all about seduction up front," adds Julie. "You have to seduce the investor with the attractiveness of your proposal, and then switch gears by revealing how you intend to execute and how you would manage the things that could go wrong." If you focus on seducing the investor with a passionate plea about your incredible opportunity but fail to explain its implementation, you may lose out. Similarly, if you only focus on how you'll execute without sharing your exciting vision, you may not gain their interest in the first place.

- **Do put a value on the investor's knowledge, experience and contacts.** They can probably offer you a great deal more than money, so ask them how they can help.

- **Do consider walking away.** If you have offers on the table that don't come close to your own valuation, you should be prepared to walk away, but only if you are sure that the investor won't add so much value that you need to revisit your original thinking. Always consider the bigger picture.

- **Don't do a sales pitch.** "You're not trying to close them and you're not trying to tell them about the product," advises Bill Morrow who has amassed data from speed pitches about what does and doesn't work. "Nobody wants to be sold to because it's an investment pitch not a sales pitch," adds Bill. "It's almost as if the product isn't necessarily that important. It's more about the revenue model that accrues from that product and the individual and team behind it."

- **Don't waffle.** Keep to the point and avoid jargon.

- **Don't be rude or arrogant.** You may know your business well and passion and enthusiasm are welcome in a pitching environment. However, you should also listen to and learn from experienced investors. If they say something you particularly disagree with, challenge them politely and make your case clearly and concisely. Don't argue.

- **Don't be afraid to create competition.** In general, you should see a number of potential investors. If they are interested, let them know that they aren't the only show in town.

Likeable and believable

Your pitch may be perfect, but investors invest in people. They invest in likeable individuals who they can believe in and who they believe they can work with.

At the start-up stage, many investors invest more in the person than in the idea itself. A healthy dose of passion along with clear evidence of sector expertise and drive may be at the top of an investor's list when it comes to evaluating an investment opportunity.

Attitude is also important here. As well as likeability, attitude comes down to confidence rather than arrogance.

"You have to convey the sense that you're giving an investor an opportunity and not come across as a supplicant for cash," advises Julie Meyer.

The right attitude is therefore a balance between passion, drive, confidence and control, mixed with a dose of realism and an awareness of what can go wrong. You'll need to convey that you're someone who continually sets goals and achieves them.

"The best entrepreneurs exude a kind of expectation of success (rather than a nauseating sense of entitlement) based on their track record of delivering," adds Julie. "As a result they have the natural confidence to say, 'I'm going to do this and no I haven't done it before and I realise a lot of things could go wrong but frankly I'm going do it whether or not you give me the money.' There's a fine line between being arrogant and being confident but, when you hit that line, it's very powerful."

Finding the right investor

Get to know them

Just as the likeability factor comes into play for investors, so it does for those seeking investment. Essentially, you are looking for a like-minded and supportive partner, someone you can relate to who engenders trust. They must believe in your vision and how you intend to build the business. Friction and finance don't mix.

"We've got a guy who has turned down six angels because he felt that the chemistry just wasn't right, that the skills that they'd bring were not the skills that he'd like. He just didn't get a good feel for them," says Bill Morrow.

Compatibility is critical and one way you might achieve this is to find an entrepreneur to back you; someone who has already built one or more businesses, who knows and understands the process. Ariadne Capital pioneered the model of entrepreneurs backing entrepreneurs. "That's our model," says Julie Meyer. "We set up in 2000. Our 53 founding investors have backed early-stage companies, so now we're institutionalising that with our entrepreneurs' fund."

Julie believes that entrepreneurs who are already successful are ideally placed to back the next generation. They understand the twists and turns along the way. "Otherwise you get investors who are not prepared for the level of panic and change and risk that happens in high-growth businesses."

Ultimately you need to do whatever you can to ensure that investors add value rather than detract from it. The only way to do this before signing a deal is to match your expectations with theirs. It doesn't always work.

For example, Piers Daniell's company, Fluidata, had to buy out its early-stage business angels as a result of a mismatch in long-term aspirations. This was despite hitting most of their targets.

"They didn't understand the business," explains Piers. "And because they were risk averse, they were trying to take as much money out of the business as possible."

This meant that the business was being choked at a time when it needed funds for expansion. By taking more money out of the business than they were putting in, the angels brought the business close to breaking point.

"That was one of the reasons that they were happy to exit," says Piers. "Them staying in wasn't helping either side."

Piers subsequently secured alternative investment which he's since paid back. The company is now debt-free and profitable. He has no regrets because, without their initial investment of £150k, the company would have struggled to get to the size it needed to be by the time his suppliers reviewed their contracts. "We would've been affected in a different way had we never had them on board. It's all worked out in the long run," says Piers.

That said, it's clearly preferable to avoid potential conflict by getting clarity around expectations and aspirations at the outset.

In some cases, entrepreneurs feel that they have had to give away too much to get the backing of their investors.

"A recurring complaint from business owners is that investors got their shares cheaply – but owners often forget that the value of their share of the business wouldn't be what it is without the investor's help," says Brian Livingston, head of M&A at Smith & Williamson. "Investment comes as a package – you should focus less on what it costs and more on where it gets you and what it allows your business to achieve."

Brian believes that good investment goes well beyond the cheque book. Know-how and opportunities can fuel a company's growth as much as cash can.

Smart money

"You should look for smart money," advises Coffee Republic founder Bobby Hashemi. "You should look for partners as opposed to mere investors; people who can genuinely add value. And that doesn't have to be operational value. It could be marketing value. It could be someone you respect who will challenge you as the business grows."

You cannot overestimate the value of a supportive and helpful investor. As founder of Angels Den, Bill Morrow says: "The contacts and the little black book that an angel comes with are more often than not more valuable than the cash. They may have put £100k cash in, but it was actually the investor's squash partner or chum at Megacorp who has brought in £1m-worth of business."

From providing mentoring and playing devil's advocate, to helping entrepreneurs negotiate better terms and thrash out better deals, the extra value that investors can bring is massive and varied. So think about what your business needs and what kind of added value you are seeking. "One man's added value is another man's interference," says Brian Livingston.

Create a sketch of your ideal investor. What experience and knowledge might they ideally have? How might they help you achieve your goals? What particular attributes would be useful to you? Is it their contacts or their industry knowledge? How about knowledge of mergers and acquisitions, marketing or operational expertise? Perhaps you are seeking a mentor?

Seek out the smart and supportive money. Wherever possible, your investors should add value, as well as passing the likeability test.

Understanding your investor

Apart from obvious research into sector focus and investment criteria, it's good to get under the skin of your investor. Find out about their core skills and experience. Do they focus on operational efficiency? Buy-and-build strategies? International expansion? Look at their other portfolio companies and work out how they help them. Find out how long they will want to be invested and what they are like in a crisis.

"Ask them if you can speak to someone else whose business they've invested in," suggests Brian Livingston. "See what the other companies have to say about them in terms of how the investor has managed the investment and how they added value. Investors don't mind this approach. In fact, a lot of them recommend you do speak to others."

Brian also recommends that entrepreneurs seeking institutional investment meet with investors with three or four different house styles. "Some, for example, are very aggressive at the first meeting and give you a real hard time," says Brian. "Others are absolutely charming for the first few meetings and then they send in the more aggressive team. Some are very hands on and want to get involved with the management and some will leave the management teams alone."

Finding the right investor with the right style and level of involvement can be challenging. Hence the importance of using experienced advisors, as they will know the house styles and reputations of most institutional investors.

Concluding the deal

Once you've agreed the principal terms with your investor you'll need to conclude and document the deal. This will normally involve further soul-searching as the terms and conditions of the investment are thrashed out. It's not just the amount and the percentage of the equity, it's the conditions that come with it.

Here are some of the issues you will probably be faced with at the time:

Board representation

It is highly likely that your investor will want a seat on the board, or the right to appoint a board member at some future time. Nick Jenkins, founder of Moonpig.com, suggests that you only give away that right to those owning more than 10% of the equity.

"What you have to be careful about is that they have the right to sit on the board but they don't necessarily have the right to remuneration," advises Nick. "Otherwise you can end up with a situation where somebody who invested for 10% of the company very early on ends up having their right to sit on the board and receive a non-executive director's fee enshrined in the shareholders' agreement, despite the fact that they've been diluted down in subsequent funding rounds."

Crucially, in early rounds of fundraising you should make sure that you don't agree to things or give away rights that are going to be difficult to unravel later on. Giving away rights to sit on the board may be one of these.

Covenants

Most investors insist on the inclusion of covenants – things that the investee company promises to do (positive covenants) or not to do (negative covenants).

These will typically cover matters that can impact on the well-being or the future of the business, such as changing the nature of the business, issuing new shares, acquiring other businesses, entering into onerous contracts, selling part of the business, borrowing money, etc. There is likely to be a list of these issues and you will be expected to seek the consent of your investor should you wish to action them.

There will also be conditions surrounding the day-to-day management of the business, such as the frequency of board meetings and the delivery of financial information.

Expect control over the costs of the business. There are likely to be limits on executive remuneration, dividends, employee hiring and costs, capital expenditure and long-term commitments. If you want to exceed agreed limits, you will have to seek consent.

Other issues

There's a raft of other issues that might come into play, and these are negotiated deal by deal. They could include the use of preferred equity, the use of mezzanine or subordinated debt, anti-dilution clauses and liquidation preferences. Suffice to say that all of these can seriously affect the size of your wallet further down the track, so maintain staying power until you have understood and negotiated all the terms.

"Think hard about the shareholding structure of the company," advises Nick. "There are all sorts of clauses you can put in that protect minority shareholders such that you treat all shareholders equally."

In many structures, the actual shareholdings don't matter because the parties enter into agreements which change the normal voting rights. In these circumstances even a small minority shareholder may have rights far beyond those which might be expected. This often happens when an early-stage investor is diluted, but his rights are enshrined in inappropriate, but still enforceable, agreements.

"Proper corporate structuring is one of the biggest lessons that first-time entrepreneurs learn," says Julie Meyer. "Many think that they can sticky tape all sorts of things together just to get investment. They create all sorts of crazy concoctions in their capital investment structure. Many don't recognise that your corporate structure can dictate whether or not you make money in a business. That's why it's so important to get good advice on tax and on funding."

Inez Anderson, share scheme specialist at Smith & Williamson, has "ten key points to include in your shareholders' agreement". These are as follows:

- Rights to appoint and remove directors.

- Terms to protect minority shareholders so that, for example, unanimous shareholder approval is required for certain company decisions.

- Restrictions on freedom to dispose of shares and, if other shareholders have pre-emption rights, at what valuation such transactions should take place.

- Restrictions on changing the nature of the business.

- Terms regulating the raising of capital to avoid diluting existing shareholdings.

- Dividend policy. But note that a stated dividend policy may affect the value of the company's shares for tax purposes.

- Waiver of dividends. Certain shareholders may agree to waive dividends for an agreed period or permanently.

- Limitations on directors' freedom of action, for example to invest in a new capital project or charge the company's assets.

- Business plan. Setting out the business plan in a shareholders' agreement may help to ensure that all shareholders have the same vision.

- How shareholder disputes should be resolved.

Investor relations

Part of the process of investment will be the agreement of future goals. "The key is to agree a 90-day plan and make sure that you are highly focused towards execution and delivery," suggests James Caan.

But once the ink has dried, successful investor relations will come down to regular open communication and updates about what's going on and what's being done and delivered (or not delivered) at any given time. A regular flow of information will inspire confidence that the business is moving in the right direction or enable corrective action if it isn't.

"Keep investors in the loop," advises Brad Rosser. "Talk to them; don't just call them when there's bad news or good news. Keep it open and honest and treat them as a partner in the business."

If there are dips and variations from the plan it's important to let investors know why and what you intend to do about it, or ask for their advice.

"Always explain why something hasn't happened within the cost base, within the time span or at the top line," advises Sir Eric Peacock. "An inclusive approach will keep your investors feeling relaxed and supportive, so they continue to buy into your long-term strategy."

But it's not just equity investment that businesses need. Chapter 7 looks at the various types and sources of finance available to growing businesses.

Top tips

- **Ownership determines outcomes.** Consider whether you really need to raise external equity or whether you can keep it in the family.

- **Plan your fundraising thoroughly** and be fully prepared. You only get one chance to make a first impression.

- **Research your potential investors carefully** to ensure that they are a suitable fit for you and your business. Consider their preferred investment size, their sector preferences and their investment style. Don't try to put a square peg in a round hole.

- **Make sure your management team is up to scratch.** If you identify weaknesses in your line-up, make the necessary changes or be prepared to explain how these will be addressed.

- **Be open and transparent in meetings with potential investors.** No business is perfect, so highlight your problems and weaknesses and explain how you will overcome them.

- **Get good advisors who care.** Listen to their advice and use them as a gladiator to help you achieve your goals.

- **Understand your financial position and forecasts.** Be familiar with regularly used phrases and financial ratios that might be important in your business. It's not OK to leave this to your finance team or your advisors.

- **Be clear about the amount and purpose of your fundraising.** Set out clearly how the funding will be used and allow for contingencies. Think long term and do not raise too little.

- **Work with your advisors to establish the value of your business.** Use a recognised methodology and do not be tempted to overvalue your ideas and achievements.

- **Think about your exit at the outset.** Explain to your investors how they'll get their money back.

- **Remember that investors back people.** Be likeable and believable, not arrogant and over-confident.

- **Be prepared for investors to carry out detailed due diligence on your business.**

- **Do your own due diligence on your investors.** Talk to other investee businesses to find out how they interact with and help them.

- **Keep your investors in the loop.** Maintain regular communication and share both good and bad news. Where appropriate, ask for their help. Always remember that you are both on the same side.

CHAPTER 7
Types and Sources of Finance

"Money often costs too much."

— Ralph Waldo Emerson

Show me the money

There is more to life than equity. Businesses will normally have access to a variety of different types and sources of finance. The trick is in learning to combine these to create financial stability and maximise shareholder returns.

It may seem counter-intuitive but, in a successful business, external equity is likely to be the most expensive source of finance. It will ultimately create value for the investor far in excess of that available from deposits or similar investments and will deprive the founder of this value. From the founder's perspective, this may represent a significant and unwelcome opportunity cost.

In addition, using equity as a sole means of funding may reduce risk but it will also reduce returns. Take the example of an investor who buys for £100 and sells for £150 – a good return of 50%. Now consider the same situation, but imagine that £75 of the investor's original investment is borrowed, leaving only £25 as the equity investment. Ignoring the interest cost on the borrowing which, admittedly, is an over simplistic approach, the equity of £25 becomes equity of £75 (i.e. £150 - £75). In this case the investor's equity return rises to 200%, a far more satisfying result.

This is known as the gearing or leverage effect, where non-equity funding can be used to boost equity returns.

In practice, lenders will not make unlimited loans, so the ability to gear the equity with borrowings will be dictated by market conditions and the assets or cash flows available to secure or service them. In addition, businesses that are highly geared (i.e. those with large borrowings in relation to their equity) are more likely to face difficulties in the event of a slowdown in demand or an unexpected loss.

As always, it's a question of balance. The equity, which is the fixed capital of the business, needs to be sufficient to support the business after all other factors have been taken into account, with sufficient headroom to weather unexpected storms, should these occur.

One well-established principle is that a business should not borrow short to invest long – for example, the use of an overdraft facility that is repayable on demand to finance property or equipment that will be used by a business over many years. If the overdraft is called in, it may be difficult to realise the assets or secure alternative finance, potentially causing the business to commit the ultimate sin – running out of cash.

"Trying to fund growth in the long term using short-term finance is not going to work," says David Molian of Cranfield School of Management. "Historically too many businesses have relied on short-term debt funding, principally overdraft arrangements from their bank, which are liable to be vulnerable in recessionary periods."

There are four main financing options: equity, debt, sales and asset financing. All of these, bar equity, involve the business taking on borrowings. In practice, most businesses will use a number of different sources over time.

Financing options

TYPE: Debt or equity
SOURCE: Friends and family

Many businesses start with funding from friends or family, aka the 'Bank of Friends' or the 'Bank of Mum & Dad'. In practice, this will often be the cheapest and easiest route to gaining early stage funding, with loans often being made on a low interest or even an interest-free basis. This is not to be confused with commercial funding.

In some cases, friends or family may consider getting involved or becoming 'sleeping partners' in the business by making loans or investing their money in return for equity. If they invest on this more formal basis, it's wise to set up a proper loan and/or shareholders' agreement to avoid the potential for any disputes later on. Remember that using your friends or family to finance your business can often affect personal relationships if the business fails or if the value of the loan or equity investment goes down.

Notwithstanding the potential difficulties, friends and family are a hugely important and growing source of funding. "It's much easier to ask family or friends to write out a cheque for ten or twenty thousand pounds than trying to find the money elsewhere," says Seb Bishop, founder of Espotting.

TYPE: Debt or asset-based finance
SOURCE: The bank

Banks represent the traditional and biggest source of finance for businesses. They are not venture capitalists but, in the good times, they can behave quite generously, often taking on risk that goes beyond the available security or lending on an unsecured basis against anticipated cash flows. In the bad times, they revert to a more cautious and measured approach. It's worth remembering this in case the environment changes at a time when you are over-exposed. The often used, and sometimes unfair, analogy is that banks are very happy to lend you an umbrella when the sun is shining, but they may want it back when it starts to rain!

Because a bank's primary function is to lend money and because of the wide array of facilities they can offer, it's often worth approaching the bank as your first port of call, even if it's only to evaluate their offerings and terms and use them as a benchmark against other potential sources of finance.

"It's worth testing your bank periodically with small requests to see what their current policies and attitudes are," advises Julia Hoare of ?What If!. "I always start with the bank because they set the bar in terms of the standard of market financing."

Your bank will typically have a view on how you should finance your business. The most likely options are overdrafts, loans, invoice finance or asset-based lending. All of these carry arrangement fees and interest charges. These are negotiable and will be dependent upon the quality of your business and the bank's assessment of your ability to repay. In addition, security will typically be required. If there are insufficient assets in the business, this may take the form of a personal guarantee, meaning that your personal assets and even your home may be at risk.

Overdrafts

Overdrafts are probably the most common form of bank lending for both individuals and businesses. In businesses, they are designed to support a variable funding requirement based on the trading cycle of the business – for example to finance debtors at a time of higher sales or to finance stock purchases in advance of sales being made. Overdrafts are generally intended to be 'fully fluctuating' facilities, meaning that the bank will expect your balance to move around within the agreed facility and even go into credit from time to time.

An overdraft is a facility, as opposed to a fixed loan. This means that an overall limit is agreed but that interest is charged only on the amount of any overdrawn balance. For this reason, overdraft arrangement and interest rates can feel expensive, as the bank has to allocate its capital even if you don't want to borrow it.

Be aware that overdrafts are repayable on demand, although a demand for repayment is unlikely to be made unless the lender believes that your circumstances have changed adversely or that your business may default.

Loans

Loans are typically used to acquire premises, finance new projects or make smaller acquisitions. They can also be used to support core working capital requirements, if appropriate.

Loans will typically involve repayments taking place from the outset, although it is sometimes possible to vary the arrangements to include a capital or capital and interest holiday for a period.

Banks follow strict processes and it is likely that you will need to jump through a number of hoops in order to get agreement to your loan. In particular, you will need to satisfy them regarding:

- the track record of the business

- the capability of the management team

- the purpose of the loan and your ability to repay it and

- the value and amount of your security.

In addition, they will typically require you to enter into a number of legally binding loan covenants, specifying their interest or asset cover or other matters, including the probable requirement to provide monthly management accounts.

Invoice finance

Invoice finance can be suitable for businesses selling goods or services on credit to other businesses. Cash is paid to you by your lender against the value of the invoices issued to your customers. Typically, lenders will advance 80–90% of the invoice value, helping you to maintain your cash flow.

Problems can arise if you have poor quality customers or a dependence on a few key customers, but the main advantage of invoice finance is that the amount available can grow as your business expands.

On the downside, invoice finance is not normally the cheapest option, and if sales are falling, your facilities may diminish, making it less viable. If things go wrong, you may also find that you are tied into a long-term contract, so it will often pay to use an independent broker or advisor to help you secure the right deal.

"Sales-linked finance facilities such as invoice discounting have been proven to help businesses grow far faster than with a more restrictive, traditional overdraft facility," says Jamie Gould, a debt advisory specialist at Smith & Williamson. "Lenders generally like a spread of good quality debtors, so businesses with just a single or a few customers may struggle to get a facility. If debtors are well spread, quality becomes less of an issue."

Asset-based lending

Asset-based lending (ABL) results in a secured loan being made against the assets of your business. These may include property, plant, machinery and stock, as well as your sales invoices.

With ABL, you will get a revolving credit facility which varies according to the amount of available security at the time. It can be particularly helpful to asset-rich businesses and is often used to help finance acquisitions or to fund ongoing growth.

People often think ABL is more expensive than traditional loans and overdrafts but this is not necessarily the case. Costs can vary, but the stronger the business, the more negotiating power you will have.

TYPE: Debt
SOURCE: Credit Cards

Financing short-term spending using credit cards can be useful and cheap, but don't use them to fund longer-term requirements, unless you are able to repay the balance in full at the end of every month. Convenience and attractive initial interest rates generally give way to far higher interest rates than those applicable to loans and overdrafts.

TYPE: Asset finance
SOURCE: Various

Asset finance enables you to acquire or lease capital assets such as vehicles or equipment. This is either done via hire purchase (HP) or via leasing (including contract hire). With HP you end up owning the asset. You make regular fixed payments each month with the transfer of the asset into your ownership taking place once you've paid off the loan in full. With leasing and contract hire you never actually own the asset, but pay a regular monthly rental over a specified time period. At the end of this period, you must return the asset. As payments are fixed and do not change with interest rates, this type of finance can enable effective budgeting and planning.

TYPE: Grants and loans
SOURCE: Government

National governments and state-funded institutions often make grants and loans to businesses in certain sectors or in particular regions. The difficulty is in determining how to access these funds and working out whether you qualify for them.

If you find a grant or a loan that fits your circumstances, there are likely to be some disincentives. These can include the large amount of paperwork and administration involved in application processes and the time-consuming task of assessing your eligibility. In addition, this type of funding can come with a number of strings attached. Some may require matched funding, whilst others may seek a share of the IP created with the funding. Each opportunity will have its unique features.

Governments typically get involved in order to create or safeguard jobs, help disadvantaged communities or to expand or modernise facilities. They also invest in the promotion of new technologies to create social, economic and environmental benefits.

TYPE: Mezzanine finance
SOURCE: Banks and venture capital funds

Mezzanine finance is a form of debt that sits between equity and secured debt, providing the lender with a higher than normal interest rate and an opportunity to share in the future success of your business. It is normally used to fund risk-based strategies, including acquisitions and expansion.

Mezzanine finance can be provided in a number of ways, often involving the issue of subordinated debt (i.e. debt that ranks for repayment after senior debt), preferred shares or convertible instruments.

From a lender's perspective, mezzanine finance carries a higher risk than senior debt and is therefore more expensive for the borrower. It is often described as a mixture of debt and equity and, due to this hybrid nature, it provides access to funding that might not otherwise be available.

Mezzanine finance is generally repaid at the end of its term in a single, one-off payment. This will help your cash flow during the period of the loan but the final pay-out will be significant. If growth or exit plans are not achieved, this can cause stress in your business.

TYPE: Private equity
SOURCE: Business angels, private equity and venture capital firms

The world of private equity consists of investors and funds that make equity investments directly into privately owned businesses. Companies that are listed on public markets do not therefore fall into this category, unless the purpose of the investment is to buy out the public shareholders and take the company private.

Private equity, by definition, includes venture capital, but the market differentiates between them. Venture capital is normally provided to early stage businesses with high growth potential, typically after the establishment of the business but before it has achieved scale. Venture capital investments, whether by business angels or funds, therefore carry high risks and generally offer the potential for extremely high rewards.

Private equity, on the other hand, is focused on more mature, established businesses, with private equity investors sometimes taking control of the business or sometimes providing growth capital in exchange for a minority interest. Private equity is often used for expansion, including 'roll-out' and 'buy-and-build' strategies.

At the lower or early stage end of the market, business angels tend to dominate the scene, as venture capital and private equity firms will not wish to spend their administrative and investigative time in order to invest small amounts of money. This is where the so-called 'equity gap' comes in, with angel investors typically investing from £10,000 at the lower end to £500,000 at the upper end, and smaller venture capital and private equity firms often not wishing to make investments of less than £1–2m.

"It takes the same amount of time and effort to invest £2m as £10m, with similar levels of commercial, legal and management due diligence required," says Brian Livingston, head of M&A at Smith & Williamson.

When it comes to giving away equity in a business, entrepreneurs fear the loss of control and strive to retain as much of their shareholding as possible. However, many realise that they can create far greater wealth by giving away equity in exchange for both money and expertise. As the saying goes, 30% of something is worth a lot more than 100% of nothing.

Although it can be expensive in the long term, there are many benefits to be achieved from equity funding. Investors are typically less risk-averse than banks and the day-to-day cost of carrying the equity investment is low.

So should you opt for a business angel or a venture capital firm?

If you are lucky enough to have the choice, your intended pace of growth is likely to sway your decision. If you are looking to grow fast and boldly and need a very significant cash injection, a VC is likely to be most beneficial. If you are looking to grow in your own time with less pressure and less investment, a private investor may be preferred. In some cases, too much money can bring unwanted stresses and strains, so make sure you are ready for the challenge.

As outlined in Chapter 2, it took Nick Jenkins and Moonpig ten years to refine the process that his greetings cards go through. Having private investors on board meant that he had the ability to expand at the rate he chose, helping him to perfect Moonpig's complex automated system in a way that alternative types of finance might have hampered.

"VCs often take the attitude that you can throw money at a problem," says Nick. "But I honestly don't think, looking back historically, that we could have thrown money at the problem in the first five years. We couldn't find a cost-effective form of customer acquisition and, had we thrown money at it, we'd just have wasted it. So the slightly longer-term private investor approach has worked better for us."

Whichever option you decide to pursue, here are some tips to take on board:

Private equity tips

- **Allocate time**. Give yourself six months to a year to source private equity. "People think they'll do it in a couple of months or need the money to pay salaries ... forget it, it's never going to happen," comments Seb Bishop.

- **Be prepared and aware of the potential bear traps**. As well as ensuring you have a compelling and well-written plan and financial data, you'll need some good lawyers on hand. "There are catches," warns Seb Bishop. "What often ends up happening is that you raise some money, they tell you that they're going to give you half a million pounds, yet, by the time you receive the money you only get £400k. That's because the legal and other advisor fees come out of the fundraising and before you know it, they've taken that money in advance and you walk away with a lot less at the end of the process."

- **Consider the impact on morale and pressure on management**. VC-backed firms often achieve high growth and high returns. But the road to success can be hard. Tough decisions will need to be made along the way. Sometimes morale can be affected by job cuts or changes, a lack of security or trust, or lower than market-rate salaries. Don't forget that VCs' motivations are driven by profit, exit and return on investment and they won't hesitate to recruit a new team of people if they feel it's necessary.

This pressure is often more intense than working with a private investor who, while motivated by financial gain, might also have additional objectives, such as giving something back or doing something they enjoy.

TYPE: Equity
SOURCE: Corporate venturing

While business angels and VCs can capitalise businesses to help them achieve their goals, companies can also get involved. They can do this through a process known as corporate venturing, where a larger company provides finance and other resources to a smaller business in return for equity.

This was the funding option chosen by Monitise, who decided to team up with Morse, the large IT services and technology company, as they needed both funding and a partner who was prepared to join them on their journey.

"An idea can be originated in a small company or in an individual's mind, but for it to be delivered to the mass market there has to be this partnership with a big infrastructure," says founder Alastair Lukies.

Working in the banking sector, Monitise needed to be taken seriously in order to achieve its success. Alastair didn't just need funding, he needed to raise perceptions of size and scale from the outset.

"The problem was, we were going into the banking industry and we needed to appear much more robust and scalable than we were," Alastair explains. "And what Morse gave us was the perception that we were part of a decent size company with £300m turnover, a FTSE 250 listing, 2,000 staff, a good plc board, plus an excellent chairman and CEO. So you could go and tell the corporate story with instant credibility."

Having started their business in a shed, Alastair and his co-founder Steve were suddenly part of a huge organisation. Alastair's business card had Morse on it. So, when the procurement team within a bank were doing their analysis and checking on the size of their organisation, everything stacked up.

"There's no way they were going to let a company of two people run infrastructure for their consumers," adds Alastair.

Additionally, and perhaps equally importantly, Morse gave Monitise something that many entrepreneurs underestimate: back office. That saved Alastair the usual start-up-issue of having to wear all the hats. So, rather than doing "all that stuff which takes up so much of your time when you want to be out selling", it was done for them. "It was fantastic," says Alastair. "At the end of the month, as the CEO of a two-person company I was getting a report from my investor setting out what our big priorities should be."

Alastair was also able to use the Chief Financial Officer's PA which gave him raised credibility when booking meetings with a senior director at a bank. "Morse definitely gave us the perception of scale. They gave us the capital and the benefit of their balance sheet but didn't try to subsume us into the Morse strategy. They let us breathe but within the incubator of a big organisation."

Monitise is now a publicly quoted company – the result of a great corporate venturing partnership.

The ?What If! Group has also been involved with corporate venturing, connecting larger companies to smaller companies with innovative ideas or taking their own ideas to larger companies and setting up joint ventures.

A good example of this is the Little Big Food Company, which was set up following a period of research carried out by ?What If!. This found a consumer aspiration for organic food but also a requirement for convenience food. "We spotted a niche in the market for frozen organic foods," explains Julia. "And, at that time, we had a working relationship with Heinz."

?What If! approached Heinz with the idea to see if they'd be interested in getting involved. ?What If! would put up the sweat equity and the know-how, structure the business and provide its leader (someone with food manufacturing experience), while Heinz would put up the cash and enable the smaller firm to piggy-back on their credit lines, providing access to suppliers that they would otherwise have been unable to source. Furthermore, Heinz enabled access to supermarket buyers, something a start-up would have struggled to do.

"They were keen and saw the opportunity, but they wanted to do it at arm's length rather than in-house and didn't want to have Heinz all over the product," explains Julia.

Ultimately, corporate venturing or corporate partnering can provide the best of both worlds – the flexibility of a small business together with the resources, credibility and connections of a large business.

TYPE: Equity
SOURCE: Stock markets

Stock markets are traditionally the stamping ground of larger businesses, although there are a number of markets around the world that provide 'lighter touch' regulation, designed for smaller, growth companies. One of these is the UK's AIM market, which the London Stock Exchange describes as its international market for smaller growing companies.

Critics may say that 'lighter touch' regulation can make growth company markets more like casinos, but they have their place in the ecosystem. The UK's AIM market has become the most successful growth market of its kind in the world.

But what are the benefits of listing on a growth market like AIM? Why would growing companies consider a flotation and what are the likely benefits? On the other hand, why do some companies who've gone to all the trouble of listing on AIM end up de-listing and returning to their privately owned roots?

Here are some of the pros and cons:

Pros

- **Creates a market valuation for the business** and enables the opportunity to raise capital for expansion, as well as the possibility of realising some of your investment.

- **Provides access to an acquisition currency and transparency around the value of the business.** Listed companies often use their shares, as opposed to cash, to make acquisitions. This can be particularly useful when implementing a buy-and-build strategy when cash can be better utilised in other areas. "If you've got an objective valuation for your shares, a target company is going to know exactly what they're getting if you offer them shares in your business," explains Dr Azhic Basirov, head of capital markets at Smith & Williamson. "The value is objectively calculated by the market. Unlike a private limited company, you don't need to try to assess the relative value of two different businesses. If you've got a valuation that's objective it's very much easier for people to see exactly what they're getting." Notwithstanding this, share prices do go down as well as up and some vendors will not accept payment in shares, although they may often form part of any purchase consideration.

- **Encourages employee commitment by rewarding them with something of clear value.** When there's no objective market valuation or ability to buy or sell shares, as is normally the case in a private company, it can be difficult for employees with shares or options to understand the value that they have been given. On the other hand, employees of listed companies who are given shares or options can see exactly what they are worth.

- **Creates a heightened public profile and improves the ability to attract high calibre board members.** "I knew from day one that, if we were going to build a successful banking technology firm, I needed to hire people much brighter than me," comments Alastair Lukies of Monitise. "Most of my executive team are all on boards of banks and have run big payment systems. To get people of that calibre into your business, being listed really helps, because they see the listed status providing a genuinely liquid incentive plan."

- **Improves supplier, investor and customer confidence and improves your standing in the marketplace.** This can help enormously if you're trying to build a global business. Listed companies have to go through a rigorous due diligence process before they can join the AIM market. The checks and balances that are carried out can lead to increased confidence, resulting in better supplier credit terms, better relationships with customers and higher valuations from investors. "I would never have got VISA to buy 15% of my company if it was a private company," adds Alastair Lukies. "Certainly not at the price I got. So because they knew that we had to govern ourselves in a transparent way it gave them the comfort that we run our company properly."

Cons

- **Accountability and scrutiny.** Public companies are public property. As such they are expected to comply with the rules of the markets they populate. Companies on AIM have to use the services of a nominated advisor (known as a Nomad), a firm or company which has been approved by the London Stock Exchange, who effectively acts as the regulator of the business, managing its listing and ensuring its ongoing compliance.

- **Undervaluation risk.** Issuing shares is not only dilutive but shares can also lack liquidity. This can undermine fundraising and acquisition activity, because there is a lack of demand for the shares. In addition, a lack of demand normally translates into a low share price, so the use of shares as an acquisition currency may also lose its appeal. On the public markets, companies' share prices are not only affected by their own performance, but by the performance of the market and the economy as a whole.

- **Cost.** The amount of management time and the significant costs associated with a flotation and ongoing listing should never be underestimated. From the process of flotation itself, which can take many months, to the time-consuming administration of regular and constant announcements (interim and final financial results, director dealings in shares, trading updates etc.) there is a lot of activity to manage. "It's quite hands on, labour intensive and time consuming," says Dr Basirov. "So it's not suitable for every business."

Suitability and timing

Stock markets like companies with strong, scalable business models and dependable cash flows. They can be excellent places to be if you can show a genuine growth opportunity, ample market size and a realistic growth trajectory.

Suitability also comes down to the level of your market capitalisation (i.e. the value of your business), your eligibility for admission and your ability to sustain the reporting obligations and general requirements of being a public company.

In terms of market capitalisation, although there is no minimum on the AIM market, businesses that are valued at less than £20m rarely float. "If you're thinking of raising around £10m with a pre-money value of £20m and upwards, you're likely to be a viable AIM company," says Dr Basirov. "Much smaller than that and your suitability will be questioned in terms of whether you will get a big enough following to generate liquidity in your shares."

Suitability also comes down to timing, awareness and readiness. The 'investor road show' part of the process will reveal whether the time is right. "If you're finding it difficult to get an audience with the institutions, it will be a clear indicator that the time is not right, either for your business or for the market," suggests Dr Basirov. Ideally companies should choose a time when the markets are stable and the business is performing well.

Finally, remember that it's the Nomad that will approve or deny you your flotation on AIM. As Dr Basirov explains: "It's an interesting dichotomy that people sometimes fail to understand, but our responsibilities are solely to the London Stock Exchange and we sign a declaration that says the company is suitable for AIM. Our reputation stands and falls on the quality of businesses we take to the market."

For that reason they will only take you to market if you are suitable and ready.

So ... about Nomads and other advisors

When you take a company to AIM you need to appoint a number of key advisors. These include:

- nominated advisor (Nomad)
- broker (responsible for matching companies with investors and generating after-market share trading by matching buyers with sellers)
- accountants (to assist with the financial reporting)
- lawyers
- financial PR.

You must retain a Nomad, a broker and other advisors on an ongoing basis once you are listed. As well as carrying out their key duties, they will produce the plethora of reports that are required, from the legal due diligence report and working capital report to the admission, marketing and research documents, investor presentation and historical financial information.

The broker will set up the 'investor road show' by arranging meetings with institutional investors over a period of a few weeks. During this time, the broker will build a book of investment, pricing shares at a level which achieves the fundraising target and, hopefully, creating after-market share demand.

"In the SME high-growth business space AIM is well served by the availability of Nomads who will take you through the technicalities of the process, enabling the management team to focus on delivering the day-to-day business imperatives," says Sir Eric Peacock.

The Nomads rule the roost on AIM. They will tell you whether your company is a suitable candidate and, depending on your objectives, advise you on the best method of entry. There are alternatives to a straightforward flotation. These include 'reversing' into an existing AIM-listed company (a reverse takeover, whereby the company seeking an AIM listing takes control of an existing AIM company) or buying an existing 'shell', a company that is listed on AIM that has no ongoing activity.

AIM case study #1

When Monitise came of age and outgrew its parent, it had to decide how to become an independent company. The choice was a demerger, where Morse shareholders received shares in Monitise when it left the group.

It became clear that AIM was the obvious route for this transaction. Not only did Monitise's customers, the retail banks, feel comfortable that they should be public and transparent but it also suited the Morse shareholder base. "We had lots of pension funds, lots of individuals, etc. So we were onto AIM by default rather than it being seen as a growth thing," explains Alastair.

The float also enabled Monitise to raise £21.4m in working capital to take them through to break even.

AIM case study #2

Business internet, mobile and telecommunications services company Daisy plc achieved a £200m AIM flotation when it reversed into AIM-listed Freedom4 Group, known previously as Pipex. The resulting company became Daisy Group with Pipex founder, Peter Dubens, becoming chairman and Daisy founder, Matt Riley, becoming CEO. This generated £50m to fund acquisitions.

In exchange for reducing his ownership from 100% to 24%, the float provided Matt Riley with £30m in cash, eight years after starting the business and two years after winning £5m in the Bank of Scotland's Entrepreneur Challenge.

Judge of that competition, retail billionaire Philip Green, told *Growing Business* magazine that he advised Riley to ensure the deal had a significant cash component: "You're not in control of your own destiny once you've gone public. You need a sum of money to stop you getting seller's remorse. We needed a deal that gave the business the capability to get to two or three times the size but at the same time gave Matt financial stability. This deal probably did both."

The public markets are not for everybody but, if you have a wide shareholder base or seek awareness and credibility (like Monitise), or if you want to create a platform for acquisitions (like Daisy), they can provide an ideal solution.

Top tips

- **Be realistic about your ability to raise finance.** Consider the attractiveness of your proposition and don't waste time trying to put a square peg into a round hole.

- Remember that, in a successful business, **external equity is likely to be the most expensive source of finance.**

- Maintain balance – gearing your business with **debt can increase your returns but will also increase your risk.**

- **Never borrow short to invest long.**

- Look into the possibility of **government grants and loans**, but beware of bureaucracy and ongoing involvement.

- **Corporate venturing activity is growing.** If your business is scalable, consider the potential benefits – including funding, credibility, administrative support and access to supply chains and markets.

- **Don't forget the public markets.** These will not be suitable for the majority of businesses, but may be ideal for some.

CHAPTER 8
From Entrepreneur to Leader

"Management works in the system; Leadership works on the system."

– Stephen R. Covey

Being an entrepreneur is a beginning, but to build a successful and sustainable business you'll need strong leadership and management. Which role will you play and how will you get there? Are you just the innovator or are you the owner-manager? Can you graduate from being the owner-manager to being a leader and, if so, what obstacles will you have to navigate along the way? This chapter considers the journey from entrepreneur to leader, examining the skills and approach you will need to succeed in this most challenging of roles.

In order to begin the journey, it's important to recognise that management is not the same as leadership. They are not interchangeable. As we saw in the first chapter, the function of leadership is to do the right things, whereas the function of management is to do things right. As author and consultant Stephen R. Covey says, "Management is efficiency in climbing the ladder of success; leadership determines whether the ladder is leaning against the right wall."

So let's start by examining the entrepreneurial journey from creator to manager to leader which, according to David Molian of Cranfield School of Management, often results in entrepreneurs being their business's "biggest asset and sometimes its biggest liability".

Reducing owner-dependency: the journey to leadership

In their book *Growing Your Business: A Handbook for Ambitious Owner Managers*, Gerard Burke, Liz Clarke, Paul Barrow and David Molian describe the owner-manager as developing across specific roles over time. These roles include 'artisan', 'hero', 'meddler' and 'strategist'.

They put forward the proposition that the majority of owner-managers start businesses in areas and disciplines in which they have a degree of expertise or skill. "A plumber who plumbs, an accountant who accounts, or a solicitor who solicits is an **artisan** [emphasis added]," explains Gerard Burke.

As they generate sales and customers, the next phase of their development involves recruiting or subcontracting to help them deliver their increasing workload. This can often be one of the busiest points in the journey. As the individual with the most skill in the core area of the business, but also the boss, the owner-manager thus evolves into the '**hero**'. Not only are they still working in the business and servicing customers, but they are also getting the business in and getting the invoices out, while simultaneously managing and training their staff.

As a consequence of this pivotal (but hopefully temporary) role, a huge part of the early-stage owner-manager's time is spent fighting fires. Everyone comes to them as the main point of contact – customers, staff and suppliers. They are the hub and the hero of the business, the person that the entire business revolves around and depends upon. This is self-perpetuating. The more problems they solve for others, the more likely they are to retain their role as chief firefighter.

Unfortunately, this period of development can be self-limiting and will often prevent the business from growing. The owner-manager is typically too busy to focus on growth, with his hands tied to turning the daily handle.

So what's the way forward? Put simply, the way to break through this frustrating glass ceiling is to begin to build infrastructure, recruiting additional management to take on some or even most of the responsibilities that were once the domain of the owner-manager. In practice, however, human nature and an all-too-common reluctance to let go can make this fundamental behavioural shift particularly difficult.

Breaking through the barrier of owner-dependency can take the entrepreneur through a transition from 'hero' to 'strategist', empowering the team and enabling the business to reach prosperous new heights. However, it can also lead to the ambitious entrepreneur unsettling the business by seeking new and disruptive levels of heroism (e.g. the introduction of new business ideas or diversification) or assuming an unwanted role; that of the '**meddler**'. Either way, the business can be held back and its growth stunted.

Unwarranted interference is dangerous. Meddling undermines rather than builds confidence, it stifles skills rather than cultivating them and it demoralises rather than motivates.

Owner-managers often feel that nobody can deliver in the way that they can and yet, in order to become good leaders themselves, they must recognise the value in helping others. They need to take a long-term view about the personal development of their team and empower them at every level. Great leaders spot potential and unlock it. They allow other people to prove their worth, progressively 'passing the ball' and generally starting by enabling others to take over non mission-critical tasks before delegating full responsibilities.

So remember that meddling has an adverse and unwelcome effect on the business. Faced with constant criticism and micro-management, the management team will give up or quit and the owner-manager will revert back to being the 'hero' who limits the business growth. Continuing to run day-to-day operations at a detailed level, fighting fires and/or meddling simply doesn't work in the long-term. Yet it can be hard for owner-managers to realise this until it's too late.

"The hardest thing for many owner-managers to take on board is an acceptance that they will contribute *more* by doing *less*," comments David Molian.

A vital behavioural change is therefore required. Delegation, empowerment and trust must come to the fore as the entrepreneur evolves and assumes the role of the **strategist**. This means thinking about what's next. It means looking forwards, outwards and upwards. It means establishing relationships to enable growth and shaping the business for the future ... in other words going from working *in* the business to working *on* it. Rather than spending time solving, checking, training, selling and doing, time should be spent thinking, trusting and – crucially – leading!

"Of the hundreds of owner-managers we meet at Cranfield, roughly 90% identify themselves as either predominantly 'heroes' or 'meddlers'," says David Molian. "Only 5% rate themselves primarily as strategists: that's to say, leaders who work largely on the business, not in the business. And it's only by working on the business that they will succeed in growing it."

To help a move towards the strategist role, David advises owner-managers to simply "get out more" – delegating where possible and divorcing themselves from the daily routine. Anything that creates space and time to ponder strategy, consider direction and gather insight is helpful. But this doesn't mean that leaders should stop working in the business altogether.

"It's all a question of balance," adds David. "The owner-manager who achieves it successfully will progressively give more autonomy to the people they've hired, buying time for him or her to spend on planning the business's development."

Trust defines leadership. And it boosts business performance. You cannot unlock the potential of your team unless you build trust and unless they feel they are in a safe and trusting environment.

"Trust is efficient," says Julie Meyer. "If you can operate on trust in a business, people will move faster and feel comfortable creating value in the organisation, rather than questioning why they should do that little bit more. Trust sets the tone of the business. Leadership, for me, is about creating those conditions of trust, while management is about holding people accountable for what they need to get done."

Management and direction

Perhaps one of the key factors preventing entrepreneurs from becoming successful managers and leaders is their lack of confidence around managing others or their lack of knowledge about appropriate management styles. But while it can be difficult for owner-manager entrepreneurs to let go and to manage other people, they are normally in a good position to do so.

As a founding entrepreneur, you've probably done just about everything. You've worn all of the hats. This gives you a great advantage. Having got your hands dirty in every area, you truly understand each part of the business and the basis of each role within it.

As Piers Daniell of Fluidata points out, "It's very difficult to manage somebody and tell them how to do their job if you've never done it or you don't appreciate how it's done or how it works."

In order to lead effectively and do the right things right you will need to assume your new role of strategist and use your unmatched knowledge of internal roles to appoint and lead others. This means that you will also need to:

- make the right decisions (to do the right things)
- hire the right people (to do things right).

Let's tackle these challenges one by one. The rest of this chapter is devoted to the decision-making processes of leaders. The following chapter will then focus on recruiting and getting the most from a management team and/or board of directors.

Making the right decisions

"In any institution, there has to be a final authority, someone who can make the final decisions."

– Peter Drucker

Good leaders are naturally decisive. They hone their decision-making ability, often relying on past experiences and in-depth knowledge of their specialist business area. Does luck come into it? Most certainly. As Napoleon reportedly said, "Don't give me good generals, give me lucky generals."

Notwithstanding the apparent ease with which some leaders reach their conclusions, decision-making is a complex process that requires a balance between listening to:

- instinct (your own thoughts and feelings)
- feedback (the thoughts and feelings of others)
- data (facts and information).

Instinct: listening to your inner voice

Business decision-making is often driven by data, insight and rationale. Yet it's as much about the ability to listen to ourselves and our feelings – our instinct. Instinct, or gut feeling, is far more prevalent in decision-making than many would give it credit for.

While our environments can encourage specific entrepreneurial traits such as risk-taking, many of these are actually intuitive and in-built. Instinct cannot be learnt. Instinct is about survival and belief, fear and greed, risk and reward. Both in nature (animals use instinct to decide on fight or flight) and in business (entrepreneurs use instinct to decide whether to negotiate or shake on a deal, whether to launch new products or enter new markets). Other factors obviously come into play, but instinct is a key decision-making ingredient. So much so that in a 2006 *PRWeek*/Burson-Marsteller CEO survey, 62% of CEOs rated 'gut feeling' as being highly influential in their business decisions.

> **"I rely far more on gut instinct than researching huge amounts of statistics."**
>
> – Sir Richard Branson, Virgin Group

Intuition and vision are borne of instinct. Many leading entrepreneurs have proved the value of instinct in their decision-making process.

"Instinct can be just as important as data and spreadsheets when it comes to making a truly innovative decision or taking a business risk," says Sir Stelios Haji-Ioannou, founder of easyGroup who, thanks to his wealthy background, admits he is not fearful of failure because he can afford to make mistakes. This freedom has empowered him to listen to his instinct. As a result he fearlessly challenged strong brands and re-engineered established processes to offer cheaper prices to consumers.

Herbert Hainer, Adidas CEO, similarly backed his instinct to acquire Reebok in a bid to compete against Nike. "I can smell good and bad decisions," says Herbert. "It is in my blood and I feel it in my stomach … When you make decisions every day you can't always draw up a business plan. My natural feelings always help and I feel my way through deals."

Strong feelings can strengthen your focus when it comes to deciding on a particular direction or path.

For example, Sir Crispin Davis, ex-CEO of £multi-billion turnover company Reed Elsevier, was advised to break the company up. However, rather than following that advice he followed his instinct when making his "most fundamental decision, to focus on four core businesses – science, legal, B2B and education". This intuitive decision revolutionised the company by safeguarding and strengthening its core sectors. Following his instincts paid dividends, subsequently earning him the nickname 'Mr Ten Per Cent', for his record of delivering double-digit earnings growth at the company.

So how reliable is your instinct? Think back to decisions you've made and whether these have proved to be good or bad. If you believe in your thoughts and feelings, don't be afraid to go against the grain. If you are clear about what you want to achieve, your instinct will help you find the right path.

Feedback: the voices of others

Sir Crispin may have decided to ignore some of the advice he was given, but he still listened before making his judgements. This is because the best leaders listen to the opinions of others, soliciting and welcoming feedback and often modifying their thinking as a result.

Good leaders understand that their valuable employees and advisors want to be heard. They operate in a world of open communication where 'not-invented-here' syndrome is banished and the best solutions are implemented, irrespective of who thought of them.

Asking people for their opinions is only half the story. You will also need to show an interest in their response, taking their thoughts seriously and making them count.

Creating an open culture where people can contribute and share opinions becomes a self-fulfilling prophecy. The more you solicit and value feedback, the more comfortable people are providing it. Furthermore, leaders who seek feedback are more approachable – people feel more confident in their presence, asking important questions or offering suggestions themselves. This ease of two-way communication will empower organisations to do the right things in the right way.

Listening to the opinions of others enables leaders to gain a wider perspective on a problem or opportunity.

For example, if sales are declining, it might be assumed that the sales team are not skilled enough at closing the deals. However, the decline may be due to a competitor entering the market or the emergence of a more appealing product. Or perhaps you are targeting the wrong niche audience with your marketing collateral. A whole range of issues could affect demand. You therefore need to think laterally when you gather information and gain as wide a perspective as you can by soliciting feedback and listening to your team. Try getting out of your office, walking around the building and talking to people. Your time will not be wasted.

Shared values

Business leaders and managers must do all they can to ensure that everyone is pulling in the same direction. This comes down to having shared values and effectively communicating those values. We'll look more at this topic in Chapter 12 when we consider brand identity and culture. For the time being, the point is that shared values create a common direction which makes decision-making far easier, because every decision can be made in line with those values.

Many companies stick motivational messages, mission statements and mottos on the walls of their offices, hoping that by reading these words, staff will automatically begin to exhibit behaviour that reflects the desired values. Unfortunately, as Enron proved with their well-packaged and promoted 'ethical' stance that was later pulled apart by the US Congress, values and actions don't necessarily correlate.

Yet strong values and a real sense of shared purpose can have a huge impact on the quality of the business and its decision-making.

Johnson & Johnson, the multi-national manufacturer of healthcare products and pharmaceuticals, are famous for what they refer to as their 'Credo'. This is a clear values statement and their "recipe for business success". It was written in 1943, long before the term 'corporate social responsibility' had even been invented. The Credo challenges staff to "put the needs and well-being of the people they serve first", and provides a guiding philosophy for responsibilities to customers, staff and the wider community. You can look it up on the company's website. It's well worth a read.

Although the language in the Credo is a little dated, it is taken particularly seriously by the company's management. It is a testament to the fact that the company is one of only a handful which has flourished through more than a century of change. The management commit to practising what they preach and do all they can to ensure that their employees do the same. From providing job security and work-life balance to enabling freedom to provide feedback, they embed these values through their actions, through a decentralised management approach and through the establishment of think tanks, affinity groups and mentoring programmes. Not only do they listen to their teams, they also act on feedback and commit to continuous improvement. There is a mutually beneficial learning process whereby leaders learn from staff and vice versa.

The examples quoted in this chapter show that leaders sometimes need the courage to go against the grain and question established thinking. Sometimes conventional wisdom needs to be broken. Instinct will no doubt pay a part, but seeking and considering team feedback can give leaders the added confidence and support needed to break the mould and gain real competitive advantage.

Johnson & Johnson embraced 'collective intuition' to do just that. Collective intuition is a group dialogue guided by shared company values which leads to a consensus among the team; a blend of feedback and intuition. The power of this collective intuition was harnessed by CEO William C. Weldon (April 2002 onwards) when it persuaded him to break from the conventional industry wisdom of focusing on a single higher-margin market to take the riskier path of focusing on a broader portfolio of products. The impact of this decision to diversify protected the company from market shifts associated with its core products. And it fast-tracked the company's growth by allowing it to focus on "providing breakthrough products that cure disease and save lives," says William. "Sometimes a leader must be able to endure chaos and appreciate it in order to discover the right thing to do."

Cisco Systems CEO John Chambers is another advocate of collaborative leadership. He has used it to transform his company. Cisco now involves hundreds of executives in making key decisions, rather than the ten top executives that the company used to rely on.

Rather than a formal analytical team meeting, collective intuition goes deeper and derives from continued discussion. As Weldon of Johnson & Johnson discovered, when a group is led by shared experiences and beliefs, it is often drawn towards a specific decision. If the vision and values of a business are strong enough, and truly embedded into the culture, groups will be guided by them.

Where unity is lacking, or where there are an insufficient number of engaged participants, it's wiser to heed your own instinct and balance that out with the feedback you glean. Too many diverse opinions can cause havoc to the decision-making process. As Steve Jobs of Apple says, "Never let the noise of other people's opinions drown out your own inner voice." This can be all too common in business. Most successful entrepreneurs will admit to regretting not listening to their inner voice at some point in their careers.

As usual, it's a question of balance. "Every good senior management team and CEO I've worked with has had a range of trusted advisors," says business author Tony Fish. "They listen to all their advice. And then they do their own thing anyway. But they balance it; they take that advice on board when making their final decision."

So what can we learn from all this?

In simple terms, whilst you should always consult your team, you should never make a decision that goes entirely against your gut instinct.

Data

Instinct and feedback are not the only components of successful business decisions. *Data* is a pre-requisite in most decision-making processes. Whether it's about the market, customers, competitors, suppliers, specific products or services or even the macro-economic environment, data and factual evidence has an important part to play.

The starting point for any plan is knowledge and understanding. That's why entrepreneurs and business leaders tend to work in businesses or industries where they already have experience, insight and understanding.

Nobody can guarantee success but decisions based *purely* on instinct, without a factual backdrop, are far more likely to fail than decisions supported by detailed research. With access to the internet and a plethora of information providers, it's not as if it's difficult to find.

All big decisions are based on fact. Facts influence instinct and intuition. And interpretation of the facts facilitates thinking and innovation. Where is the gap in the market? What is the impact of technology? Why would the expansion of your product or service range be beneficial to your business and your customers? Who are the competition and what are they doing? If you've got a big new idea, what are the barriers to entry? These questions, and many more, can be at least partially addressed through research and a careful analysis of the facts.

Data and intuition are both a fundamental part of the decision-making process, with decisions being influenced by the head (data) and the heart (instinct). David Molian of Cranfield School of Management suggests that decision-making should be based on instinct, data, evidence and detailed debate and questioning.

Says David, "The managers in the business need to have the discipline of building and presenting an evidence-based case for whatever it is that they want to do. That evidence can be quantitative or qualitative. But both types of evidence need to be subjected to challenge before decisions are made."

"It's not enough for everybody around the table to come to a consensus very quickly that this is the right thing to do," adds David. "That can actually be quite a dangerous thing. It is better that somebody round the table is given the specific role of playing devil's advocate, with the decision being talked through quite vigorously before the consensus is reached."

Here's a five point plan to help you create a robust decision-making process:

1. Be clear about your objectives and goals.

2. Gather data from multiple sources.

3. Encourage internal debate and listen.

4. Identify a devil's advocate to challenge your thinking.

5. Base your decision on instinct, feedback and data – but *never* go against your instinct.

Once the decision has been made, the devil will move to the detail. Make sure that your planning and implementation processes are up to scratch. It could be the implementation of the decision, rather than the decision itself, that will determine your eventual success.

Top tips

- **Encourage proactive thinking.** When, as leader, you are asked, 'What shall we do?' Turn the question back on the enquirer and ask them, 'What would you do?'

- **Clarify role definitions and expectations.** Ensure that everybody understands their role and is adequately qualified and trained to carry it out.

- **Develop trust through delegation.** Don't be a hero or a meddler. Trust in people to make decisions and allow them to do their job.

- **Build mutual confidence.** Pass over more and more responsibility as your confidence builds in your team and their confidence builds in themselves. Be interested and supportive – don't abdicate your own responsibility.

- **Go away.** Get away from the daily routine of the office operations: network, meet potential partners and customers; take time out to strategise.

- **Consider your instinct.** Always pay attention to your first thoughts, your instant responses.

- **Actively seek out and consider the opinions of others.** There is always more than one view. Be flexible and open your mind to the wider possibilities.

- **Balance thinking and debate with data.** Carry out your detailed research and base your decision-making on firm foundations. Try to be objective and unbiased.

- **Use collective intuition.** Have group discussions based on your company's vision and values. Use these discussions to advance your thinking and to reach a group consensus.

- **Never defy your instinct.** Think of a time when you ignored your instinct. Remember how it felt and what happened.

CHAPTER 9
The Board and Management Team

> **"If you limit a company by its structure or by the people in the company, you will, by definition, limit the full potential of that business."**
>
> — Michael Dell, founder of Dell

Hitting the glass ceiling

The average early-stage business doesn't spend a lot of time thinking about management teams and board structures, but instead focuses on carrying out the immediate and necessary task in hand, whatever that may be. As the business begins to grow, however, increased resources will be required. This means that more and more people become involved and a pattern of working emerges. As a result, a rudimentary management process begins to take shape.

In these early stages, natural talents and capabilities tend to become apparent, with individuals taking responsibility for different disciplines and roles. These informal and unstructured arrangements can often be surprisingly long-lasting and perfectly satisfactory to take a business through its formative and early growth phases.

The 'board' in these businesses will often consist of the founders, or perhaps a husband and wife team, with no formal meetings and no real agenda. Suffice to say that this is a perfect stamping ground for entrepreneurial heroes and meddlers who, unchecked, will typically go on to run small, often family-dominated, businesses.

For many, successfully establishing and running their small business will be both satisfying and satisfactory. However, there are some who will recognise that, whilst capable of more, they and/or their businesses have hit a glass ceiling. This chapter is for those who want to break through this invisible, yet sometimes seemingly impenetrable, barrier.

Breaking through

You've recognised that something needs to change. It may even be you! But before you throw the baby out with the bath water, you may want to consider the most typical and potentially most beneficial starting point – getting help in understanding your finance function and using this to strengthen your overall financial position.

This may sound strange, but the finance function in a growing business is typically under-resourced and under-qualified. Getting the right resources, including the part-time or full-time expertise of an experienced finance person, can unearth a host of opportunities.

"We find that most small businesses don't understand their finances and the opportunities they present", says Sara Daw, managing director of the FD Centre, an internationally established business providing part-time finance directors (FDs, aka chief financial officers or CFOs) to growing businesses. "When we get asked in we can often use our experience to suggest operational changes that improve both profitability and cash flow."

Experienced finance people have often 'seen it' or 'done it' before, so they can prove to be a valuable sounding board on a host of business issues. Getting the right person on board may well transform your view of your business and its potential.

Once you've sorted out your finance function, you can start thinking about other roles in a more formal way. There may be some major challenges at this stage, as you realise that the people who fell into senior roles during the formative stages of the business, and who have supported you loyally ever since, may not be the right people to lead the business forward. Sometimes it will be possible to retain them in the business, but most will not enjoy being passed over in favour of more experienced, external recruits.

Unfortunately this can be a recurring theme – nothing is forever and the skills you recruit at a particular stage in your business's development may need to be reviewed as the business continues to grow.

This includes you. Typically, you have been chairman, chief executive officer (CEO), managing director (MD) and chief operating officer (COO). You may also have been sales director (SD) and chief technology officer (CTO). So what's your own role going to be in the future of the business?

This is often when the concept of a board of directors starts to take shape – the time when the business starts to move away from being entrepreneur-centric to being more reliant on key executives with proven experience and expertise. This certainly doesn't mean you shouldn't be involved, or that you should step back from the business, but it does mean thinking about what your future role should be.

And the last step, often not present in smaller or privately-owned businesses, is the appointment of one or more non-executive directors (NEDs). NEDs sometimes get bad press, as in the old joke:

Question: 'What's the difference between a non-executive director and a supermarket trolley?'

Answer: 'You can get more wine in a non-executive director.'

Nothing, of course, could be further from the truth! NEDs can bring a wealth of experience and contacts, often taking the role of non-executive chairman or heading up board committees. Consider the benefits they might bring in one or more of the following areas:

- an objective perspective on your business, seeing opportunities that you may otherwise overlook

- expert insight or knowledge in your particular business sector

- contacts and relationships with potential customers and suppliers

- business intelligence and knowledge of your competitors

- strong relationships with external advisors, matching relevant skills to your particular business needs.

These ignore the valuable input that NEDs might have for your strategy, and the risk management skills they might bring to bear to help you stay in business. As Jonathan Hick of Directorbank says, "You're less likely to go wrong with a good handful of non-execs around you. Non-execs are cheap, plentiful, fantastic value and each one of them brings 25 years' business experience. It doesn't matter what business they've been in, they've seen the problems of running out of cash, of a customer unexpectedly going bust on you, problems with employment; whereas executive management won't necessarily have seen those things before."

Evolution, not revolution

It's a case of evolution, not revolution. It's worth remembering that all these people will need to be paid. So, except in unusual circumstances (perhaps a VC-backed or very high-growth business), it will probably take years to develop a strong and compatible management team and a board of directors with the right mix of executive and non-executive skills.

Here are some of the more common mistakes that are made along the way:

- trying to do everything at once

- the easy and convenient appointment of friends and family

- over-promoting people before their long-term value to the business is known

- giving away equity too early or to people that will not have a long-term role in the business

- trying to put square pegs in round holes – e.g. taking your top salesman and promoting him to a management role

- failing to look in-house for top talent

- poor internal communication – don't forget to tell people what's happening

- lack of clarity over roles and job descriptions

- poor recruitment, interview and induction processes

- lack of training.

Identify the skills and qualities

Building a management team or a board of directors means that you must first identify the skills, disciplines and qualities you are seeking. I divide these into five areas: corporate necessities, business disciplines, leadership qualities, personality and track record. Let's look at each of these in turn:

Corporate necessities

Management apostle Peter Drucker, aka 'the father of modern management', saw management as "the organ that converts a mob into an organisation, and human effort into performance". In order to maximise performance and organise that 'mob', teams require a set of complementary, but often very varied, skills.

These skills should include a balance of attitudes and opinions, a balance between believers and challengers.

We've already discussed the importance of building a strong foundation and broad base. That goes for the leadership too. For example, Alastair Lukies of Monitise says that you need to be able to look to your right and your left and, "as far as you can see both ways, be able to see people who believe in your vision and then set off together. My board has set my horizons much wider, rather than much taller".

However, your believers shouldn't just march blindly beside you. They should challenge you too.

"Too many people I know set up a board comprised of their great mates who ultimately aren't going to challenge them at all," continues Alastair. "Then it's like the Pied Piper of Hamelin; you all end up running into the sea together."

Irrespective of the number of people in your team or on your board, it's generally beneficial to have at least one dreamer, one doer and one cynic:

- **The dreamer** – often the entrepreneur, the initial instigator and CEO. This individual's vision will drive the business, giving it its character and culture and garnering support in the market. Think Richard Branson at Virgin, or Steve Jobs at Apple.

- **The doer** – often the COO or MD and the trusted confidante of the CEO. This is the individual that makes things happen, the person with the drive and organisational skills to bring ideas and concepts to fruition and manage the efficiency and effectiveness of the wider team.

- **The cynic** – often the FD and the voice of reason in the team, challenging the thinking and considering the risks, both financial and otherwise, to the security and well-being of the business. This may also be a role for a non-exec who can often bring an objective, third-party view.

Having a team with these core traits means that your business will benefit from healthy debate and a filtering system where each person has to be convinced that a particular decision, strategy or action is the right way forward.

Business disciplines

Successful businesses need to cover the bases in terms of disciplines. These will vary based on the activities of the business, but may include research and innovation, production, sales, marketing, distribution, IT, finance and administration. If you are recruiting for a particular role, make sure you understand the intricacies of the role and the specific skill sets required.

In early-stage businesses, individuals may carry out multiple roles. The challenge for a growing business is to create the need for dedicated and skilled resources in each of the key areas, thereby professionalising the business (and hopefully maintaining profitability and cash flow along the way).

When assessing an individual's capability to carry out a particular role, consider their qualifications and whether these are appropriate. Finance is a particularly easy area to assess, as there are a number of recognised qualifications. The same applies to other areas, although the qualifications are often more varied.

Leadership

Their qualifications may be perfect, but members of your management team or board should also possess strong leadership and communication skills to inspire and motivate your wider team. If they can't do this, they shouldn't win the role.

Here are some desirable attributes of leaders to help you assess whether your candidates are likely to measure up:

- visionary (particularly important for a CEO)

- self-starter, enthusiastic and passionate

- good communicator, listener and networker

- accessible and approachable

- supportive of staff; able to build trust and empathy

- confident decision-maker and troubleshooter

- supportive of the company's core values and direction

- knowledgeable about the industry and the business

- insightful about process and politics

- accountable, ethical and responsible.

Do you have people with these qualities in your team or will you need to bring them in from outside?

Personality

Personality is too big a subject to go into in any detail here. However, it's worth having an awareness of the 'big five' factors, also known as the 'five factor model'. These factors, discovered and defined by several independent sets of researchers over many years, have been found to contain most known personality traits and are now assumed to represent the basic structure behind all personality traits. The factors are:

1. openness – inventive and curious as opposed to consistent and cautious

2. conscientiousness – efficient and organised as opposed to easy-going and careless

3. extraversion – outgoing and energetic versus shy and reserved

4. agreeableness – friendly and compassionate as opposed to cold and unkind

5. neuroticism – sensitive and nervous versus secure and confident.

If you are interested in this subject you may also be interested in Raymond Cattell's 16 personality factors and the 16PF personality questionnaire.

These factors are relevant in the areas of job performance. For example, research has shown that extraversion is a valid predictor for occupations involving social interaction (e.g. management and sales), whereas one might expect conscientiousness to be a valid predictor for a finance director. Similarly, one might expect openness and extraversion to be key traits of a successful CEO.

Hopefully, your recruitment and interviewing processes will enable you to get a good feel for the personality of your candidate. At the end of the day, the likeability factor must also be taken into account. Remember that you and your team are going to have to work with your new recruit, so avoid high neuroticism and low agreeableness at all costs!

Track record

Track record is often a useful predictor, but has a number of disadvantages. Firstly, people who are seeking new roles generally talk up their past achievements, claiming the success of others for themselves. That is not to say that they did not play a part, but claims of huge successes should generally be validated rather than accepted without question. Secondly, many excellent, but younger, candidates simply do not have the track record to demonstrate their suitability for a particular role.

In these circumstances, judgements will have to be made. Track record is, therefore, a variable predictor of future success. Where it can be helpful, however, is in understanding the general background and culture of an individual and their likely suitability for a role. Take, for example, a successful sales executive of a global brand who is looking to perform a similar role in a smaller, unknown business. One might find that the individual's former success was due to the power of his company's brand, and that the idea of actually have to sell something, rather than simply manage the process, is all too challenging.

From management team to board

There comes a time in the development of a business when it is often beneficial or deemed desirable by the shareholders for a distinction to be made between the role of the management team, which is focused on running the day-to-day activities of the business, and the board, a more strategic grouping which is focused on making sure that the interests of the shareholders and other stakeholders are well served. As businesses grow, this two tier structure, which is an accepted feature of the public company sector, will normally emerge.

A board of directors is elected by and accountable to the shareholders, whereas the management team is chosen and appointed by the board of directors. The board of directors will typically include senior members of the management team, for example the CEO, CFO and COO (the 'executive directors'), and a number of external directors who are not part of the management team (the 'non-executive directors' or NEDs).

An important point to note from this structure is that the board is unlikely to be populated by the management team as a whole. It is only the key members of the management team that are likely to be represented.

The role of the board

There is a clear distinction between the role of the board and the management team. In general, the board works on the business, whilst the management team work in the business.

The board is the most senior committee of the company, the steering group that agrees the vision and values of the business and sets its strategy. It is about adding value. Those who sit on a company's board should be able to benefit the business through their collective expertise, experience, knowledge and contacts.

The board's responsibilities are wide, but key areas include:

- establishing the vision for the business, guiding its operations and communicating its culture and values

- evaluating present and future opportunities, as well as identifying threats and weaknesses

- setting the strategy for the business

- ensuring that the structure of the business will enable it to pursue its strategy

- appointing and reviewing the performance of the company's CEO

- evaluating the quality and capability of the management team and their performance in implementing and executing strategy

- monitoring the performance and liquidity of the business

- approving budgets and keeping proper accounts

- communicating with shareholders and other stakeholders.

The board should be proactive rather than reactive. Members should not only have a firm understanding of the core strategy and values, but should also have a good knowledge of the business KPIs, customer base, operating costs, financial and market position so that they can identify and flag up areas of vulnerability or highlight threats and opportunities.

"In the smaller growth business the board should be pretty hands on," suggests Jonathan Hick. "They should have met all the employees and maybe know key customers. They should have touched the coalface in the working year, and, at the very least, be aware of and have approved the strategy for the business."

While the COO/MD (if one exists) should manage the business, it is generally the role of the CEO to manage the bigger picture. The CEO should therefore work on the business, exploring new avenues, evaluating current priorities and focusing on the future direction and growth of the business. As a matter of record, neither the board nor the senior executives should be forced to micro-manage.

"As a board, we put together a strategy document and a budget document every year and, provided that the management team is operating within the strategy and is on budget, we let them get on with it," says Nick Jenkins, Founder and Chairman of Moonpig.com. Moonpig's board has four NEDs, two executives (the MD and FD) and Nick Jenkins who has moved from CEO to Chairman. In Moonpig's management team (at the time of writing) they also have an IT Director, Marketing Director and Production Director, none of whom sit on the board.

Board committees

As businesses grow and become increasingly complex, more formal procedures are adopted. This often leads to the creation of 'committees of the board' to deal with specific areas and issues. The most common board committees are the nominations committee, the remuneration committee and the audit committee.

Nominations committee

This committee leads the process for board appointments. It is normally led by the chairman, unless it is the chairman's role that is being considered.

Remuneration committee

This committee considers the packages needed to attract, retain and motivate executive directors and, frequently, other senior staff.

Audit committee

This committee considers internal financial controls, working with the auditors and monitoring their independence to ensure the integrity of the company's accounts.

Individual roles

The role of the chairman

It is the role of the chairman, whether executive or non-executive, to lead the board and advise on direction and strategy to help the business grow. As well as determining the board composition and organisation, the chairman must manage the board meetings and agendas and develop its overall effectiveness. A strong chairman is often invaluable in holding a company and its strategic vision together, aligning the focus of the key board members, chairman, CEO, COO/MD and CFO (or, if the business has no board, the lead managers), who form the heart of the team.

The role of chairman therefore tends to be a blend of advisor, adjudicator, regulator and mentor.

Sir Eric Peacock chairs a number of growth businesses and has his own views on the role of an effective chairman:

"A multi-faceted chairman's role is:

- "to ensure that the board has created a strategic and tactical delivery plan to achieve its objectives

- "to ensure that the control systems within the business and the key performance indicators are relevant to the plan

- "to ensure that the board operates within its fiscal and compliance responsibilities and

- "to act as a mentor to the CEO and the other executive directors on the board."

The chief executive of the Directorbank Group, Elizabeth Jackson, said that a recent survey revealed near universal agreement that the skills required to be a company chairman were very different from those of a CEO and that a non-executive chairman can add great value to a business.

"There are significant benefits attached to a chairman coming into a company with no baggage and an entirely fresh perspective," says Elizabeth. "And that is every bit as true for a family business as a plc." Interestingly, the directors surveyed also felt strongly that the roles of CEO and chairman should not be combined – 85% said the two roles should always be kept separate.

The role of the CEO/COO

David S. Thompson, author of *Blueprint to a Billion*, has an interesting observation on the differing roles of CEOs and COOs. He recommends "Inside-Outside Leadership" when it comes to the roles of effective leaders. This involves a "strategic leadership pairing in which one leader (or team) faces outward toward markets, customers, alliances, and the community with the other leader (or team) focusing inward so as to optimise operations."

This is the approach adopted by many billion dollar companies, from Microsoft and eBay to Yahoo. The CEO often faces outside with the COO (and/or MD) facing inside. This type of leadership structure also helps to prevent the 'meddling' we discussed in the previous chapter.

Seb Bishop, one of the youngest presidents of a NASDAQ-listed company (appointed to the role at the age of 31), echoes the importance of the outward facing CEO.

"A lot of entrepreneurs I speak to don't like to spend time outside the company," he says. "Yet, behind every great CEO there's a great COO, CFO and MD. The truth is that you need a really good COO to help guide the operations of the business. The CEO should hardly be in the office. He should come into the office to inspire, but he should be outside in terms of drumming up business. He should lead from the front, he should be the talisman, your number one salesman; leading by example, talking to all the customers and learning what's needed."

Board composition

To get the best from your board, you'll need to consider its dynamics. Monitise's board, for instance, consists of a number of high calibre individuals from the banking, technology and telecoms world.

Alastair Lukies advises, "To keep your board focused you should match them off with peers who they see as challenging. It's no good having one great FTSE 100 CEO type and surrounding him with early stage non-execs."

At the time of writing, Alastair's board has Colin Tucker, founder of 3 and a co-founder of Orange. He "bounces really well" off John Braun who's the CFO of BT. "So, you've got a fixed-line expert with a mobile expert," says Alastair. "You've got Peter Radcliffe who was CEO of First Data in South East Asia and he bounces off Jan Verplancke, who's the CEO of Standard Chartered Bank. You've got a bank and a payment processor, so there's a natural tension."

"If you can get people on the board that will agree and disagree regularly then your job as CEO is just to keep throwing items up for debate and then listen. It's really just a listening game," adds Alastair.

Monitise is a public company with a board full of luminaries. Whilst it's ideal to find such high calibre and experienced board members from outside the company, businesses should adopt a 'horses for courses' approach. In general terms an ex-CEO or chairman of a blue-chip company, who is used to formality and extensive reporting, may not be an ideal fit for an earlier-stage business. Finding individuals that suit the resources and culture of your business and who can be passionate about its development is therefore paramount.

Board behaviour

Board behaviour is an important and challenging area. Susan Stratton, the owner of Leading Edge Mentoring, a governance and leadership consulting firm based in Michigan, has identified five manipulative board types – The Dominator, The Clueless, The Waste of Space, The Flame Thrower and The Naysayer. The descriptors say it all. Her view is that if you look round your board, you'll probably spot at least one of these disruptive types. She recommends that the chairman or one of the NEDs, rather than the CEO, is despatched to correct these behaviours!

There is no doubt that a 'well behaved' board will achieve far more than one that is constantly infighting or pursuing personal agendas. In terms of board effectiveness, and ignoring the need for expertise and capability, my experience identifies three key attributes to look out for in smaller companies with less experienced boards. These are dominance, bullying and yes-men.

Dominance

It's very easy for a board to be dominated by one or two individuals, leaving the others in the 'Waste of Space' category identified by Stratton. This may happen because of ineffective leadership, or because the wrong people have been chosen to sit on the board. In most cases, it is likely to be the former. Think about whether you, as the entrepreneur, are the culprit. If so, consider how you can modify your approach to include your full team.

Bullying

Dominance can lead to bullying, a particularly unpleasant boardroom practice that happens far more often than one might think. A combination of dominance and aggression come into play here, often accompanied by a blame culture. Part of the problem may stem from the fact that a number of the board members are reliant upon an intellectually powerful and/or dominant board member, perhaps the owner, for their livelihoods. Bullies do not suffer so-called 'fools' (i.e. people who disagree with them) gladly and board members or managers may therefore be loath to put their heads above the parapet in case their views are unwelcome or found wanting.

Do not allow fear to permeate your board – it will do nothing to enhance your business success. The solution is to ban aggression and encourage openness and equality in the board.

Yes-men

The professionalisation of company boards, increased regulation and the decline of the 'old boys network' means that there are fewer of these about than there used to be. Yes-men are people who add little or no value to the board's proceedings and who usually owe their appointment to a dominant shareholder or board member.

Remuneration may also be a driver, even for NEDs. There are obviously many independent and objective NEDs, but none so independent and objective as those that love the job and don't need the money!

The simple rule is that if a member of your board is not contributing in a meaningful way, offering his or her views in a constructive manner and adding to the overall debate, he or she should not be on your board.

Board evaluation

It is quite normal for staff to be evaluated on an annual or more regular basis, but many boards still don't evaluate their individual or collective performance. Arguably, as the board is the architect of a company's vision and strategy, which in turn determines the success or failure of the business, it should be subjected to regular review and assessment.

Monitoring the performance of the board and its individual members should be the responsibility of the chairman. This should not be considered to be intrusive by the members of the board, although it probably is! On the contrary, they should welcome such an assessment for the benefit of the business and the shareholders.

Making meetings work

"Not everything that can be counted, counts; and not everything that counts can be counted."

— Albert Einstein

Meetings are the perfect place to waste time, so if you want to be productive, make sure that yours are properly organised with well-thought-out and relevant agendas.

Meetings are often dominated by a standard agenda, with the same issues being discussed month after month. The same ten items come around again and again, like baggage on a conveyor belt. Sure, there's a place for standing items on an agenda. But they don't generally require endless discussion, especially if meeting papers have been circulated in advance. Try tabling these items and only discuss them if attendees have particular issues to raise. Report by exception rather than by rote.

There's a difference between management meetings and board meetings, as the two committees have different purposes. Management meetings will be operationally focused, with updates on activities in key areas. Board meetings will consider the bigger issues, as well as monitoring the business and the management's performance.

Having covered the basic business of the meeting, always try to include fresh items for discussion. It's best to try to get to these before the meeting is exhausted or out of time, so the chairman should set a brisk pace. Where discussions get bogged down, they will rarely involve everyone in the room. In these circumstances, the chairman might suggest that the matter is considered by a smaller group outside the meeting, rather than wasting valuable meeting time.

"Meetings are not problem-solving sessions, they are to share information, to make sure that you are a team, that you are doing stuff fast enough and that you are communicating," says business author Tony Fish.

How to maximise the effectiveness of your meetings

- **Use management and board meetings constructively and use the time effectively.** "Get the issues out onto the table and try to use the people in the room to fix them or exploit opportunities," advises Brad Rosser, with his experience of several Virgin subsidiaries. "Minimise the time spent solving problems," suggests Tony Fish. "That can be done elsewhere between the few people affected."

- **Control the agenda.** Consider the objective of every meeting. What do you hope to get out of it and why?

- **Minimise box ticking and the listing and reporting of results and minutes.** People should have read these, so only discuss the matters arising, rather than reinventing the wheel. Instead, use the opportunity to maximise action points that will drive the company forward. "Unless there's a crisis", says Brad, "it's far more crucial to identify things to do, next steps, what action point you're going to do next. I think that's the fundamental difference between a well-functioning board and a poor board."

- **Keep things simple.** "Don't be afraid of asking silly questions," suggests Jonathan Hick. "If you can't get a straight answer, carry on asking. It should be about everybody understanding the company, where it's at at the time, where it's going and doing their best to help it on its way. And the executives have a responsibility to make sure that the non-execs have all of the information to do that."

- **Make them regular and well-documented.** Documenting meetings is essential for a host of important reasons. In some cases these will be required to demonstrate compliance with regulations, but at the very least there will be action points requiring follow up.

- **Take meetings seriously.** Meetings are held for a purpose, which is why they need to be well planned, executed and recorded. Tony Fish recommends taking it a step further: "Get an external person in to every senior management meeting that happens. If an external person comes in, everybody tends to take it more seriously."

At the end of the day, some meetings will be more successful than others, just as some organisations will be better managed than others. As Peter Drucker said, organisations are "complex human systems". Which explains why, in order to manage a successful organisation, you need to look at the people you employ and the interaction between them.

┌── Top tips ─────────────────────────

- **Have you hit a glass ceiling?** Consider the management changes you should make to overcome this.

- **Don't underestimate the importance of a senior finance person** or FD.

- **Identify the role that you will play** in the future of the business. What gaps will this leave and how will you fill them?

- **Don't try to build your dream team overnight.** Take your time.

- **Cover the bases** in terms of disciplines and, where possible, recruit qualified people.

- **Don't forget to take the likeability factor into account.**

- **Consider areas where NEDs could bring benefits to your business. Get a great chairman.**

- Remember the personality types. **Don't suffer dominance, bullying or yes-men.**

- **Regularly evaluate your team** and the individuals within it.

- **Don't waste time** in unproductive or poorly planned meetings.

CHAPTER 10

People Management – Part One: Talent Recruitment

**"A business is absolutely nothing without its people!
Success is a team effort."**

— Peter Jones, investor and entrepreneur

It's all about the people

You've heard all the clichés – 'people are the lifeblood of the business', 'the business is all about the people', 'people buy from people'. They are all, as clichés tend to be, true.

This means there is no single more critical asset in a business than its people. Without good people, an entrepreneur can have the best idea in the world and yet be unable to execute it. An idea is simply an idea, a business in waiting, until it is implemented by a team of talented people with a common vision and complementary skills.

Successful business leaders understand this. "You can come up with loads of ideas but if you haven't got the people in place to make them happen there will be a logjam," says Nick Jenkins of Moonpig.com.

"My ex-bosses, Sir Richard Branson and Alan Bond, provided insight into the business and the spark to get it going. Then they'd hire fantastic people around them to make it happen," comments Brad Rosser, ex-right hand man to both business leaders.

It's people that make things happen. They bring their knowledge and expertise and they deliver capability. They create a culture, building your brand and your corporate values in the process. Some products and services may 'sell themselves' but, ultimately, it is people who conceive, create and market those offerings.

Having the right team will enable growth and reduce owner dependency, the repetitive curse that we've discussed in earlier chapters. As David Molian of Cranfield points out, "Unless you can recruit, retain and motivate talented people, you will never buy yourself the time to free yourself from doing the operational stuff. That has to come first. Successful recruitment will allow the owner-manager to spend a significant amount of time in creating and fashioning the business of tomorrow."

There can only be one conclusion. Sourcing the best talent you can find and then cultivating, motivating and harnessing its potential is the most vital ingredient of business success. And because recruiting and training talent is such a costly and time-consuming exercise, it's important to get it right first time.

The trials of hiring

It sounds simple, but recruitment comes with its own set of challenges. For starters, according to a Chartered Institute of Educational Assessors (CIEA) survey, one in three job seekers lies on their CV. In addition, as the world of business has shifted from a focus on processes to people and the working landscape has moved from 'jobs for life' to more flexible 'serial career' working practices, talent has become less loyal, more demanding, and invariably more difficult to secure and hold on to. The very nature of work has evolved and become more fluid and individualistic.

The reality is that businesses no longer have the luxury of relying on training and longevity to manage the gaps in their talent pool. They can't afford to carry excess resources, nor do they have the luxury of time when trained executives leave or are lured away.

These shifting trends mean that companies will often need to recruit the best and most suitable ready-made talent – people who are already equipped with adequate competencies – to help them lead their businesses. In order to do this they will need to stand out from the crowd. This may be because of a reputation for excellence or an outstanding remuneration package, or perhaps because of a deep commitment to diversity or work-life balance. In practice, a host of factors will be taken into account.

An essential part of the process is to create a stable environment to enable individuals to shine, nurturing and prioritising their development, keeping them informed and aware about how they can contribute and enabling them to work harmoniously together.

Happy people are secure people, and happiness takes many forms. To build and retain a dream team, today's employers need to pull out all the stops.

Talent is king

In order to succeed and grow, a business must:

- recruit the right people to deploy in the right roles – and at the right time
- develop reliable and cost-effective recruitment policies and processes
- create an open, inclusive and stimulating environment that fosters team spirit and celebrates success
- unlock and develop individual potential, whilst offering attractive rewards.

The first two points come into the 'recruitment' bracket so we'll cover them in this chapter. We'll examine the latter two points in the next chapter on talent retention and reward.

Recruit the right people

Building a dream team is not simply about recruiting the right people in the right roles. Successful growth also comes down to hiring those people at the right time.

According to entrepreneurial expert and writer, Mike Southon, making the transition from 'sapling' (up to 25 people) to 'mighty oak' (over 50 people) requires businesses to hire 'grown ups'. These are people with real and proven business experience of managing projects, teams and even whole companies.

If you can't change the people, change the people

It's unfortunate, but there's almost no doubt that changes to your management team will be required as your business transitions through growth.

A key challenge that CEOs face is managing the replacement of people who are unable to take the business to the next level. Hard decisions will have to be made. Loyalties forged from long involvement can make changes problematic. And yet, as Sir Eric Peacock says, "having the right people on the bus is mission critical."

"All too frequently a business has grown faster than the people within it," adds Sir Eric.

Julie Meyer's comments mirror this experience. "One of the biggest things I see is companies that start with a team that can't get it to the next level."

Bill Morrow, founder of Angels Den and previously an accountant at Virgin concurs. "For me the biggest lesson I've learned on the growth side is the understanding that your staff are going to have to change. So, just because Betty was with you when you started, the skills that Betty has as you grow might not necessarily serve you all the way."

Your instinct will tell you when you need to take action to change or upgrade your management capability. When it does, consider the following approach:

- Be objective about having the right people in the business. You need a balanced team that covers all the key disciplines and competencies for the current growth phase. And, if possible, beyond. It may be helpful to seek advice from a mentor or external advisors.

- Review your team to identify the weak links and any skills gaps that will need to be filled. Consider how you might help the existing team to step up to the plate. Perhaps training and mentoring, or support from external advisors or sub-contractors, may be the answer.

- Be honest and up front with people about your expectations, about the natural evolution of the team and how, realistically, roles will have to evolve or disappear once the business reaches a certain stage.

"Some people are good at getting companies going and other people can help them scale and get them across the finish line. It's important to recognise that not everybody can be there on the finish line," explains Julie Meyer. "The more you can be up front with potential employees and the more you can articulate the milestones that they have to achieve to get to the next level, the less ambiguity there will be."

It may be that certain individuals are capable of being on the bus but don't want to sign up to the journey. Julie Meyer continues: "To succeed in a growth business, everybody needs to be on the same bus. If the bus is going 70 hours a week, you can't have people getting off at 45. Everybody's got to be working at the same pace to avoid resentment. So you have to be really up front about what the journey is. If the journey is that you're going to work hard for five years and aim to make a load of money, or at the very least make some money, learn a lot and become more valuable as individuals, some people will want to sign up for that journey. Not everybody will."

Embrace diversity

"It were not best that we should all think alike; it is difference of opinion that makes horse races."

— Mark Twain

Optimising your team to take a company through each level of growth boils down to assessing exactly what skills are required at any given time.

New competencies should be complementary to existing ones, but different. A common mistake can be to hire people in your own or a stereotypical image, duplicating skills, limiting diversity and innovation and, ultimately, growth. While you want to hire people that you and your team will like – people who fit in to your culture – this does not mean you should seek out 'more of the same'.

It's not just skill sets that should be diverse. The ideal team should be a mixture of personalities, backgrounds, genders and cultures. Today's global marketplace is increasingly diverse and competitive, so our workplaces should reflect this.

Creating and maintaining a culture of diversity is a key differentiator which benefits everyone in the workplace and the marketplace alike. Diversity enables businesses to tap into the creativity and vitality of their employees, while gaining a better understanding of the needs of the varied markets they serve.

For example, if you serve a broad spectrum of different communities within your target market, or if your market is multicultural, or even if it is merely a mixture of male and female or young and old, having a diverse workforce that connects with these communities will give you a better understanding of their needs. In addition, it may provide increased access and distribution for your products or services.

Employing people from a diverse mix of ethnicities, abilities, ages and genders will build trust and engagement both inside and outside your business. The ethical companies of today embrace diversity and, in doing so, often top the lists of 'Best Companies' to work for. Accolades such as these result in a plethora of free PR coverage and attract top talent – isn't that what we're all looking for?

Verizon, the global wireless communications leader and one of the top ten US employers, is one such company (named in *Working Mother Magazine*'s list of best companies to work for the eighth consecutive year in 2008). It has become a $100 billion revenue business. It almost certainly couldn't have done so without a diversity-embracing culture.

With 59% of their workforce being female and ethnic minorities making up 35% of the Verizon global team (double the average of US companies), this is hardly surprising. Many hold top management positions.

"Diversity is not a game of quotas or head counts," says Verizon CEO, Ivan Seidenberg. "It's a way of seeing – a broadening of the corporate vision to encompass a wider and more varied employee and customer base."

Through employee affinity resource groups, Verizon is educated about issues that concern diverse communities. This aids innovation and drives competitive advantage.

"The most powerful solutions come from the widest range of thoughts and ideas," says Seidenberg.

Sourcing staff – the recruitment process

Develop reliable and cost-effective processes

Recruitment processes need to be responsive and fluid in order to access talent quickly and strategically. However, it's important to understand how long it takes and how much it costs to bring new people into the company, as well as to induct and train them. These 'time-to-hire' and 'cost-per-hire' metrics will be influenced by the type of staff, their role and the methods used to recruit them.

Define your needs

Not every role in your business requires a full-time employee and not every function has to be carried out in-house. Your business-planning process should determine the broad parameters, but the detail will be driven by your day-to-day business needs.

There are plenty of options. Whilst most management team members will be permanent employees, there may be roles that are more suited to temporary or freelance resources, providing increased flexibility around commitment and cost. Similarly, certain activities might be outsourced, enabling the business to manage its costs, reduce its internal headcount and focus on its core activities. In certain circumstances, part-time resources might also be appropriate – the example of a part-time FD to give you sound financial guidance at a fraction of the cost of a full-time employee.

Types of staff

The type of staff you need will depend on the seniority of the role, the nature of the work, how long it will last and the number of working hours required. Options include:

- **Permanent employees** – full-time or part-time, they have an open-ended contract. You have obligations to them but they will be an investment for your business.

- **Fixed-term contract employees** – have a contract for a predetermined time period. Useful for specific projects. Your employer obligations last only for the duration of the contract.

- **Temporary staff** – your contract is typically with the agency that supplies you with staff, but you still have certain legal responsibilities towards the worker.

- **Self-employed freelancers** – your employer obligations with consultants and contractors are minimal, assuming that the individuals concerned are truly self-employed and not employees in disguise.

- **Corporate freelancers** – some people run their affairs through personal service companies. Their company therefore contracts with you to provide the services of the individual.

- **Zero-hours contracts** – enables you to have people on call to work whenever necessary. You're not obliged to offer work, and they're not obliged to accept.

Groundwork and preparation

Once you've decided on the type of staff you require, you'll need to clarify and define the job role and the type of person you need to fill it. A clear job description and person specification will help you streamline the recruitment process by attracting only suitable applicants with the right skills and experience.

Remember that staff will want to be motivated, so widening their experience and offering opportunities for personal development will increase the attractiveness of the role. You are not just looking to find the right person for the role but also the right role for the person.

Here's a potential process:

- **Create a job description** that includes the job title and summarises the role and responsibilities. Include details of expectations and milestones, if possible. Also include details of the person (and role) to whom the new employee will report. Detail the working arrangements, including hours, location, salary and benefits. Once you've created a job description you can refer to it when writing your job advertisement or agency brief. Use it once you've filled the position to give your new member of staff clear objectives.

- **Create a person specification** that defines the skills and experience that the job will require and the type of person you are seeking (e.g. qualified, organised, numerate, analytical). Include details of the character traits you are seeking (e.g. open, outgoing, sociable, conscientious). In an increasingly competitive world, raw skills and character traits are only part of the package, so set out the kind of experience you would expect the successful candidate to have.

- **Define your employer brand**, i.e. the public persona of your business and how it is communicated to the marketplace. This helps to reinforce brand values. It also provides potential candidates and new recruits with a consistent and accurate perception of the company, including its culture and ethos, ahead of any contact.

- **Create a job advertisement** or instructions for an agency which includes details about how to apply for the role and the deadline for submitting applications. Avoid advertising during holiday periods and decide how you'll deal with responses.

- **Ask candidates to go the extra mile.** In order to generate a better quality of candidate, ask them to complete a one-page account of why they want to join your company.

- **Remember that you want a diverse mix** of personality types from varying backgrounds with a range of complementary skills. For example, if you are seeking sales staff, you might look for a confident extrovert who is motivated by money and success. A financial or technical role might suit someone with a quieter personality who is highly organised and analytical. During the interview stage your person specification will prove useful as a checklist to ensure you get the right mix.

Finding your candidates

Once the role and type of person has been considered and clarified, you need to think about how and where you'll find the right person. It may be that you have existing managers who are ready for internal promotion, or that you need to take on fresh, external talent.

As your business grows, mistakes in recruiting can prove to be ever more costly. However, there is no right or wrong method of recruitment. Some people recommend using professional recruitment agencies and headhunters, whilst others advise against it.

"I recommend finding someone whose judgement you trust, such as a professional headhunter or recruitment agency who really understands your business and what you're looking for," advises David Molian of Cranfield School of Management.

Jonathan Hick's experience has led him to use his own extensive and trusted contact network to find his new recruits.

He should know. Having run a multitude of companies over the 23 years he's worked for himself as a serial entrepreneur, it was the realisation that teams of people with complementary skills are core to business success that led Jonathan to establish his latest firm, Directorbank – Europe's leading provider of senior directors to private equity and venture capital-backed companies.

"My experience is not to advertise," says Jonathan. "It's to ask contacts if they know anyone suitable and always be on the look out for good people. We've recruited as much that way as we have in any other traditional way," he adds.

"Probably the least successful method we've found is if we have a specific job and we've advertised it or tried to headhunt people. That's never worked for us in any of the businesses I've worked in."

Perhaps that's why James Caan, who made millions from establishing and selling leading recruitment firm Alexander Mann, suggests using a variety of methods to attract talent, rather than sticking to one avenue or source. "Use every source available to you," advises James. "From recruitment agencies and advertising to online job sites and referrals; not one method exclusively, but all of them."

Recruitment sources include:

- hiring through internal contacts, recommendations from your existing team or through your network of industry contacts

- using a recruitment or headhunting agency, particularly if you don't have the time or knowledge to recruit in-house or are seeking temporary staff

- using social media such as LinkedIn, Ecademy or Facebook to post openings, either via your own company page or profile, or through your own personal networks and groups

- advertising in local newspapers and magazines or trade press if you wish to reach a specific audience within a trade sector or locality

- searching an online database of CVs for suitable candidates

- posting your ad on a job website or freelance directory to reach a large or targeted audience who may have requested alerts when specific opportunities arise.

The role of internal/external HR professionals

Some people argue that headhunters and recruitment agencies often recommend the least objectionable, rather than the most talented, people.

This may be because they are risk-averse and incentive-driven. Certainly, before the transformation of human resources in the 1990s, many HR professionals saw themselves as career advisors, rather than strategic decision-makers, with no real need to understand the core business or vision of the companies they were hiring for.

This has all changed now. With human capital being valued more highly than ever before and the retention of talent becoming as important as the recruitment of talent, HR has reinvented itself. Its leaders are involving themselves in organisational strategy, culture, reward, internal efficiency and morale building. Some even see themselves as change leaders.

Many companies, particularly larger ones, have their own in-house HR departments, another topic that has encouraged fierce debate. Some commentators say that accountability for results should rest with the people responsible for delivering those results, i.e. the department heads or line managers who should know more about the necessary skills and their value than a HR department might. One such commentator, Robert Townsend, author of *Up the Organization: How to Stop the Corporation from Stifling People and Strangling Profits*, went as far as to say that HR departments should be scrapped entirely, handing over salary issues to the accounts department, with core training requirements going to external institutions, and internal managers providing 'on the job training'.

Others suggest that companies with internal HR departments should give the head of HR a seat on the board. This would enable them to be fully conversant with ongoing strategy and core business issues. That knowledge would then trickle down to the rest of the department and better align recruitment and HR policy with the strategic direction of the company.

I wouldn't wish to concur with any particular opinion. However, it's clear that – whether HR departments are in-house, outsourced or non-existent – those involved in recruitment should:

- gather and provide continuous feedback about required skills and roles on an ongoing basis

- stay informed regarding strategy and growth plans and how they will impact on the business's needs as it expands

- develop expertise in building diverse, collaborative teams where cultural differences are celebrated and respected.

If you do contemplate using an agency, consider this: recruiting independently may be far cheaper than using an agency, but is far more time-consuming. With a multitude of available agencies in every major economy there are plenty to choose from. Many will only charge if they place a suitable candidate with you, operating on a 'no win, no fee' basis. But you need to know exactly what you're going to be paying for.

So before appointing an agency, look at client testimonials, terms and conditions and credentials of individual consultants. Consider whether they have a relevant track record of recruiting for the role you need filled and whether they carry out background checks on their candidates. Finally, find out about the amount of control and contact involved in their process – and, crucially, what criterion triggers the 'win' fee.

The decision to hire

Once you've decided to hire, set your sights high. Don't just fill the vacancies; go for the best, most seasoned, top-notch recruits you can afford.

Start-ups simply can't afford to make mistakes. Early-stage entrepreneurs need to be very particular and mindful of what new recruits will cost them and how each person will add value. Growth businesses should take recruitment just as seriously in order to avoid wasting potentially serious amounts of money.

So as well as reviewing a candidate's skills, experience and track record via their CV and references, it's also important to consider their attitude and motivation. Once all of the boxes have been ticked, the decision to hire will probably come down to chemistry – a mixture of instinct and likeability.

Here are some suggestions to help you whittle down your shortlist:

- **Use the same questions for all candidates** so that you can compare answers directly. Deal with the mechanical part of the interview first – background, skills, qualifications, etc.

- **Find out what makes them tick.** Is it money, security, recognition, independence, responsibility, teamwork? What results have they achieved? Was it really down to them or were they part of a wider team? How have they dealt with past mistakes? Dig deep to try to get to know them as individuals.

- **Try psychometric testing.** Give candidates questionnaires where they select words that most or least describe them. The results can define their personality type and provide a deeper assessment that interview questions may not provide.

- **Involve existing staff** in the decision-making process. Use a panel of people who will be working alongside this person and then listen to their views.

- **Use instinct** to decide if you can work with the candidate, as well as evaluating the skills and experience discovered at the interview stage.

Once you have made the decision to hire someone, either best practice or law dictates that you should:

- **Inform each candidate** about the outcome and, if feedback is requested, provide a factual response to avoid unwanted discrimination claims. (Under UK law, for example, discrimination on the grounds of age, gender, ethnicity, race, sexual orientation, or beliefs is prohibited.)

- **Make the job offer in writing** and ensure you have a legally compliant employment contract in place that includes a probationary period. A UK employment contract should include: the name and address of the employer and employee, commencement date, job title and description, working hours and salary details plus pay frequency, holiday entitlement and sick pay, notice periods, details of disciplinary and grievance procedures, pension scheme details and contract duration, if applicable.

"When you're hiring somebody, try to understand their situation and what they might want out of the job," advises Nick Jenkins of Moonpig.com. "Sometimes it's not just a question of getting the best-suited person for the job, it's also finding the best job for the person. If a candidate is fantastically well qualified and evidently able to do the job, but this isn't really their dream job, you're not going to get longevity. So you have to consider whether this job is going to be the dream job for this candidate and if there is enough room for them to expand and to satisfy their ambitions for the next five years. There has to be a good match both ways – that's important to remember."

If you've made a two-way match and provided a clear job description, new staff should be fully aware of their role and function in the business. This should be supplemented by a suitable induction process where the individual is welcomed into the business and educated in its ways. The company culture should be explained and the new recruit should be given ample opportunity to experience it for themselves through a detailed introduction to workmates, as well as a full tour of the environment and amenities.

A positive induction process should not be rushed – new members of staff will be far happier and more productive if they feel that adequate time has been devoted to welcoming them into the company and showing them the ropes.

The next stage is keeping the momentum going; keeping your new recruits motivated once the novelty of their new jobs wears off! We'll consider this in detail in Chapter 11.

┌─ Top tips ─

- Always remember that **your people are your business's most important asset.**

- Recruiting and training talent is a costly and time-consuming exercise, so **plan it carefully to get it right first time.**

- **Regularly review your team** to identify any weaknesses or skills gaps – the right team will help you drive growth and reduce owner dependency.

- **Create and maintain a culture of diversity in your business** – a mix of people and skills.

- **Maintain flexibility** by using a mixture of permanent, part-time, freelance and outsourced resources.

- **Always prepare a clear job description and person specification** before recruiting.

- **Use every recruitment source available** to you – friends, contacts, referrals, advertising, job sites, social media and recruitment agencies.

- If you use recruitment agencies or headhunters, **select them carefully and understand their terms.**

- **Develop robust interview techniques** and involve your existing staff in the decision-making process.

- **Don't skimp on induction** – make your recruits feel secure and happy from the moment they arrive.

CHAPTER 11

People Management – Part Two: Talent Retention and Reward

> **"My business success has been built on recognising the importance of people."**
>
> — James Caan, entrepreneur and investor

What everyone wants

Finding the right people at the right time may be difficult, but holding on to them can be even more challenging. Good talent can be lured or, sometimes, even driven away. But keeping it is essential, reducing the disruption and costs associated with high staff turnover and providing strong foundations on which to build your future business.

People create more value than any process or procedure ever can. It is the actions and attitudes of your people that will really make a difference to your success. When people feel valued and secure, they are more creative and innovative, so you should do everything you can to create and maintain this happy state. It will add value to your business for employees, customers and shareholders alike. Put simply – it's what everyone wants.

Creating a 'total reward' strategy which is aligned with your business culture, vision and strategy should therefore be seen as an investment, rather than an expense.

Here are the key issues to focus on:

- **cultivation and inclusion:** unlocking and developing potential by creating an environment that fosters teamwork and learning, whilst encouraging ideas and innovation

- **motivation and reward:** motivating people with the right incentives and rewards and by understanding what makes them tick

- **shared vision:** creating a collective culture and purpose that makes work a pleasure rather than a chore.

We'll cover the first two in this chapter and look at shared vision as part of the next chapter on brand identity and culture.

Cultivation and inclusion

To successfully cultivate plants you need the right tools – a spade or a fork, a hoe and a rake – along with a supporting cane or trellis. You also need to create the right conditions for your plants to thrive and reach their full potential – an environment with the right soil and with plenty of sun, water and air.

Cultivating the potential of talented people and their ideas is no different. You need the right tools and the right environment to encourage and support their growth.

Start with the office

Many small businesses operate without offices, using technology to work from home and visiting clients in their own premises, or in hotels or clubs. You may be in this situation, but as your business grows, you will probably want and need a more permanent gathering place – a hub for your operations and a home for your team.

A working environment is defined both by its infrastructure (e.g. its office space and equipment) and its atmosphere – the 'vibe' of the workplace. If you want to keep your people, it's best to work on both.

Some companies go the extra mile when it comes to building a fun and innovation-inducing environment. Google, for instance has a yellow brick road installed in the 'Googleplex' and provides free scooters, free food and volleyball courts for its staff.

?What If! were given the accolade of the EU's best place to work in both 2004 and 2005 by the Great Place to Work Institute. Their reception area doubles up as a meeting hub, with praise for employees written across the walls and ceiling. Pixar's working environment includes colourful huts for its creative teams while Red Bull's futuristic London offices include a slide for people to use to go down to the next floor.

We don't all have budgets like Google's, but we can all do something to enhance the atmosphere in our workplaces. Some people may do it with design and colour, others by creating workplace activities or celebrations. Whatever you choose, a pleasant and stimulating environment will boost both energy and morale.

Celebrate success (and have fun!)

Feel Good Drinks, for instance, have Feel Good Days. "We celebrate every success and will spontaneously declare a day or afternoon a Feel Good Day. That's when we tell the team to drop everything, and we go out and do something fun for a couple of hours," explains co-founder Dave Wallwork. "Whether that's taking people to a spa and having massages, or taking them out to lunch somewhere or having cocktails after work – it's all about keeping the guys positive and buzzing in the team, and making sure they're passing on that feeling to customers."

At Ariadne Capital, Julie Meyer is also keen to celebrate success. The Ariadne team do this by sharing their "wins for the week" every Friday afternoon, whether that's the creation or implementation of a new idea or the addition of a new client, "so everybody feels that they're here to win," says Julie.

"It's important that individuals feel that they're participating in a group win, that they can establish their own contribution to the overall team. So I try to create a culture of celebration."

While upbeat surroundings and activities encourage creativity, productivity and loyalty, having a laugh can also encourage staff retention. An Ipsos study revealed that staff who consider their managers to have an 'above average' sense of humour are 90% likely to remain in their jobs and still be there a year later, while employees with managers rated as having an 'average' or 'below average' sense of humour deemed the chances of remaining as 77.5%.

The Great Place to Work Institute says that, in great workplaces, employees experience both a friendly, welcoming atmosphere and a fun, enjoyable spirit. They add that employee perceptions of their workplace as a fun place almost exactly mirror their trust in their employer. There is an extraordinary correlation. In the 100 best companies, approximately 81% of all employees experience high levels of trust and think their workplaces are fun places to be.

Entrepreneur James Caan, who started his own executive recruitment firm, Alexander Mann, in 1985, reinforces this point about the importance of workplace fun.

"If you're having fun you perform better and achieve more. Making the office fun meant the staff were incredibly loyal in an industry where staff turnover is pretty high," says James in his book, *The Real Deal*.

From making pop videos in a shopping centre booth to closing early on a Friday to create sketches, perform in a band or simply go to the pub, James created a fun environment which nurtured trust and camaraderie.

"At Alexander Mann I started the AM Sound Band and justified my belief that in any organisation with hundreds of people, finding four with karaoke fever, drum or guitar yearnings, is not too far a stretch," James told the *Sunday Times*. "The AM Sound Band subsequently played at our conferences and fostered a sense of belonging, company-wide."

"It was a huge success," adds James. "In no small part thanks to one band member who was adept at changing the words to well-known songs. Imagine the impact at a sales meeting when the lyrics to Queen's Bohemian Rhapsody, "Mama, I've just killed a man" is replaced by "Jimmy, I've just placed a man." It was highly appropriate and had the audience in fits of laughter. No amount of money can buy that sense of team spirit. With a little research, similar opportunities will present themselves in most organisations and the team will grow from the experience."

Ultimately, the workplace environment needs to be enjoyable and fun; not a place where people sit slumped at their desks, bored or frustrated, but a place where people can be inspired and energised to voice their opinions and thoughts.

It's a team game

Successful entrepreneurs realise that there is no monopoly on good ideas. They are open and receptive, rather than closed and controlling. They encourage and embrace innovation by fostering an environment of inclusion. They make it safe for employees to participate and contribute. This gives employees a sense of shared ownership in decision-making processes and, ultimately, the vision and direction of the business.

Companies that fail to encourage inclusivity will not only lose ideas but also the people that have them. They will simply leave and set up on their own or join a competitor who not only listens to their ideas, but puts them into action. You really don't want the best ideas walking out of the door with your best people.

Says James Caan, "If your working environment promotes the sharing of good ideas and early identification of potential threats, then the probability of success is increased and the risks to your business reduced."

In *The Real Deal*, James recalls an idea that an employee had which "changed the direction of the recruitment industry" and led to the resulting division "generating revenues in excess of £380m today". If James hadn't listened to the woman who approached him with that idea, he would not only have missed out on that revenue, but would probably have lost the employee too. "The idea would certainly have spawned an important competitor, instead of an asset," says James.

"You've got to have an atmosphere where your workforce feels that their ideas can thrive," says Julia Hoare, company secretary of ?WhatIf! – a great business that helps its clients become more profitable by releasing creative potential in their people, products and brands.

She suggests creating an environment in which anyone in the business can have an idea and an avenue to put that idea forward.

"From the newest junior person right through to the most senior member of the board, no idea should be crushed, because one of them will turn into the next area of growth, which we've seen time and time again," adds Julia. "We call that greenhousing."

Greenhousing, valuing the input of individuals from the ground-level up, can have significant positive effects on growing businesses. Apart from uncovering opportunities, it will create an energetic and positive atmosphere which builds loyalty. Loyalty means lower staff turnover and better results.

"We're very keen on making everyone feel good about us as a business," says Dave Wallwork. "And that's got to start with your own team. So we involve everyone in everything – when we're developing new products, everyone has a taste and an opinion, which creates a good team atmosphere."

Valued team members become great brand ambassadors. NASA famously values every function of every team member at every level. They see every role as vital to their overall performance. Ex-US president Bill Clinton once visited the supremely clean space facility and bumped into a man with a broom. When asked what his role was at NASA, the man told Clinton, "I take people to the moon."

Managing change

Fostering an inclusive culture delivers another valuable benefit – it facilitates change.

According to various surveys by the Chartered Management Institute, the majority of managers experience some form of organisational change on at least an annual basis. Managing change is, therefore, what managers have to do. Yet not all managers manage change well.

Change creates opportunities and opportunities create change. Handled well, change can empower and invigorate your employees. But the fear of the unknown can also create an unsettled and uncertain workforce that feels fearful, stressed and threatened. With trust and loyalty potentially under attack, how change is managed is crucial to the well-being of your business. It follows that staff shouldn't merely be kept informed; they should be empowered and included, contributing to and participating in the change conversation.

Inclusion in the change conversation

In Chapter 3, we briefly touched on how Antonio Perez, CEO of Kodak, famously tackled a hierarchical culture which bowed to the omnipotence of leadership. When he joined Kodak in 2003 he found a company in denial about the impact the digital revolution was having on their business. Not much was being done to address this issue or harness the power of digital technology. People simply hoped that they might be able to slow down the shift to digital through marketing activities.

Crucially, Perez realised that, as leader, nobody would challenge his opinions. The hierarchical culture instilled in the company was so strong that innovation was being stifled. He needed to take drastic action to revitalise the organisation.

His method was to set up what he called the R (Rebel) Group, a committee made up of the most sceptical people within the organisation. This was due in part to his belief in 'the rule of thirds' which states that while a third of staff will happily support change, another third will not, while the final third are open to being convinced. He decided to empower the third that would be most unwilling to embrace change.

He invited the R Group to suggest ways that the company could commercialise its technologies to provide new digital services. The ensuing discussions informed the Kodak strategy, which helped to turn the company around.

Not only did Perez succeed in winning support from the most sceptical group in the company, but he instigated a culture where people were included in the conversation. Motivated by Perez, the R Group embraced and drove change, whilst spreading the word about their belief in him as a good leader and influencing opinion across the workforce.

How to improve innovation and manage change

- **Invite employees to board or management meetings.** Involve them in the strategic and operational decision-making process, especially when those decisions affect them, and then let them spread the word about their inclusion.

- **Establish an 'R Group'** to encourage employees to participate in the change conversation.

- **Hold regular meetings to provide a platform for ideas and feedback**, particularly from customer-facing employees. Throw ideas around; discuss client challenges, new campaigns and research, future objectives and goals … the more insight you can gain from the wider perspectives of your workforce, the more gems you'll uncover.

- **Spend time explaining why change is needed.** Involve key people in the process and deal with any fear before it arises. "Communicating why, how, and when are really important," advises Liz Jackson of Great Guns Marketing, whose business has grown at more than 50% a year. "At that rate you get used to change," says Liz. "Communicating the benefits and finding out what will motivate people to want to change is important. Inflicting and pushing change is a lot harder, so it's better to lead with the carrot and entice people into the new way of doing things than it is to push them into it."

- **It's a team game, so celebrate success by having fun** and letting people know that they have all contributed to the big picture.

Stimulate to innovate

Julia Hoare of ?WhatIf! suggests that one of the best ways to encourage and cultivate ideas is to get people to venture outside their normal environment or comfort zone. "Much of the stuff that we do is getting people out of their normal routine and shaking them up a bit within a safe environment, just to get them out of the rut and let them develop by doing things differently. It's about trying to get people away from behaviours that tend to stifle innovation."

Jonathan Hick, who has started ten businesses from scratch, admits that the idea for every single one of them was conceived in a bar or a restaurant rather than in an office or boardroom. "You need to take people out of the work environment and relax them and that may be going for a walk over the hills, taking a day away from the office or it might end up in a pub or a wine bar where people can relax and want to contribute ideas."

"The worst thing is to have a culture where ideas only happen in the boardroom and the boardroom door is shut, with no communication either way," he adds. "That's a dreadful environment. A good company should have a real interchange of ideas. Going away from the office ensures that happens."

Here are some ideas to help you stimulate and empower your people:

- **Establish hot-desking or stand-up meetings somewhere different** to where you'd normally work. "Move your team around. Go and sit or stand somewhere else," recommends Julia Hoare. In 2008 Procter & Gamble took this approach to the extreme. They not only swapped desks, but swapped companies. They swapped employees with Google so that each set of teams could learn from each other's approach and culture.

- **Set up cross-team or cross-functional idea forums and incubators** to encourage communication and debate across entire teams or departments.

- **Stage 'innovation jams',** as IBM do: brainstorming events that provide people from every corner of the company with the chance to put their ideas forward.

- **Hold annual innovation awards** to celebrate and reward the ideas and efforts of individuals who are thinking outside the box.

The level of staff satisfaction and the level of innovative output can be interdependent as people enjoy being part of a ground-breaking organisation.

Here are some examples of innovative companies and how they've empowered their teams to think creatively.

Through the looking glass

Due to some restructuring at ?WhatIf! there were two new offices created with plain glass walls that needed some livening up. At their Christmas party they staged a competition where the person who came up with the best idea to decorate the new offices would be provided with a £1k budget to do whatever they wanted. The rest of the company then voted for the winner.

"We had three finalists who had to deliver their ideas to the room. People could suggest anything, there was no limit to what they could do and we provided them with the budget to do that," Julia Hoare explains.

The winner was a relatively junior member of staff who captured the staff's imagination with his Alice in Wonderland 'through the looking glass' idea. "He was passionate about his idea and engaged others in it," adds Julia. "So we provided him with the resources to bring his idea to life."

Thinking outside the box

Nintendo's CEO, Satoru Iwata, thought outside the proverbial 'X' box when he gave his creative teams free reign. The Wii game console and intuitive motion-sensitive wireless controller were the result. Rather than focusing on creating a bigger, more powerful, faster and flashier console, as is the games industry norm, teams diverted from the established path and focused on the users' emotional experience. Nintendo subsequently opened up the console world to an untapped market of non-gamers.

Come fly with me

Even lone inventors need sounding boards and creative teams. Southwest Airlines employees are empowered to innovate in teams by their CEO, Gary Kelly, who says, "Our people are our single greatest strength and our most enduring long-term competitive advantage." He's a strong advocate of organisational innovation in order to provide customers with more choice.

Innovations such as ticketless travel, unmatched aeroplane turnaround times and online boarding passes are the result of SWA team-led innovations.

"In a maturing industry, you must continue to find ways to be innovative and creative and grow," says Gary Kelly. "People don't stand still and neither do companies."

Game changer

Shell continues to promote its award-winning GameChanger programme, a system for encouraging and funding technical innovation.

For example, when a Shell engineer spotted a foam toy in a toy shop that swelled when immersed in water, it kicked off a train of thought that made him think of a use for this material that could help solve a growing problem for the oil industry – water seeping into the well and mixing with the oil. He thought that if the material, or elastomer, could be wrapped around well pipes, it would swell up in contact with water and prevent it from getting into the well oil. He was right, and the resulting technology – Expandable Zonal Inflow Profiler (EZIP) – is now being used in wells around the world.

Management style

If people are going to stay, it's critical that they enjoy working in your business. In order to get the best from your staff, you need to manage them in the right way.

Back in 1960, Douglas McGregor devised the Theories X and Y in his book, *The Human Side of Enterprise*. The domineering autocratic style of Theory X was founded on the belief that humans have a natural inclination to avoid work which management must negate. Conversely, the more cooperative style of Theory Y assumes that people are engaged with the objectives of a company and can implicitly motivate, direct and control themselves in order to reach them. The role of management in this instance is to maximise that commitment.

McGregor himself was a supporter of the self-motivating notion of Theory Y as the only motivational method to encourage high achievement. While much has been written about both theories, it is apparent that people are more likely to be committed to their work if they enjoy it, if it enables them to achieve their own goals and if it stimulates their needs. If their work meets those requirements they are less likely to need 'prodding' and are more likely to work hard and remain in their role over the longer term. They are also less likely to want to take unnecessary time off.

"We've had a couple of managers who've taken a fairly disciplinarian approach and we've had to tell them that it doesn't fit with our way of doing things," says Nick Jenkins, founder and chairman of Moonpig.com.

"It cuts both ways though," adds Nick, "so if you have employees who respond to a fun and encouraging environment over a ruthless one by taking too much time off and taking liberties, you have to remove them too. It's about creating an atmosphere where people feel as though they're able to do as much as they're capable of doing and a place where they enjoy turning up in the morning."

Management practices have moved on significantly in the last 50 years. McGregor's Theory Y is now more of a default than an exception and there is little tolerance for an authoritarian, control-oriented working environment.

High staff turnover and/or high levels of sickness absence are generally signs that management styles or practices need review. If you are suffering from either, consider all the facts to establish what's happening.

Even if there's no endemic problem, there are many reasons why staff take time off: because they are stressed or ill, because they are bored, because they feel undervalued or because they simply don't enjoy their work. It's important to notice and address these issues to minimise any damage or disruption to your business.

It should be obvious if your staff are unhappy, so consider the following potential solutions:

- **Enable work-life-balance** in your business by reminding staff that life should consist of work, family and themselves. While hard work, dedication and persistence are the cornerstones of success, a tired, stressed and burnt-out workforce is wholly counterproductive.

- **Be supportive and considerate.** Understand and comply with your legal obligations and have clear and appropriate policies in place for employees and managers to follow. Consider the possibility of home or flexible working to ease pressures and ensure that regular holidays and breaks are taken.

- **Introduce return-to-work interviews** to highlight and expose any underlying issues or problems. Consider how you can assist in resolving these.

- **Reward those covering maternity or sick leave** by providing an 'acting-up allowance' for the duration of a colleague's absence. Pay can revert to normal when the colleague returns and the employee's usual role is resumed.

Motivation and reward

As well as creating the right environment, you need to engage and motivate employees through other means. How much people are prepared to give depends on how well they are understood, appreciated and treated. And the more employees you have, the greater the impact that motivation, or the lack of it, will have on your business. The better you treat your staff, the better they'll treat your customers and you as a business.

As Gamal Aziz, president of one of the most successful hotels and casinos in Las Vegas, the MGM Grand, told *Business Week*: "Imagine taking 10,000 employees and each and every one of them wanting to give more. That's really the difference between [us and] a company that has its employees just punching the clock and trying to get through the day."

According to Don Lowman, the former MD of Towers Perrin and co-author of *Closing the Engagement Gap*, the number-one factor that engages employees more than anything else – more than pay, relationships or career development – is management's interest in their well-being.

System Concepts, an ergonomics consultancy, has taken their staff's well-being quite literally. They implemented healthy-eating programmes and energetic outdoor team-building exercises. Investment in their well-being programme reduced staff turnover from 20% to 7% in just one year. They also slashed the number of days taken off, saving sick pay and down time.

All growing companies want to improve performance, productivity and efficiency; the right motivation enables all three. Yet many companies lack an explicit reward strategy and haven't considered what incentives their employees respond best to.

You can only nurture and engage your high value personnel if you know them; if you have a genuinely deep understanding of what it is that really motivates them. "It's not always cash," says Julia Hoare. "In fact very rarely is it cash. It's more likely to be recognition from peers, across the business."

"Motivation and well-being is about relationships," concurs Liz Jackson of Great Guns Marketing, who also pays her team well and gives shares to "really make people a part of the business." A big part of her focus is on making sure that her staff members are interested in what they're doing.

"It's about really getting to know each person and getting to know what makes them tick. Why do they get out of bed in the morning? What are their passions and interests? What motivates them?" continues Liz.

With today's organisations far flatter in terms of hierarchy than the multi-layered businesses of yesteryear, there are fewer opportunities for promotion through the ranks. This means that business leaders need to seek out alternative methods to motivate their people to stay.

Theories around motivation have been widely documented. Industrial psychologist Frederick Herzberg quantified the theory of factors that cause discontent and factors that create fulfilment. Money, he says, causes dissatisfaction if it's inadequate but adds nothing to satisfaction once the member of staff believes they are being paid fairly.

What is satisfaction?

For Herzberg the factors that create satisfaction are achievement, recognition, the nature of the work, responsibility, advancement and growth.

Maslow's hierarchy of needs theory about the way in which people are motivated also points to these factors, whilst noting that people need to fulfil certain basic needs first before they can be motivated to do anything else. For example, people are unlikely to be motivated to earn the respect of peers or achieve goals until they have satisfied their basic physiological needs of eating and sleeping.

Human beings are complex creatures and are often likely to find themselves at all levels of the hierarchy of needs simultaneously. However, Maslow, along with most other commentators on 'motivation', says that people tend to share certain criteria for satisfaction. We can probably group these into four key areas in order to maximise the potential of our people.

Key motivational factors

1. Financial security

2. The nature of the role and work

3. Learning and development

4. Recognition, appreciation and reward

A company's 'total reward' offering may encompass each of these areas and include salary, bonuses, share awards, benefits, pension, life cover, training, career development, company culture and environment.

1. Financial security

Although money is not always the most important consideration when deciding to join or stay with a business, Maslow's hierarchy of needs shows that we need to be able to afford to pay our bills, put food on our table and feel adequately secure before we can be motivated to achieve more demanding or superior objectives. Financial security, often defined by an individual's basic salary or entitlement, is therefore a key motivating factor.

Pay scales vary according to industry or sector, location and reputation. The best companies to work for and the most interesting jobs don't necessarily offer the best salaries, but there may be a host of reasons for their popularity. Supply and demand, particularly where specific skills are required, will also play its part.

If you are looking to retain and motivate your staff, make sure that you're competitive. It's not difficult. A simple internet search will uncover a host of salary surveys and details of businesses offering salary benchmarking or even the tools to carry this out yourself. Recruitment and search agents will also be able to advise you on the range of salaries applicable to a particular role.

Rather than eating into your profits, paying the right people well can have the opposite effect, not only by encouraging loyalty and reducing staff turnover, but by boosting motivation and performance.

Some roles include elements of both fixed and variable pay. Examples include sales commission, performance bonuses and profit-sharing based on the achievement of specific objectives or results. Whilst these are often necessary and desirable, they need to be structured to encourage both individual and team performance.

Businesses should realise that performance is a team game and that organisational success should be properly and widely rewarded. Similarly, assuming overall results permit, an outstanding performance made by an individual team member should be rewarded, irrespective of the performance of the team. Too often, employers use the excuse that a poor team performance caused by a difficult market should be penalised, whereas those operating in easier or more profitable markets take all the rewards. In many cases the former will be far more deserving than the latter, often even contributing to the latter's success!

In order to avoid these potential bear traps, businesses need to consider what is important to their longer-term objectives. It's all too easy for businesses to shoot themselves in the foot and damage their long-term success by underestimating the importance of a competitive and fair salary structure.

How to motivate with money

- Pay a fair basic salary. Use benchmarking to ensure that you are competitive.

- Base your performance or profit-related bonuses on the achievement of individual, team and company-wide results. Don't create a culture of 'us and them'.

- Penalise poor performance, not poor results. If your results are poor, the reasons are likely to be management or market driven. Don't take this out on your employees.

- Regularly review roles and responsibilities and look for opportunities to promote from within.

- Realign salaries and bonuses as and when promotions take place.

Where pay is concerned, there are no secrets, so always consider whether your actions are even-handed and fair to the workforce as a whole.

2. The nature of the role and work

In most instances it's the job itself that's the source of true motivation.

In order to function well and be fully engaged, employees need to be interested in and inspired by the roles they play, the projects they are involved in and the tasks they carry out. They also need to know what is expected of them, how they fit into the wider organisation and how they will contribute to its overall objectives and performance.

Staff that are truly inspired by their roles often become driven, taking an almost personal responsibility for the future success of their area, or of the business as a whole. They will be amongst the best attenders, the hardest workers and the biggest achievers. They will always be positive and busy, either working at their role or developing their ideas for the future. They will never be bored and they will show extraordinary commitment. Lucky are the businesses that can identify these individuals, empowering them and encouraging them to succeed. They are worth their weight in gold.

How to motivate through the nature of the role

- Ensure that people are working in roles that interest and inspire them.

- Provide clear objectives and the resources to do the job properly.

- Never give responsibility without authority.

- Don't underestimate the importance of regular support and encouragement.

- Keep your staff informed. Tell them what's going on in the business and include them in the conversation.

- Dig for gold – identify and promote the staff that will help you drive your business forward.

3. Learning and development

We live in the information age and, for most of us, the more we learn about the world and the opportunities it presents, the more demanding we become. As information and knowledge spreads, it levels the playing field, opening the door to advancement and personal development – people want to achieve their dreams.

Businesses that ignore these trends are unlikely to retain their employees. It is part of the employer's role to help their staff learn and develop in order to maximise their career opportunities, whether in their current organisation or somewhere else. Failing to facilitate this, or even deliberately trying to prevent it, will quickly destroy motivation, creating both resentment and dissent.

Businesses that commit to promoting learning and development will gain far greater commitment from their staff. Employees who identify a supportive approach and a long-term opportunity in your business are much more likely to stay.

Good practice means holding regular appraisals with your staff to discuss their performance, as well as their learning and development needs. These should take place at least biannually and should include discussions around career progression and advancement.

How to motivate through learning and development

- Help people to achieve their dreams. How can you help them realise their career aspirations within your business?

- Invest in learning and development. Help people develop and exploit their talent.

- Hold regular appraisals to discuss plans of action and the future needs of the business. Don't forget to consider career and training needs.

- Focus on developing people's strengths rather than fixing their weaknesses.

- Deal quickly and fairly with underperformance.

4. Recognition, appreciation and reward

They say that variety is the spice of life. The same could be said about total reward schemes, which are designed to include everything that employees value in the employment relationship. By everything, we include business environment, culture and values, quality of work, monetary rewards and benefits, work-life balance and future development. Some incentives reward individual performance while others, including share-based awards and payments, will ultimately depend on the performance of the business. Some rewards are monetary and others are not. From sending 1lb bags of pistachio nuts to salesmen who have sold a new machine, as Hewlett-Packard have done, to treating staff to massages or trips away, there are plenty of ways to reward good performance.

Piers Daniell, MD of Fluidata, provides a mixture of rewards, including high commission to sales staff and bonuses on company-wide performance for the rest of the employees. There is also a share option scheme to create share ownership and other benefits include company-sponsored health insurance, dental cover and gym membership.

"I think it's very important that everyone benefits from the success of the company," says Piers.

"We organise company events every three months and I ensure that extra 'gifts' are awarded for excellent work, such as a bottle of champagne or shopping vouchers," he adds. "We also give extra days' holidays and prizes for effort. I expect everyone to work as hard as I do but also to benefit from their efforts."

How to motivate through recognition, appreciation and reward

- Recognise achievements by praising, rewarding and promoting individual and team-based performance. Hold regular employee events including dinners, award ceremonies and parties to congratulate and thank your staff.

- Develop a range of performance-related incentives to align efforts with organisational objectives. From gift or childcare vouchers to gym memberships and discount cards, and from trips abroad to group away days.

- Facilitate total reward by offering flexible benefits, including buying or selling annual leave, providing dental or health insurance, pensions, life assurance and cover for critical illness.

- Provide staff with the opportunity to share in the success of the business by offering shares and share options for encashment on exit or at some specified time in the future. This gives people a vested interest in enhancing the value of the business, whilst encouraging their retention.

- Develop clear and transparent measures of performance so that you'll know when bonuses or incentives have been earned. Performance related rewards are only effective where performance can be tracked and measured.

Share schemes and awards

Once upon a time shares were a rarefied incentive, used for a small number of senior executives. Nowadays, however, the opportunity to participate in the ownership of a business is often extended to all employees.

The decision to use share options or share awards as incentives should not be taken lightly. First, the prospects and intentions of the company need to be taken into account and, second, the perceived value of the award to the employee requires consideration.

The company's prospects and intentions

The main purpose of an incentive is to reward staff, whilst encouraging their retention. Handing out shares in the business may well achieve this, but only if there's a clear and identifiable opportunity to cash the shares in at some future time.

Publicly quoted businesses (i.e. those whose shares are traded on a recognised stock exchange) often use shares to incentivise their employees. This can make great sense, as it encourages inclusivity and focuses employees on the behaviours needed to build long-term value. In a publicly quoted business, employees know that they are building a store of value and that, at the appropriate time, they will be able to turn this into cash by selling their shares in the market. They can even calculate the value of their award by checking the price of their shares in the newspaper or online.

Contrast this with a small, privately owned business. In this case, the company may be relatively unstable, with no market in the shares and a value, if any, that is extremely difficult to ascertain. Combine this with a lack of clarity over the future direction of the business, such as the principal owner being uncertain about whether to exit the business or keep it in the family, and the benefit of owning shares may be very questionable indeed.

These are two extremes, with multiple scenarios in between. In a smaller business, however, the general advice is that the shares should be held more tightly and, where possible, kept mainly in the hands of those that manage the business on a day-to-day basis.

Perceived value

If you're contemplating widening the share ownership in your business, it's important to consider the perceptions of your employees. There is no point in giving out shares or share options to your employees if these are not valued by the recipients.

Reverting to my earlier example, shares or share options are likely to be a valuable part of any package offered by a publicly quoted business whose shares are readily saleable on a stock exchange, but what is the perceived benefit of owning 1% (or much less!) in a privately owned business with an uncertain future?

To counter this problem, private companies that wish to use shares to incentivise their employees will often create an internal market. This may enable shares to be sold to other employees or bought back by the company itself. In these circumstances, the value of the shares will need to be ascertained and companies will often use external valuers to assist with this process.

At the end of the day, businesses need to consider what will motivate their employees. Many will prefer the immediacy of cash rewards to the uncertainty of share ownership and this will need to be taken into account in the design of your total reward scheme.

A winning formula

Cultivation and inclusion, motivation and reward – these are the keys to building a strong and sustainable workforce. If you care for your staff, they will care for your business, becoming ambassadors for your brand and promoting your success in an ever-changing business world.

Top tips

- **Create the right environment for your employees.** Focus on maximising the benefits of your infrastructure and the vibe of your workplace.

- **Regularly celebrate success** and remember the importance of making work fun.

- **Encourage inclusivity** and participation. It's a team game.

- **Change is unsettling**, so involve your employees in the change conversation to reduce unnecessary fear and uncertainty.

- **Encourage innovation and new ideas.** Reward original thinking and **make it safe for your employees to contribute.**

- **Make sure your management style is open and supportive**, not closed and controlling.

- **Take the well-being and advancement of your staff to heart.** Mentor and train them to help them achieve their goals.

- **Place people in roles that interest and inspire them.**

- **Recognise achievement** by praising and rewarding individual and team performances.

- **Use benchmarking** to ensure that your salaries and benefits are competitive.

- **Consider the benefits of** widening your company's ownership through **share participation.**

CHAPTER 12
Brand Identity and Culture

> **"Business must be run at a profit, else it will die. But when anyone tries to run a business solely for profit … then also the business must die, for it no longer has a reason for existence."**
>
> — Henry Ford

Creating a meaningful brand

In the modern world of consumerism and enterprise, we are fast developing an immunity to brands. Information overload and incessant marketing have desensitised people to brands and the messages they churn out. Today's business must therefore be smart when creating its brand identity and culture. Successful brands must be associated with memorable and evocative feelings, with a purpose, a personality and clear values.

Profiting with purpose

Brands are about capturing hearts and minds. If you want your brand to be noticed, you'll need a purpose that people will embrace and buy into.

Both internal culture and external identity begin with purpose. Why are you in business? What do you stand for? What is your function and relevance in society?

Purpose shapes the vision and values of your business – the inherent promise that you make to your staff, customers, suppliers and partners. It also defines the mission and the strategy, guiding your actions and behaviours. Ultimately, these combine to create your culture and brand identity.

While businesses need to make profits, that's not their only purpose. Yet businesses with a strong purpose often end up making the biggest profits:

- Apple's purpose is to innovate, to create a positive user experience and design aesthetically pleasing products.

- Google's purpose is to organise the world's information and make it universally accessible and useful.

- Gap's purpose is to make it easy for people to express their personal style throughout their lifetime.

- Skype's purpose is to revolutionise telecoms by providing an alternative via free and low-cost calls over the internet.

- Smith & Williamson's purpose is to help people create, manage and preserve their wealth.

- The Body Shop's purpose is to support community trade, defend human and animal rights and protect the planet.

- Avon's purpose is to "empower women one woman at a time to learn how to earn".

The importance of values

Liz Jackson, MD of Great Guns Marketing, has recently had her logo redesigned to reflect how they've moved on as a business. But branding, she says, is not just about imagery and logos. "For me branding is not really what we look like, it's more about who we are," says Liz. "For me, brand is more like the blood in your body that pumps around, it says so much about your company. It's how you answer the phone, your values and your culture."

Values – what you stand for – affect how you are perceived, how much custom you bring in, how your workforce perform and, ultimately, how successful your business will be.

In the rest of this chapter we'll look at how your purpose and values can attract customers and unite your workforce. We'll also consider how they can benefit the wider community, adding to the success of brands that act both ethically and responsibly.

How to attract customers

People buy from people, but they also buy from brands that they trust. Brands create trust in many ways – through product or service excellence, creativity, reliability, safety, value for money, etc. They can also build trust by establishing reassuring familiarity (which comes through raising brand awareness) and through affinity. The main way to create affinity with a brand is to make sure it stands for something.

Values are a set of ideals, attitudes and ways of doing things. They are indicative of a company's purpose – what it stands for. They enable people to see how a company ranks the importance of certain things, positioning the company according to its values and, in turn, attracting a following that relates to and concurs with those values.

As Brad Rosser, formerly of Virgin, says: "the company rather than the individuals should become known as expert and become well-known for whatever it stands for, so it becomes a 'come to' business."

Becoming a 'come to' business means that people will seek you out – your brand becomes their logical choice and destination. Rob Frankel, branding expert and author of *The Revenge of Brand X*, says: "Branding is not about getting your prospects to choose you over your competition; it's about getting your prospects to see you as the only solution to their problem."

Brands that recognise this identify and focus on their strengths. If people want innovative, stylish products they 'come to' Apple. If people want high quality audio and televisual solutions they 'come to' Bang & Olufsen. If people want value for money solutions they 'come to' easyGroup.

Purposeful businesses

Sir Stelios Haji-Ioannou created a budget brand that stands for making customers' lives easier and saving them money. His easyGroup brand values are visible and widely appealing, enabling him to expand his brand into a group of complementary businesses (easyCar, easyMusic, easyMoney, easyInternetCafe, easyHotel …). All of these share the same strong identity as his first business, easyJet.

"In easyJet I had two assets, the airline and the brand," explains Stelios. "[T]he name meant something to people, so I separated the brand from the airline."

The brand name – 'easy' – makes it clear that its purpose is to make people's lives easier. Its bright orange logo is bold and suggests affordability – reflected in its strap line, "more value for less". Every part of its brand identity is tied closely to its purpose and values.

Another good example of a 'come to' business is Saga, whose messaging clearly defines its strengths and purpose: "Saga Zone is the biggest online social network for people over 50." Saga's strength lies in focusing on a specific demographic, understanding the needs of the target audience and offering it reliable, value-for-money services. It then markets to them direct.

Saga has carved out a trusted, familiar and strong 'come to' brand across a number of different product offerings. Having started out by offering holidays, the Saga brand now offers cruises on its own ships, insurance and financial products, along with a magazine and radio station.

Nike's purpose is to encourage sporting activity. Its personality is energetic and driven. This is reflected in its name (Nike was the winged goddess of victory in ancient Greece), its logo – the infamous swoosh (positive, affirming and victorious), and its strap line ("Just Do It" – direct, encouraging, active).

Nike's strengths, the things it does really well, are product design and marketing. The brand actually transcends its products. In general, people wear Nike running shoes to look cool and feel motivated, rather than to improve their performance. They are also buying into a brand which invites them to join a community of athletes and a culture that spreads the gospel of sport.

Personality, name and image

Whilst purpose and values define a business, they are not the only elements that attract customers. Human beings are attracted by what things (and people) look like – their personalities, what they do, what they stand for and how they behave. So, as well has having clarity of purpose, strong brands must be brought to life with clearly recognisable and relevant characteristics.

People are drawn to brands with strong identities and identifiable, appealing attributes. Personality and purpose work together to create the backbone of a brand. These should be captured in the brand's name, logo and slogan, all of which should be featured on every piece of promotional material, publicity, advertising and packaging.

A good example of this is the 'Apple' name and logo, which symbolises the fruit that famously fell from a tree beside Isaac Newton and inspired his formulation of the theory of gravity. The Apple image and name suggests freshness, creative thinking and innovation.

As well as clearly representing the purpose and personality of the organisation, the brand name and logo must also position the brand correctly in the marketplace and consider its target audience and distribution.

When establishing recruitment consultancy, Alexander Mann, James Caan needed to find a name that suggested respectability. He'd already bagged a Pall Mall address – a bit of a broom cupboard but nevertheless a prestigious location in London's Mayfair. He now needed an up-market name. "It mattered what I called the business because it had to feel like a brand that clients and candidates wanted to associate with," says James. He set himself the exercise of imagining his business as a person and listing desirable characteristics: "having integrity, smart, dynamic." He then considered what this person might be called: "I came up with Alexander and wanted a short word to go with it. I chose Mann because it was masculine, which fitted my executive market," says James in his book, *The Real Deal*.

Similarly Nick Jenkins of Moonpig needed a fun and engaging brand name that was original, short and easy to remember. "If you have a consumer brand you need it to be passed on by word of mouth so you shouldn't use a word that's difficult to spell or forgettable," he says.

He also wanted a name that would generate minimal results on internet search engines. As it happened, his school nickname was Moonpig, so he tried that out. "When I started the company, if you entered Moonpig into Google nothing came up at all," an ideal scenario for a business that trades entirely over the web. The name also leant itself to a catchy and successful TV advertising jingle which boosted brand awareness.

How to unite your workforce

"A business has to be a community of people working together toward a common goal."

– Doug Richard, entrepreneur and investor

Culture goes to the heart of a business. If your purpose and values inspire your people, the likelihood of growing a great business, as well as a great brand, increase exponentially. People are proud to be associated with businesses that value 'meaning' as well as 'money'.

Alex Cheatle, the founding entrepreneur and CEO of Ten Group, the fast growing lifestyle management company, espouses this philosophy. He argues that companies that are built purely with money in mind lack depth and longevity and fail to engender loyalty from staff or other stakeholders.

Ten's values inspire its staff, who focus on satisfying and exceeding their members' expectations, fostering an environment of continuous improvement, being trustworthy and keeping their word, and, last but not least, being innovative and open to change.

These strong values are spread across the business and Alex attributes Ten's success to his workforce. "The heroes in our business are the lifestyle managers which is why we need to recruit really, really good people, then coach and train them, giving them complete autonomy to do their job, whilst supporting them."

When it comes to growth, Alex believes that it has to be earned. "Our growth is driven by a very honest and basic driver which is: the better we get, the bigger we get. If we don't get good we don't get bigger," he concludes.

In a hyper-competitive world where products and services can be instantly replicated, the only element that can't easily be imitated is the culture of an organisation.

"Your brand is only as good as its touch point at every stage of the customer journey, so focusing on culture is mission critical," says Sir Eric Peacock.

Like Alex, Sir Eric believes that giving people a cause and a purpose creates a culture that people want to be a part of, a reason to engage, interact and go the extra mile.

"From purpose comes vision and from vision comes values," adds Sir Eric. "What are the values that we hold dear as a business? What are the stakes in the ground which are non-negotiable? What are the values we fall back on when we have difficult decisions to make? What can we be held to be accountable for? From values and our behaviours against the values comes a whole area around engagement. How do we get our people to go the extra mile? Because, in going that extra mile, they deliver awesome service and have amazing relationships with our supply chain and with our customers."

Many benefits accrue from a workforce that's aligned around a shared purpose and vision. In particular, a united team is generally:

- **Harmonious.** Keen to work together to achieve a shared objective. This limits the likelihood of conflict or confusion, making it easier to reach a consensus and making coming to work a pleasure rather than a chore.

- **Productive.** People put more effort into work they enjoy and a purpose they believe in. Shared goals promote positive thinking and valuable activity.

- **Flexible.** Staff who share a vision and are embedded in the business are often better able to understand and facilitate change.

- **Loyal.** Staff are less likely to leave a team if they have a strong sense of camaraderie and purpose.

Unity of purpose and culture will be of particular importance if you are expanding your business in new locations or across borders. Ensuring that your brand stays true to your values as you grow can be challenging. Yet, if a single global culture is aligned across departments and locations at both business and group levels, it will be easier to implement new ideas, integrate teams and run an efficient and scalable organisation.

Who cares, wins

At the end of the day, the culture of a business will be determined by its leaders and managers. If they care about the business and its future, they will value both meaning and money.

How to build your brand in the wider community

It's clear that branding goes much deeper than a company's name, logo or strap line. Ultimately, branding is about the people in a business and how they, and the organisation, behave. The culture of a business determines the stature of its brand – success will not be achieved by preaching one message and practising another.

So businesses should practise what they preach. The business purpose forms the backbone of the brand, creating confidence and focus in the knowledge that 'this is the way we do things around here'. Only when the purpose and the actions of a business are aligned will the perception of its brand be favourable.

As businesses grow, it's important to consider their impact on the wider community. In particular, they should consider how they interact with and contribute to it. Implementing responsible policies and pursuing economic, environmental and social objectives simultaneously are rewarding ways to build and sustain trust.

> **"There is no more powerful a stimulator in society than business. It is more important than ever before for business to assume a moral leadership in society."**
>
> – Dame Anita Roddick, founder of the Body Shop

A responsible purpose – what is CSR?

Corporate social responsibility (CSR) is the deliberate inclusion of the public interest in business decision-making. It's about contributing and giving back to the wider world through local or global initiatives. It's also about considering and measuring a 'triple bottom line' (also TBL or 3BL) that includes profit, people and planet, a phrase coined by the founder of SustainAbility, John Elkington.

A TBL involves measuring how environmentally, socially and financially responsible a company is over time. This enables a business to:

- gain a truer understanding of the full cost of doing business

- focus more attention on the areas that are being measured and monitored

- become known as a company that cares.

It's the erosion of public trust and confidence that has propelled the cause of corporate social responsibility into the mainstream. Corporate malpractice and exploitation, child labour scandals, childhood obesity, environmental disasters and a host of other issues have all led to a sceptical and questioning public, resulting in companies having to do more to protect and manage their reputations.

Nike's nightmare

Nike is an interesting branding case study because of its corporate social responsibility record. Over the past decade it has been scrutinised, exposed, boycotted and then forgiven and celebrated. Following a public backlash and some major protests against Nike's poor working conditions, ex-CEO Phil Knight commented in 1998 that the brand had become "synonymous with slave wages, forced overtime and arbitrary abuse".

While other clothing kingpins also outsourced production to factories in developing countries, Nike was the company with the most global brand awareness and thus the company most investigated and spurned by the public. In 1998 a radical shake up was announced that included a six-point plan to set and monitor targets to improve working conditions. In 2005 the company's second corporate responsibility report revealed all of its production locations and labour policies, auditing hundreds of thousands of workers across hundreds of factories.

Over a decade later, Nike now sees corporate responsibility "as a catalyst for growth and innovation, an integral part of how we can use the power of our brand, the energy and passion of our people, and the scale of our business to create meaningful change". It has outlined a global strategy for creating a more sustainable business which includes improving conditions in contract factories, designing for a better world, achieving climate neutrality and unleashing potential through sport. It also has a renewed purpose of using sport as a powerful movement for social change by building networks of social entrepreneurs, for example, by working with Grassroot Soccer in Africa. As such, CSR has now become part of Nike's overall purpose. (Details of its purpose, approach, performance and targets are available for all to see at **www.nikeresponsibility.com**).

As CEO Mark Parker says, "Sustainability is our generation's defining issue." It therefore makes perfect sense to champion that issue. And so Nike has.

Sow and ye shall reap

Businesses that embrace CSR can boost both their reputations and their profits. By acting in the best interests of the wider community or by supporting local projects, businesses can have a big and positive impact. This will be rewarded in terms of positive PR, happier and more loyal staff, better relationships with suppliers and partners and, ultimately, more customers and profits.

You reap what you sow, so efforts to implement CSR in your business should not become an exercise in box-ticking. To be effective, CSR should be embedded in your day-to-day operations – part of your culture.

Here are some ideas to help you build your programme:

Give money and time

- Identify your CSR champions and empower them across different locations and teams.

- Establish charitable funding initiatives and get your staff involved. Ask them what causes they would like to support.

- Make volunteering a part of your culture. Create schemes that enable staff to participate in local or overseas volunteering initiatives, taking them out of their daily roles and making them proud of their role and contribution.

- Provide free services or products to selected not-for-profit and charitable organisations.

- Involve customers and suppliers, as well as staff, in your initiatives.

Save the planet

- Put energy-saving and CO_2 reducing initiatives into action. Aim to make your company as carbon-neutral and energy-efficient as possible.

- Minimise waste. Make a concerted effort to reduce the amount of materials and consumables that you throw away.

- Recycle paper, plastics, cans, water, food waste – everything from coffee machine cups to office furniture. Use packaging materials that are recyclable.

- Reduce paper consumption: avoid printing e-mails and other documents that can be stored and accessed over a computer or online network and reduce the number of mailings and paper catalogues that you distribute.

- Fix or donate damaged or redundant equipment. Fix goods that are returned, where possible.

- Avoid using plastic bags for packaging or plastic bottles for water.

- Encourage staff to lift-share or cycle to work.

Sell, source and produce ethically

- Create socially and environmentally responsible and sustainable products and add them to your range.

- Source products from fair trade or organic suppliers to ensure that what you sell is produced and traded fairly.

- Work with local producers to develop sustainable, local supplies.

- Use healthy, non-fattening ingredients if you produce or source food or drink.

- Create a production code of conduct and stick to it.

- Check that workers across your entire supply chain are treated fairly and responsibly.

Communicate honestly

- Tell your customers your story. Share details of your materials and processes so they can make informed decisions.

- Be transparent about your operations – how and why you do what you do. Encourage feedback by opening channels of communication and then listen and respond accordingly.

- Collaborate with customers, competitors and suppliers within your industry to improve communication, encourage innovation and establish shared ground rules.

- Commit to ethical targets and report on your progress. For example, Marks & Spencer has an electronic ticker in its London HQ which indicates its progress towards achieving 100 CSR targets over a specific time span which is monitored by a 'How We Do Business' Committee. "The company will help to give 15,000 children in Uganda a better education; it is saving 55,000 tonnes of CO2 in a year; it has recycled 48 million clothes hangers; it is tripling sales of organic food; it aims to convert over 20 million garments to Fairtrade cotton."

Some shining examples

The following companies prove that being a good business is also good for business:

- **Toyota** has championed environmentally friendly, responsible motoring, not only by introducing new models, such as the Prius hybrid, but also through lobbying the car industry to change its ways and find alternatives to the existing fuel-led standard.

- **Comet** have trained people who have been unemployed for long periods of time to strip down and fix returned goods and donate or sell them at a discount to disadvantaged local families. In doing so they are saving waste and serving their local communities.

- Ice cream maker **Ben & Jerry's** grew from a headquarters in a renovated petrol station to a company which was sold to Unilever in 2000 for $326 million. It did this while having an ethical purpose at its core, giving back to the community, promoting peace and acting responsibly. Through a social enterprise initiative called the PartnerShop Programme, the company waived its franchise fees to help establish community-based non-profit organisations. They also promoted environmental campaigns through the creation of new ice cream flavours such as One Sweet Whirled, introduced the first unbleached paperboard 'eco-pint' carton to the ice cream industry and supported family farms and rural communities. Additionally they donated 7.5% of their pre-tax profits to non-profit organisations through their own charitable foundation.

- **Levi Strauss** set his corporate values as empathy, originality and integrity. These values remain today. Back in 1968, Levi Strauss pioneered the idea of employee volunteer programmes by establishing Community Involvement Teams. Over two decades later the company became the first worldwide company to create an ethical code of conduct for its manufacturing and finishing contractors.

┌───┐

── Top tips ──

- Determine your purpose and values. **Be clear about what you stand for** in order to become a 'come to' business – a logical choice and destination both for customers and staff.

- **Use images and words that evoke feelings** and capture your purpose, ethos and personality.

- **Communicate your vision and purpose** regularly. "We communicate our vision monthly in a company meeting that everyone attends, including new recruits. And we have a social at least once a quarter," says Liz Jackson.

- Create a template and style guide to **present your brand consistently**. Use this at every opportunity – in your communications and on your packaging.

- **Ensure you have an internet domain for your brand**. "There's no point in coming up with a brand that is already booked on the internet," says Nick Jenkins of Moonpig.com, "so Google it to ensure that there are no conflicting brands."

- Always practise what you preach – **success will not be achieved by preaching one message and practising another.**

- **Take corporate social responsibility seriously.** Staff, customers and even suppliers want to work with businesses that attach value to 'meaning' as well as 'money'.

- Create time and space for social and environmental projects. **Encourage local and international projects, charitable giving and volunteering.**

- **Source your products responsibly** and ensure that what you sell is produced and traded fairly.

- Recognise that **environmental responsibility goes hand in hand with good management** and that it usually reduces your costs.

└───┘

CHAPTER 13
Sales and Marketing

"We miss 100% of the sales we don't ask for."

– Zig Ziglar, motivational speaker

What customers want

As one of my colleagues once said, life would be easy if it wasn't for the customers! He was right. Customers can be fickle and demanding, slow to praise and quick to criticise. That's why you've got to get it right.

Before you can think about selling, you'll need a well-developed product or service that people want or need, together with a clear market positioning.

Think about Amstrad's E-m@iler telephone, launched in 2000, or Sir Clive Sinclair's famous C5, an electric- and pedal-powered tricycle launched in 1985. In terms of sales, neither were commercial successes, despite strong awareness amongst the general public.

In Amstrad's case, their combined land-line telephone and emailer was poorly priced and badly timed. Notwithstanding the fact that it was aesthetically unattractive and (apparently) a pain in the asterisk to use, it may have had more chance of success if it had been launched five years earlier. By 2000, it was already past its sell-by date, with home computers well-established as the default means of reading and sending email.

Sir Clive Sinclair is a brilliant inventor, but the Sinclair C5 was an extraordinary looking machine, with handlebars underneath the driver's knees and a top speed of 15mph (designed to avoid the need for a driving licence). Other problems included a tendency to overheat when going up hills, an exposed driving position and concerns about safety. The safety issue (due to the C5 being so low to the ground and potentially invisible to other road users) was addressed by putting a reflector on top of a tall pole! It had its fans but the media, and just about everyone else, ridiculed it.

If you've got the right product or service, positioning will impact on your business success. Darren Shirlaw, founder of fast-growing international coaching company Shirlaws, says that businesses need to be clear about what they are offering to their customers. To ensure customer loyalty and maximum profitability, he says it should be one of the following:

- product focus – for example Apple, with its iPad

- market focus – for example Saga, targeting the over-50s

- service focus – for example Amazon, with its personalised product recommendations

- price focus – for example easyJet, with its low cost flights.

"Lack of focus makes a business weaker and more susceptible to the threat of competition and market price pressures," says Darren.

How to discover what customers want

'Build it and they will come' is the well-known mantra, but there's more to this than guesswork. You need to ask questions, and then listen, to identify your customers' needs.

Here are some ways to do it:

- **Get your offer out there to get it tested.** "The only people who can tell you whether or not your product or services are right are your customers," says Brad Rosser, formerly of Virgin. James Caan agrees: "A question often asked in the *Dragons' Den* is 'Has the product actually been sent to your target market?' Too often the negative response indicates that people overcomplicate their marketing strategy and don't simply identify the customer and put the product into their hand."

- **Gain insight from customers and user groups.** Invite customers to join your advisory community to identify and test positive and negative experiences. Uncover why things did or didn't work, why you've gained or lost custom, met or missed targets. Dig out problems to identify solutions. Learn from your mistakes and put them right. "Every deal we don't get we always return to the prospect and ask why they chose someone else to find out how we can improve our approach next time," says Liz Jackson of Great Guns Marketing. Additionally, you can gather success stories. "We have a client club which meets bi-monthly where our clients come along and share stories. Nobody else does that in our industry," says Liz.

- **Get feedback on your marketing and sales efforts.** This will improve conversion rates. "If I think an ad is going to work, I perfect it as best I can without spending too much effort and get it out there. I then listen to feedback and adjust it," says Brad Rosser. "When it's been tweaked to perfection and the conversions and analytical side are working out, I'll throw everything I've got at it."

- **Source intelligence from competitors' customers.** Ask them why they buy competing products, but don't try to sell to them. They will probably be more open and less diplomatic than your own customers will.

- **Think about the future.** It's not just about today. Successful businesses like Apple think about people's future wants and needs in order to gain and maintain their competitive advantage. And as Henry Ford once pointed out, if he had just asked what people wanted, they would have said a faster horse.

Choosing the right model

You may have the right product and positioning, but have you got the right business model? Having the wrong model may mean that it's difficult or impossible to sell your product or service at a profit, or at all.

Many businesses have been caught by innovation. As we saw earlier, Kodak was unprepared for the digital revolution, forcing it to change its model and approach. Other good examples include the travel industry (online travel agents), the publishing industry (online books and directories) and the banking industry (online banking).

And let's not forget the manufacturers. They haven't had it easy either. Technology and globalisation have opened up intense competition, with large buyers moving their allegiance from developed countries to emerging economies to take advantage of lower labour costs and, often, more efficient production capabilities. Many of those who failed to adapt are no longer in business. There's an important factor here that we'll examine in more detail when we look at social media – another technology-induced pivot point that may force slow-moving or non-believing companies out of business.

All things being equal, if you've got the right products and services, the right market positioning and the right business model, you'll have every chance of success. It's time to look at your marketing.

Marketing – what is it?

In its simplest form, marketing is about doing the things that will make customers want to do business with you. It therefore extends far beyond your product or service, encompassing brand, culture, reputation and orientation. It depends on values like trust and quality. It takes account of design and price. It worries about production methods and considers social and environmental impacts.

It follows that there is almost no part of a business that is exempt from the process of marketing. As a consequence, marketing should be seen as one of the key components of business management – a promoter and guardian of your brand and a fundamental business driver.

Marketing is different from selling. Theodore C. Levitt was a former emeritus professor at Harvard Business School. He said that "selling concerns itself with the tricks and techniques of getting people to exchange their cash for your product. It is not concerned with the values that the exchange is all about. And it does not, as marketing invariably does, view the entire business process as consisting of a tightly integrated effort to discover, create, arouse and satisfy customer needs".

Perhaps it's not as simple as it first appears. In the past, marketing was seen largely as a creative industry, a support function dealing with advertising and doing a bit of PR. Times have changed. Marketing is now recognised as a science, encompassing psychology, sociology and anthropology, mixed with a good dose of economics and finance. In today's world, marketing will often lead, rather than support, a business.

And finally, there's internal marketing, the process by which employees engage with the brand and deliver it to external audiences, encouraging both customer acquisition and retention. We have already looked at what motivates people. Giving them a clear understanding of the business purpose and values and training them to deliver these in your target markets will make all your staff into valuable brand advocates and do wonders for internal morale.

A professional game

Too many businesses play at marketing, using inexperienced staff to carry out one-off and, often, pointless tasks. The emergence of marketing as a real business driver, combined with advances in technology and the realisation that marketing lies at the heart of nearly every successful business, means that marketing is no longer a game for amateurs. Professionals are now required.

There are various skill sets needed, all of which deserve careful deliberation to build a unified and effective team. Key areas include marketing communications (Marcomms), public relations (PR), business development (BD), database and customer relationship management (CRM), events and, last but certainly not least, website management and development. Other specialist skills, such as research, e-marketing, copywriting and knowledge of social media may also be required.

A good marketing team needs an enthusiastic, commercially aware and driven leader – a person who keeps the team fully informed about key priorities and initiatives as well as focused on working together. This person needs to be 'connected' (i.e. wired in) to the business and will either be on or close to the board of directors, using his or her detailed knowledge of marketing and the market to influence direction and strategy as new trends and technologies emerge.

Marketing team leaders need strong support from the CEO and senior management of a business. They offer a different skill set so, not only do they need a voice, they also need to be allowed to experiment to help drive the business forward and stay ahead of its competition. Too often, management teams dismiss the importance of a fully functioning and coordinated marketing team, relegating it to the sidelines. They do so at their peril!

Back to strategy and planning

In order to run a successful marketing function you'll need a strategy (the 'how' that determines the big picture that you need to paint) and a plan (the 'what' that you need to do on a day-to-day basis to achieve your strategy).

For example, Smith & Williamson's marketing strategy is based on its business strategy – that of helping clients create, manage and preserve their wealth. This central purpose gives way to a set of essential values – trust, expertise, responsiveness, empathy, quality of service – that make Smith & Williamson a 'come to' brand for private clients and entrepreneurs seeking support to either grow or manage their wealth.

Everything that Smith & Williamson does is designed to create and strengthen relationships and maintain and build on its reputation for expertise and quality across a variety of financial disciplines. This might range from advising the founders of an insightful start-up business to managing the wealth of already successful entrepreneurs or other high-net-worth individuals.

For Smith & Williamson, then, the marketing strategy is about developing relationships – finding ways to make people aware of the firm's existence and services, meeting them, keeping them informed, earning their trust, helping them understand their financial and business affairs and, wherever possible, relieving them of their financial uncertainties and worries. This is achieved through a marketing 'plan' that consists of a mixture of offline and online communications, thought leadership, entering (and often winning) awards for excellence, client testimonials, public relations, technical updates, seminars and networking events, as well as through building strong relationships with complementary, non-competing, organisations.

Every business has different needs. At the end of the day, developing a marketing strategy will ensure that energy and resources are deployed effectively and consistently to increase sales and achieve a sustainable competitive advantage.

It's all in the mix

Good marketing is never 'one-off' or reactive – this kind of approach will get you nowhere. Instead, it is a coordinated and sustained mixture of activities that position your business where you want it to be.

The term 'marketing mix' was coined in the 1950s, when the role of marketers was considered to be that of a 'mixer of ingredients', sometimes following established recipes and sometimes making it up and trying new ingredients as they went along.

This marketing mix evolved into the 'four Ps', standing for product, price, place and promotion, representing the key ingredients required for successful customer-oriented marketing. If any of the four Ps is functioning incorrectly or is absent from the marketing mix, competitors can supposedly muscle their way in and cause a fall in demand.

Theodore C. Levitt talked about 'marketing myopia'. According to his theory, most businesses fail to reach their potential because of their myopic (i.e. short-sighted) approach and their failure to be customer-oriented and to understand the business they are in. He used the railroad industry as an example.

Railroad businesses, he argued, did not stop growing because the demand for passenger and freight transport declined. In fact, demand increased. They stopped growing because the need was filled by others – cars, trucks and aeroplanes – who successfully competed for and won their customers. They let others take their customers away from them because they incorrectly assumed themselves to be in the railroad business, as opposed to the transport business.

The customer is always king!

Marketing fundamentals

Having identified the business you're really in, you'll need a few more ingredients before you can write your marketing plan. Remember that marketing is about doing the things that will make customers want to do business with you, so you'll also need to think about:

- your value proposition
- your audience
- your messaging.

Your value proposition

A value proposition is a statement that summarises the particular benefits that a customer will receive by buying your product or service, as opposed to anyone else's.

The best value propositions are normally easy to summarise. For example, easyJet's value proposition is that their 'no frills' service will get you from A to B more cheaply and more efficiently than anybody else and that they'll do everything in their power to ensure that their planes leave on time.

Some value propositions can even be summed up in a single word, e.g. 'safety' (Volvo), 'price' (Walmart) and 'search' (Google).

Similarly, businesses with a disruptive business model, aka 'game changers', have no problems articulating their value proposition. Think of Skype's disruption of the telephone industry, or eBay's redefinition of the second-hand goods market.

For most businesses, the luxury of disruption is difficult to achieve and businesses that can achieve it are in the minority. That doesn't mean we can't all run successful businesses, with or without disruption.

According to David G. Thomson, author of *Blueprint to a Billion*, there are three kinds of value proposition:

- 'Shapers of a new world' – businesses that truly create a new market for their products and services.

- 'Niche shapers' – businesses that follow new world shapers with products or services that redefine and address a specific market segment.

- 'Category killers' – businesses that optimise a market by attacking the existing incumbents with a better, faster, cheaper value offer.

"I initially thought that the greatest number of Blueprint companies (the 5% that have IPO'd since 1980 and grown to $1 billion in revenue) would be shapers of a new world," says David. "[But] I found over 43% of top Blueprint companies to be either niche shapers or category killers. This finding counters the notion that most great companies require new innovation waves or eras in order to grow."

Whichever category you're in, or even if none of these categories fit, you'll need a value proposition to enable you to create marketing messages for your target audience. As Sir Eric Peacock advises, "I don't think businesses spend sufficient time on developing and articulating their value proposition and integrating that value proposition into all the stages of the marketing plan, from targeting to after-sales."

Your audience

Having a great product or service is only part of the equation. You'll also need to identify the customers who will buy from you, and why. This is an area where entrepreneurs are often overcome by their enthusiasm, thinking that they can sell everything to everybody, but it's difficult to make a meaningful splash in a giant ocean.

It's even more difficult to make that meaningful splash in a short time, with plenty of potentially great businesses running out of cash or failing because they underestimate their time to market, relying on over-optimistic and wholly unrealistic sales projections. This is one of the principal reasons why investors are wary of pre-revenue start-ups – just how long does that piece of string need to be?

Working out who is going to buy your products or services, and why, is an absolute priority before you spend a penny on marketing. In order to do this you need to carry out some form of market research, positioning yourself against your competitors and understanding what will motivate potential customers to buy from you. There's no point in entering a market that is already well served by respected operators unless you can demonstrate some extra or different value. Perhaps your product or service is more suited to a particular niche market, or perhaps it's better, faster or cheaper? Perhaps customers using your service will benefit from more experienced advisors or a range of additional benefits not available from your competitors?

Remember that, unless you are truly disruptive, any differentiation will always seem more meaningful and relevant to you than it does to your (potential) customers.

All of this means that you need to measure your thinking and focus on the opportunities that are likely to generate the cash and profits that will sustain your business, cover your overheads and enable your growth in the future. Here are some ways to help you evaluate your audience:

- **Identify the pain.** What pains are your potential customers suffering from and how will your offering ease or cure them?

- **Study your competitors.** Look at your successful and unsuccessful competitors. Who is buying from them and why? Can you win their customers and take their market share?

- **Consider customer traits.** Are there any particular traits displayed by your potential customers in terms of age, gender or ethnicity?

- **Look at buying habits.** Make sure you understand how your customers buy the products or services you want to sell and then structure your business model accordingly.

- **Remember that business buyers are different.** Selling to businesses rather than consumers involves a wholly different dynamic. Businesses often have established supply agreements that are difficult, or take time, to change.

- **Target a niche.** For many businesses, clear focus on a specific market is often the best way to achieve profitable growth.

- **Identify the low-hanging fruit.** It will often be easier to sell more to existing customers than to win new ones.

- **Don't try to be all things to all men.** Identify your critical path and focus on your strengths.

Defining you target audience is an essential part of the jigsaw. By understanding which customers you should be targeting you can identify the best routes to market and tailor your marketing messages to suit their specific needs.

Your messaging

In today's world we are bombarded with marketing messages. On the street, in newspapers and magazines, on the radio, on TV, on the internet. As intelligent human beings we have learnt to ignore much of this 'noise', so that the majority of what we see or hear is filtered out and, effectively, invisible to us. Because of this innate filtering process it's only the messaging we want to hear that gets through.

As David Frey, author of *The UK Small Business Marketing Bible*, says in his five-step formula for creating your marketing message: "The biggest marketing message mistake I see is companies communicating 'What-We-Do' instead of 'What's-In-It-For-Me.' If these were two radio channels (i.e. WWD vs WIIFM), which one do you think your prospect would rather hear? While you are playing WWD on your radio transmitter, your prospect is looking for the WIIFM station. In order for your message to match your market you need to be broadcasting WIIFM."

Theodore Levitt, Harvard professor, agreed: "People don't want to buy a quarter-inch drill. They want a quarter-inch hole."

Perceived wisdom says that you have 30 seconds or less, the proverbial 'elevator pitch', to capture attention and build rapport, whether that's over the phone, online, or face-to-face. You therefore need to ensure that your messages and communications get to the point quickly.

"As an ad man, the ads I used to enjoy writing most were the big 48-sheet poster billboards," says serial entrepreneur Jonathan Hick. "20-feet wide and the optimum number of words for the speed of cars passing is nine. If you can't sum up your business proposition in nine words with an accompanying picture, you've got to rethink it," advises Jonathan. "Clarity of message is absolutely crucial."

Your messaging should:

- **Spell out what's in it for the customer**, explaining in as few words as possible exactly why the problem is important and how your offer is going to meet their needs.

- **Differentiate yourself from your competitors.** Explain why your product or solution adds more value.

- **Back up your claims.** Provide proof and/or examples of the benefits associated with your product or service. Use testimonials from satisfied customers.

- **Include a call to action** by telling the prospect what to do next to take advantage of this opportunity.

- **Facilitate contact** so they can continue the conversation with you.

"A good sentence is like architecture," says Jonathan Hick. "A well-designed building doesn't necessarily cost any more than an ugly building but it has ten times more aesthetic value. And that's true of a piece of marketing. Whether it's a piece of advertising, packaging or marketing literature, well-designed and well-written marketing messages don't cost any more than bad ones, so there's no need to suffer the consequences of bad marketing."

Marketing – how to do it

By now, you should have all of the information you need to develop an insightful and effective marketing plan. To summarise what has gone before, this will include:

- a product or service that people need or want

- a business model that will enable profitable growth

- a marketing strategy – the big picture that you want to paint

- a value proposition that highlights the benefits your customers will receive

- a target audience that you believe will be receptive to your advances

- a message that tells potential customers what's in it for them.

With all of these in place, you can move forward and build your detailed plan.

Begin at the beginning

Before you start, you are going to need to determine how much you have available to spend on your marketing. This should include your staff costs as well as your direct costs. Growing businesses rarely have all of the resources they need in-house, so outsourcing costs may also need to be considered.

Once you've determined your available spend, you'll need to consider the mixture of activities that you want to carry out. These are the day-to-day tactics you'll deploy to achieve your marketing strategy.

It's important to note that marketing should never be a series of one-offs, but a coordinated and sustainable activity that will continuously move you towards the centre of your market, building awareness and enhancing your reputation along the way. This will never happen overnight, so remember the old chestnut: 'Success by the inch is a cinch, success by the yard is hard!'

Consider all the elements

A mixture of activities will normally be required to successfully take your products or services to market. There are many to choose from, so all you need to do is to select which ones to pursue and how to combine them to find the perfect marketing balance. Simple? No, it's not!

As Lord Leverhulme (1851–1925, founder of Unilever) famously said: "Half the money I spend on advertising is wasted and the problem is, I don't know which half."

At the end of the day, you have to find ways to test and measure every aspect of your marketing, but this can only be done after the event. Experimentation, hopefully using small and affordable steps, is therefore required.

Here is a summary of the key elements for you to consider:

- **Brochures, leaflets and flyers.** Most businesses use a brochure or hand-out to provide general information about their activities. These typically include key information, including the business name, contact details and addresses, philosophy and value proposition, details of products and services and biographical information about the management and staff. Leaflets and flyers can also be used to highlight particular products, services or offers or to update the market on important changes e.g. technological developments or new legislation.

- **Website.** This is no longer an optional extra. Nobody is going to believe that your business is credible without a well-designed and informative website and you can be sure that anyone who is thinking of dealing with you will look. The real question is how far you need to go. Do you want a commercial website that enables you to sell your products or services, or do you want a website that simply provides information? Or perhaps a hybrid of the two? You'll need to decide how interactive you want to be and whether to include extras like newsrooms, blogs and chat rooms.

- **Advertising and advertorials.** Advertising has its place in the marketing mix but smaller businesses may be right to question its effectiveness, especially if it's carried out on an ad hoc basis. Advertorial, say in a trade or professional journal, may be more rewarding as you'll get the opportunity to position your business as a commentator or leader. The more that advertorial looks and feels like editorial, the better. For some businesses, advertising is a cost of sale rather than an overhead. Examples of this are businesses that sell 'off the page' in newspapers and magazines, with sales being measured against the cost of the specific advertising.

- **Posters and billboards.** These advertising techniques are typically used by larger businesses to draw the attention of the general public on buildings and by the roadside.

- **Sponsorship.** Sponsorship is widely used and generally associates a business with particular sports or causes. Sponsorship can be used by businesses of all sizes, from a local business sponsoring a village fete right up to sponsoring individual motor racing teams in Formula One, where annual sponsorships often cost tens of millions of dollars.

- **Thought leadership and public relations (PR).** This is the cheapest and, arguably, the best way to get publicity for you and your business. Both your national and trade press need to fill their pages with interesting content and will be happy to talk to you if you can provide this. Remember that a story about you will also reflect on your business – Richard Branson of Virgin is the king of PR, gaining publicity from things like his ballooning and powerboating exploits.

- **Newsletters.** A traditional form of communication to help educate and keep your customers and prospects up to date. These can be sprinkled with information about what's happening in your business and highlight any special offers or opportunities.

- **Direct mail.** Direct communications sent to targeted lists of potential buyers, introducing your business and delivering a specific offer. Also known as junk mail – the spam of the offline world.

- **Catalogues.** Magazines or books filled with products of all descriptions, enabling customers to choose and buy products from the comfort of their own homes.

- **Online and email marketing.** Everything that can be done offline can also be done online – often with better or more extensive results. The beauty of online marketing is that it can be easily tracked and measured, as well being visible to search engines and therefore available to a much wider audience. Online marketing includes search, affiliate marketing, email marketing, online networking, link development, viral campaigns, display advertising, blogging, podcast and/or online video creation, online prize draws and other methods of directing leads to your website or selling over the internet. We'll consider the power of the internet and its impact on marketing and consumption later in this chapter.

- **Social media.** An increasingly powerful medium which uses web-based and mobile technologies to turn communication into interactive and collaborative dialogue. Social media allows the creation of user-generated content which can easily go viral, reaching millions of people. It's inexpensive and accessible, and a revolutionary marketing tool.

- **Seminars and conferences.** Traditional event-led, face-to-face marketing enabling dissemination of information and direct interaction with both clients and prospects. Useful for customer care as well as new customer generation. The online version is webinars, which disseminate information without creating the same level of social interaction.

- **Networking and entertaining.** You can build relationships with prospects and clients by creating networking opportunities and entertaining them. This can range from a one-to-one coffee or lunch, to offering your clients and prospects (expensive!) hospitality at prestigious events. In today's world, the latter tends to be the preserve of the larger corporates.

- **Telemarketing.** Direct communication with customers and potential customers to alert them to a particular opportunity or offer. Making unsolicited calls is a long and arduous business and there are specialist call centres that you can employ to do this on your behalf. In-house telemarketing can be useful to ask people to attend events, or to follow up afterwards. Many countries have rules about cold calling, so be aware of these.

- **Awards and testimonials.** Awards and testimonials from satisfied clients can give your business credibility. It's far better to have third parties endorse the excellence of your products and services rather than shout about them yourself. Awards can be publicised through PR, on your website and on all written communications issued by your business. Personal awards, such as entrepreneur of the year, even if only at a local level, will raise your awareness and profile.

- **Case studies.** Prepare case studies for use in your marketing materials and on your website. These will show your expertise or the effectiveness of your products in real-life situations.

- **Trade shows and exhibitions.** A place to see and be seen. As a visitor you can find out about your competitors. As an exhibitor, you can meet and entertain customers and prospects on your stand. Event businesses will typically build a 'package' for their exhibitors. This may involve giving them tickets to give to their clients and prospects or providing speaking opportunities at the event. These activities are normally trailed and supported by online and offline marketing before, during and after the event.

- **Vouchers and incentives.** Techniques used to attract customers to your brand, such as promotional samples or gifts, competitions and prize draws, guarantees and warranties, time-limited special offers and loyalty schemes, vouchers and points systems.

- **Public speaking.** A great way to build your personal and business brands. The three key ingredients are expertise, opinion and the ability to stand and deliver. For most people, it is the last of these that generally causes the problem!

- **Alliances and affiliations.** Think collaboration, not isolation. There are many opportunities for complementary, non-competing businesses to work together. Relationships like these can help your customers by providing them with access to a wider range of products and services. At the same time, you can extend your marketing reach by accessing and influencing customers served by your alliance partners.

It's only through experimentation that you'll find out what works best for your business. However, taking a campaigning approach tends to work best for most businesses. This means that, when you want to promote your products or services, you need to think about using a variety of different marketing techniques to help you achieve your aims. In this way, you can coordinate and focus your resources and get the best bang for your buck.

The impact of the internet

This is a huge topic and I will only touch on it here. However, once or twice in a lifetime, momentous things happen. In my lifetime, the post-war emergence of a youth culture in the 1960s, personified by the Beatles and 'flower power', was one of these. The other has been the emergence of IT and the internet.

Technology has changed our lives in both good and bad ways. On the plus side, technology has helped to create a level playing field and has been a primary driver of globalisation. We now know what's happening almost everywhere in the world, even as it's happening. This open architecture has already led to a transfer of power to the people and even, to some extent, the fall of unpopular dictatorships. It has also led to opportunities for smaller businesses to take their fair share of national and international trade. The internet is a great enabler and an almost limitless source of information.

On the downside, technology has changed individual behaviour, often reducing face-to-face communication and encouraging workers to use email and search, rather than speaking to each other or picking up the phone. You only have to go into an office to find the evidence – silent roomfuls of people staring at computer screens and/or mobile phones.

But, just like the cultural revolution of the 1960s, the internet is creating a great divide. As new techniques such as social media emerge, many are being left behind. These are the people that either don't or don't want to get it. This may be because they don't want to spend their days staring at their mobile devices or because they simply don't understand the sea change that is happening – a move to a more engaged world where online collaboration creates opportunities and influences behaviours.

From a marketing perspective, we are moving away from broadcast marketing to engagement marketing. At the click of a button, blogs, wikis and search enable us to find out what we need to know about the products or services that we buy. Social networks create the opportunity to seek advice from an almost unlimited audience. Poor products and unscrupulous or ineffective suppliers are uncovered in an instant.

How can we describe this change? Think of a marketing funnel. Our old 'broadcast' mentality involves inundating the market with information about our business and our products, getting leads and pouring them in to the top of our funnel. As we progress, some leads die away but others go all the way, becoming new customers as they drip out of the bottom of our funnel.

Now think about turning the funnel upside down, and feeding a drip of information into its narrow, inverted end. As that drip of information passes through the funnel, it opens itself up to being found on the world wide web. If it's interesting enough, it may be found by thousands, or even millions, of people. This is the phenomenon that is the internet.

The internet is here to stay, yet many businesses, both large and small, still regard it as a way of displaying their online brochure, using a platform that's now focused on engagement for a lowly broadcast purpose. If you're on the wrong side of the divide, it's time to wake up and smell the coffee. Every business needs a digital strategy to enable it to create and maintain meaningful relationships with its target audience.

Businesses that fail to recognise this trend will slowly lose ground to their more enlightened competitors. And no business will be exempt.

From marketing to sales

Effective marketing may be crucial to the success of your business, but sales are your ultimate goal. It follows that the main function of a sales person or sales team is to capitalise on the good work done by your marketing team, turning prospects into customers and building your top line.

In smaller businesses, everybody should be a sales person. As businesses grow, however, they may need to organise their sales functions more formally, building a professional sales team or considering other distribution channels to make the best use of the leads and opportunities that the combined marketing and sales functions produce. After all, there is little point in spending time and money generating opportunities, only to have them negated by an inexperienced or, even worse, inept sales team who upset your prospects, deliver the wrong messages or fail to deliver on their promises.

In the rest of this chapter we will look at elements of the sales process and consider how you can take your products and services to market.

Customer relationship management

We've talked about the importance of identifying and targeting your audience, but not how you manage your interaction. As a small business, you'll probably know your customers and prospects intimately, but as you grow it will become harder to keep track of what's happening. This is where customer relationship management (CRM) comes in.

CRM is a process that uses technology to manage and monitor your interactions with your customers and prospects. It's not just there to track and manage your pipeline, but also to help you manage your wider contacts and relationships.

Many existing businesses struggle with the implementation of modern CRM systems. The task of planning and building a CRM system that suits an organisation's needs and then converting tens or even hundreds of thousands of records can be time consuming, expensive and more than a little daunting. Some management teams see this as an unnecessary or even superfluous expense, preferring to maintain short-term profitability rather than investing in the tools that will enable efficiency and growth in the future.

Because of the costs and complexities, some businesses attempt to improve existing, often proprietary, systems whilst others implement standalone systems to enable individual departments to satisfy their needs. The former generally means that your business is likely to remain behind the curve, eventually spending more to get less than a business that grasps the nettle and invests in state-of-the-art solutions. The latter means that you will not have an integrated system, resulting in exposure to adverse reputational risks as one arm of your business blindly pursues a prospect or existing customer without understanding the often complex and sensitive relationships already in play elsewhere.

Systems that start off in a disorganised or fragmented way tend to stay that way. With state-of-the-art technology being both available and affordable, there is no need for growing businesses to fall into this trap.

Channels to market

Having identified who your customers are or will be, there are a variety of ways that you can access and sell to them. These are known as channels to market. Your channels to market may be direct or through partnerships, with you as the originator of a particular product or service, or as a reseller of someone else's product or service.

Here are some of the most typical routes to market:

Direct

- **Face-to-face** – this type of selling is typically used for high value or complex sales, or where the selling is part of a consultative process. It is generally the most time-consuming and expensive method of selling.

- **Direct mail, telesales and e-commerce** – there is a strong overlap with marketing and we have already discussed these methods earlier in this chapter.

- **Off the page** – some businesses use off the page advertising to sell their products. To do this successfully, you'll need to create a winning offer. Experts say that full page advertisements generally outperform half pages and that advertising a single product is typically more successful than offering multiple products.

- **Wholesalers and distributors** – many businesses sell to wholesalers and distributors who then on-sell their products. These may be businesses that sell products like telephone systems, photocopiers, furniture and consumables to other businesses, or businesses that sell to retailers for onward sale to end users. A variety of commercial arrangements may come into play. These may range from the outright sale of stock, to sale or return or even consignment stock arrangements where stock is simply loaned pending its future sale.

Agents

Sales agents are people or businesses that sell your goods or services on your behalf, generally in return for a sales-based commission. They can often help you win business in specialist markets or in geographical locations which might otherwise be difficult to access.

Agents can also be helpful where you lack the resources to reach all your potential targets, acting as a specialist, results-based, salesforce.

If you are considering appointing an agent, there are a number of issues to consider. These include:

- **Track record** – look at the track record and trading history of the agent. Are they financially secure? Don't underestimate the damage to your reputation if they go bankrupt or let you down. Take references and carry out credit checks before proceeding.

- **Knowledge and expertise** – ensure that your agent has the relevant knowledge and expertise to sell your product successfully in the market.

- **Competition** – make sure that your agent is not representing other businesses with products that compete with your own.

- **Enthusiasm** – consider how enthusiastic the agent is about your product or business. Don't give exclusivity or valuable territorial rights to an agent who will only half-heartedly represent your business.

Joint ventures and partnerships

Consider working with other businesses to help you increase your sales. By collaborating with non-competing, complementary business, you can increase your firepower and reach. We'll consider this in detail in Chapter 14.

Franchise

If you have a profitable business with a distinctive format, then franchising might be a quick, efficient and cash-flow friendly way to increase your sales and revenues. A franchise is a method that enables an individual or business to buy in to an established brand name and operating system, enabling both the franchisor (in this example, you) and the franchisee to run independently owned, profitable businesses.

Under a franchise arrangement, a franchisee will typically pay the franchisor for the right to operate the franchise. This is likely to involve an up-front payment covering the agreement, designs, training and other set-up costs. Once the franchise is in operation, the franchisee will usually pay a percentage of turnover to the franchisor, with the franchisor providing marketing, branding and other advice and guidance to help the franchisee build a successful and profitable business.

Note that franchisees run their own businesses at their own risk – the arrangements between franchisor and franchisee are purely contractual. Under a typical franchise agreement, they will pay for the set-up of their operations (e.g. premises and fit-out costs), manage their own resources and benefit or suffer from their own profits or losses.

Running a sales team

They used to say that sales is an art, not a science. In today's environment, it's both. The enthusiasm and passion that drove the salesmen of the past is just as important now as it was then. But now we have a plethora of psychology, technology and science to complicate the process!

Part of the problem is choice. Bearing in mind that potential customers are bombarded with sales and marketing messages, why would they choose you as their supplier?

If you're running a sales team, you're in the business of creating and maintaining relationships with customers and prospects. This activity has to set the right balance and tone of voice for the business that you are in. Consultative selling techniques will, for example, be different to product-selling techniques.

Building and training a sales team, if you have one, is therefore a challenging process. Touch, feel and tone of voice will need to be combined with product or service knowledge and expertise. One will not work effectively without the other.

Here are some tips on running an effective sales team:

- **Recruit the right people** – sales people are natural enthusiasts. In order to take the inevitable knocks they need to be 'loved'. Their entire life is about relationships, so if you treat them badly or even just ignore them, you risk de-motivating them. Support and encourage your sales team at every opportunity – celebrate their success.

- **Give them confidence** – if you've chosen the right people, give them a proper induction as well as sufficient training and the tools to do the job. Both soft skills and product or service skills will be required, as will mobile support and reporting. You can drive them hard, but keep in touch with them and give them every chance of success.

- **Incentivise performance** – consider your remuneration and reward structures to strike a balance between basic and incentive pay. Make incentive pay both achievable and worthwhile. Consider extra rewards for high margin sales or new customer acquisition.

- **Agree targets and KPIs** – work with your sales team to establish budgets and to set targets for individual accounts. Allocate target and customer responsibilities to individuals and teams. Consider KPIs such as calls, visits and conversion rates. Don't forget customer care and how this is built in to the role.

- **Monitor performance** – complete regular activity reports, hold regular meetings and encourage sales staff to share customer comments and complaints. Identify what's working and what's not. Focus on the weak links and how you can fix them.

It's worth remembering that not everyone can sell and that, for many, the prospect of selling can create emotional stress and anguish. Luckily, business is a team game, so while sales may oil the wheels, there is plenty for others to do to help you manage your activities and bring your product or service to market.

It's time to consider your supply chain and partnership management.

Top tips

- It's your products and services, market positioning and business model that will determine your long-term success. **Don't start your marketing until these are tested and in place.**

- **Identify your target audience** and develop your marketing strategy to reach and influence them.

- **Create a value proposition** that clearly sets out the benefits of buying your product or service.

- **Develop your messaging.** Remember that customers are not interested in what you do, but in what's in it for them.

- **Build your marketing plan using a range of activities and media.** Use a sum-of-the-parts approach to coordinate the various marketing elements.

- Remember that one-off marketing activities rarely add any value, so **develop a sustainable programme**.

- **Consider the impact of the internet.** How can you leverage the online world to promote engagement with your business?

- **Use customer relationship management** (CRM) to manage and monitor the interaction with your customers and prospects.

- **Identify your channels to market** and consider how to access these using your own or third party resources.

- **Marketing and sales are central to your business.** Recognise this in the way you develop and structure your teams.

CHAPTER 14
Supply Chain and Partnership Management

> **"Success in the modern world depends on the real connections you have."**
>
> — Reid Hoffman, founder and CEO, LinkedIn

Collaborate to accumulate

The road to growth is paved with partnerships – successful businesses rarely operate alone. They collaborate with other businesses and people within and outside their supply chains to establish mutually beneficial alliances. They do this because they know that partnering can leverage their own competencies and those of others to help propel their growth.

Strategic alliances are nothing new. Accenture, the management consultancy, says that Fortune 500 companies have an average of 50–70 alliances each. In this chapter, we'll examine how to work with alliance partners and build robust relationships with suppliers in order to improve your efficiency, productivity and results.

Collaboration is a watchword for the 21st century. We have discovered that working together and engaging with complementary, non-competing businesses is always more powerful than working alone – we collaborate to accumulate.

As Neal Gandhi points out in his book, *Born Global*: "It's no longer a case of working with someone from a different department to create something innovative or high quality. It's about opening our doors to working with people and organisations outside the four walls of our traditional HQs, from different corners of the globe. That's how value is created in today's economy – through collaborative networks that provide more access to talent, skills, knowledge, information and ideas. Sharing opens up a wider resource pool."

Network thinking

Thomas and Penny Power are the founders of Ecademy, an online business network for entrepreneurs and small business owners. They talk about the difference between 'institutional thinking' and 'network thinking'. The former, which is 'closed, selective and controlling' is bumping up against the latter, which is 'open, random and supportive'.

They accept that both styles are required, depending on the situation and scenario, but say that network thinking is gaining ground against institutional thinking, with its evolution presenting real challenges to executives in both large and small organisations.

For me, network thinking is all about collaboration. If you are open to sharing and collaboration, you can create a community that is more engaged and inclusive, more active and participatory. In the online age, it won't pay to hide yourself away.

There are many businesses that are fearful of adopting a network approach. They are worried about giving away their trade secrets or losing their competitive advantage. In most cases, they are wrong. If they won't collaborate with their customers, suppliers, distributors and others, their competitors surely will.

"Growing up, the world was defined by the conflict between a democratic, free-market West, and a totalitarian, command-economy East," says Jasper Westaway, CEO of software collaboration platform oneDrum. "Most companies persist with an industrial age model that resembles the latter and not an information age model that favours the former. We are by default closed [and that means] we are closed to success," he continues. "In practice, organisations never fail because they are too open; they fail because they are too closed."

Take the Body Shop, for example. A great deal of its success comes down to the strength of its partnerships at every level and its ability to build strong relationships with all of its stakeholders. These include suppliers (fair trade cooperatives), others in its supply chain (NGOs and charities) as well as its distributors (retail partners and 'at home' consultants), all of whom champion the Body Shop's causes.

Other companies, such as pharmaceuticals giant Eli Lilly, have entered into joint ventures in order to compete with first-to-market companies such as Pfizer, while Pepsi have focused their strategy on developing a high quantity and quality of retail partnerships, as opposed to Coca-Cola's focus on brand advertising.

Network orientation

So, what exactly should be brought to the collective table in this mutual back-scratching world? It's a two-way street. Bigger companies often bring reach, audience and distribution, while smaller companies may bring the technology, products, services or other means to leverage the monetisation opportunity. One company may provide the back-end infrastructure, regulatory processes and resource; the other might provide cutting-edge innovation and creative talent. One company may provide the other with credibility and market intelligence, while the other might offer the opportunity to fill portfolio gaps, increase margins and enter or serve new markets.

In recent years there has been a move towards what Julie Meyer calls "network orientation", an ecosystem of aligned businesses.

"The big thing that's happening right now in businesses is network orientation," says Julie. "Companies that win know their place in the ecosystem in which they operate and, crucially, align the economics for the entire ecosystem," she explains.

For example, established media companies have reach via their database of registered users. Essentially they need to leverage that. "They don't even need to spend money in leveraging their audience, but allow companies that have enabling technologies to access the reach that they can provide," Julie suggests.

And they can do so in exchange for a share of the revenue created. Both companies potentially get to profit from what each brings to the table.

"Where those alliances can fail is when the big media company thinks that they can impose their business model on the small start-up and the small start-up is probably undercapitalised and wants the big media company to pay them an up-front fee for use of their clever monetisation, so it just kind of breaks down," adds Julie.

This can be avoided if both parties:

- consider the revenue opportunity that's being created by virtue of the larger company's reach and the smaller company's innovation, and assess fairly how the risks and rewards can be shared to their mutual satisfaction

- understand that the collaboration can work if roles and expectations are clearly defined and the revenue creation process within the ecosystem is properly managed.

"It needs to work for everybody in the ecosystem," says Julie. "For the big media company, for the small start-up or growing business and for the consumer. So there's a triangulation there."

Julie describes coming across the idea of ecosystem economics and seeing how successful it could be thanks to the CEO of mobile banking service Monitise. Alastair Lukies was determined to make mobile banking work for everyone involved – customers, banks and mobile operators. Other attempts at mobile banking had failed because they had a dominant player in the ecosystem who was biased or who practised institutional, as opposed to network, thinking.

"The people who are winning in this current stage of business are the people who are organising the economics of these new ecosystems," explains Julie. "Why is Google winning? Not because they are organising the information of this new world, but because they're organising the economics of the world's information. And so if you can be the person who can architect the business model for the new ecosystem that you're in, whether it's music or publishing or broadcast, then you're in a very powerful position."

How to collaborate effectively

When alliances go wrong, it can be a costly exercise. Take BT and AT&T's joint venture, Concert, which offered telecom services to multi-nationals. It was once described as one of the most ambitious global alliances in the telecoms industry. Under the break-up announced in 2001, it was reported that 2,300 of Concert's 6,300 people would lose their jobs and that the two companies would write off a total of $7 billion – a very painful outcome.

So how do you collaborate effectively and ensure the success of your strategic alliances?

- **Identify potential partners.** Look for partners who are complementary rather than competing. Seek out revenue, supply or service opportunities that you or they can fulfil, along with like-minded individuals in prospective partner businesses who might advocate the proposed relationship. Remember that alliances are structured for mutual gain and that a win-win situation is required.

- **Understand key objectives and benefits.** These may be financial (e.g. revenue growth or cost savings) or non-financial (e.g. filling a service gap or improving your customer experience). The drivers and benefits may be different for each partner.

- **Consider cultural compatibility.** "Unquestionably look for a DNA match when partnering," advises Alastair Lukies. "Do they believe in your vision, do they believe in you? Are they your kind of people?"

- **Be transparent and open.** Share your strategy and vision. Be honest about threats and weaknesses, as well as opportunities and strengths.

- **Clarify mutual expectations.** Avoid unbalanced relationships and lopsided benefits. Consider how both parties will prioritise and contribute to the alliance. "See things from the other partner's point of view and make sure that the deal works from both sides if you want any kind of long-term cooperation with somebody," advises Nick Jenkins of Moonpig, whose strong partnerships with card publishers have made his business particularly resilient against its competition. "If it's something that you know is going to work very well for you but not very well for them, it'll collapse," adds Nick.

- **Get the formalities right.** Some alliances will require written agreements and some will not. In a formal alliance, you'll need an agreement that identifies the parties, the objectives and the respective obligations, as well as how potential disputes will be resolved.

- **Build and maintain strong communication channels.** Business partnerships need to be worked on, so keep on top of relationships and results. There may be teething problems and how well you deal with these will impact on the long-term success of the partnership. Arrange networking opportunities with your partners to identify opportunities and build trust.

- **Be prepared to restructure and change.** "A deal that's good for a couple of years might not be good in year three or four," says Brad Rosser, who worked at McKinsey before going on to work for Sir Richard Branson. "You assess what's in front of you at the time, and what your business objectives are."

- **Treat others as you wish to be treated.** Always treat your partners with respect and think about how you can bring additional benefits to the relationship.

- **Celebrate success.** Don't let successes pass unnoticed. Communicate them widely and congratulate all those involved.

Supply chain management

The supply chain is an ideal first port of call when seeking mutually beneficial alliances. By looking up and down your supply chain, from your suppliers' suppliers to your customers' customers, you may find people or businesses who would make ideal strategic partners.

But identifying and managing collaborative partnerships is just one element of the all-encompassing management of a supply chain, which involves the organisation of a network of interconnected businesses and covers the origination, processing, movement, storage and delivery of goods from the sourcing of the first component through to the point of delivery to the end customer, whilst managing inventories and cash flows along the way.

Or as the Council of Supply Chain Management Professionals (CSCMP) defines supply chain management: "Supply chain management is an integrating function with primary responsibility for linking major business functions and business processes within and across companies into a cohesive and high-performing business model."

Supply chain management is all about efficiency and performance optimisation. It focuses on removing bottlenecks. It lowers costs. It improves throughput and satisfies customer needs. And it does all this through engagement and collaboration with suppliers, service providers, channel partners and customers. It's a team game that increases the visibility and velocity of inventory for the supply chain as a whole.

The open supply 'web'

Supply chain management has been through an evolutionary process in the past few decades. Originally we had a model where, broadly speaking, each member of the chain knew and cared little about other participants in the chain and only sought to maximise their own revenue and interests. We have now moved to the development of best-of-breed, mutually beneficial and accessible supply chain networks and interconnected supply 'webs'. These readily exchange information between businesses, keeping supply chain members abreast of market fluctuations and changing customer demands.

Such advances mean that it is now possible for each organisation in a supply chain to add value and optimise the entire chain rather than merely serve their own interests. This results in improved production and distribution, lower costs and better control for all of the businesses in the chain.

From 'lean manufacturing' which aims to preserve value with less work by eliminating waste or anything that the customer would not be willing to pay for, to 'just-in-time manufacturing' which aims to minimise stock levels by matching production and demand, optimisation techniques have enabled efficiencies in the management of all the resources in the supply chain.

At the end of the day, supply chain management depends on communication, coordination and collaboration. By working together and leaving no stone unturned, businesses can source, produce and deliver more cost-effectively and efficiently than ever before.

How to manage supply chains effectively

The increasing number of partners in supply chains and the incremental loss of control were the triggers that created the need for formal supply chain management, whilst advances in technology have enabled it. Although simple in concept, it can be complex to organise and control, so here are some tips on how you can make your supply chain more effective:

- **Keep your eyes on the chain** from your suppliers' suppliers to your intermediary agents and distributors, right through to your customers' customers. Be aware of every element of your supply chain and remember that supply failures that are three or four times removed will be just as effective at stopping your production, revenues and cash flows as events that occur much closer to home.

- **Choose your supply chain partners carefully.** Focus on reputation, capability, quality and performance and remember that having too many cooks can often spoil the broth.

- **Streamline your supply chain** to create agility and flexibility and to ease the challenges of management. Whether this means replacing a variety of small facilities with larger distribution centres or lessening the length of the chain using vertically integrated suppliers, this will enable you to be more responsive to customer demands.

- **Define expectations clearly.** Agree and document deliverables. Consider timescales, communication channels, service levels, payment arrangements and how to proceed in the event of a dispute.

- **Use real-time communication and tracking technology** to enable and organise supply chain participants. Schedule production and delivery schedules to minimise your inventory, lock-up and cash requirements.

- **Use in-house or outsourced logistics experts** who understand national or international distribution and can get to grips with the complex procedures at the delivery end of the supply chain. Look at routing, load sizes, packaging, transportation and insurance. Consider tariffs, duties, sales taxes and payment terms.

- **Focus on customer demand and service.** Ensure that everyone in the chain from buyers and suppliers to producers and distributors all collaborate for the common goal of meeting or exceeding customer needs and expectations.

Finally, don't let distance and national boundaries be a barrier to effective supply chain management. We'll consider the international aspects further in Chapter 16.

Supplier relationships: core strength or sore spot?

Supply chains start with your suppliers' suppliers and end with your customers' customers, but what characteristics should you be looking for in your direct suppliers? The answer is that it depends on who you, and they, are.

"In terms of obstacles to growth, suppliers would probably be our most challenging aspect," says Piers Daniell, MD of Fluidata who works with various large telecom carriers, from BT and Cable & Wireless to Telefonica.

"They frequently change their strategy and their plans with huge consequences to our business," adds Piers, although he has found it easier to get his company's voice heard as his business has grown and become a bigger customer for its suppliers.

Working with large corporates can sometimes be challenging, as your business is likely to be a small cog engaging with a big wheel. Although these suppliers are likely to be financially secure, changes in policy or direction, or decisions to cull partners or focus only on larger accounts, can sometimes leave smaller customers in the cold. In these circumstances, it often means that customers, rather than suppliers, need to adapt their model.

To protect its supplier relationships, Fluidata treats others as it wishes to be treated by paying its suppliers in full and on time. "We behaved like a big business so that when they came to review decisions about cutting partners, we retained those relationships because they said it was easy business for them dealing with us; we weren't a thorn in their side."

Outside the larger corporates, there may be different challenges with your suppliers. Financial security can be a particular worry, as the goods or services you buy depend upon your suppliers' continued existence.

Here are some of the things that you should look out for in your suppliers:

- **Reliability and service.** Suppliers who consistently let you down with faulty goods or late deliveries need to be replaced. Mistakes happen, but life's too short to have to put up with this on a regular basis.

- **Quality.** The quality of what you receive will be reflected in the quality of what you deliver. Decide where you fit into the market and select suppliers who fit your proposition. You can't make a silk purse out of a sow's ear.

- **Empathy.** We generally show empathy to our staff and customers, but what about our suppliers? To have good relationships with suppliers, both you and they need to be empathetic. "It's unusual to have empathetic relationships with suppliers," says Traci Entel of New York management consulting firm, Katzenbach Partners. "For most companies, such relationships are built on contracts and service-level agreements. But we think it's highly important to have long-term relationships with your business-to-business partners, given that they are responsible for so much of your business."

- **Flexibility.** Try to choose suppliers who are flexible and who are willing to help you in an emergency. Being able to place small orders or return unused stock may be particularly valuable attributes.

- **Value for money.** Value is in the eye of the beholder and the judgement of value is based on a range of variables. There is a balance to be struck between quality, cost, reliability and service.

- **Financial security.** Understand the financial strength of your suppliers to assess the security of your supplies. Watch for any signs of distress and be aware of alternative options.

Getting added value from bankers and advisors

Bankers and professional advisors are an important part of your supply chain and their appointment should tick all of the same boxes as your other suppliers. There is a difference, however, in that these suppliers are rarely involved in helping you get your product or service to market. "Those relationships tend to be on a need-to-know basis rather than a fundamental part of the grand plan to deliver growth," Sir Eric Peacock points out.

Sir Eric looks for other qualities in these kinds of supply relationship. "When it comes to service supply such as banking, tax and audit, I'm looking for additionality," says Sir Eric. "So what do these relationships bring in addition? Do they bring a flow of new clients, do they introduce me to interesting other businesses; maybe where there's no business to be done but where these businesses are doing exciting things that could inspire my business? Do they partner me with other entrepreneurs from whom I can learn something? For me, that makes the difference, because all of the rest is a given and that's what I'm paying a basic fee for. I want added value from these supplier relationships."

In other words, how much do they care?

Whether you are talking to your suppliers, managing your wider supply chain or collaborating with alliance partners, access to knowledge and information will be critical to your success. The next chapter examines how you can leverage technology to enable new and innovative ways of working.

┌───┐

— Top tips ——

- **Consider opportunities** for alliances and collaborative partnerships. **Successful businesses rarely operate alone.**

- **Adopt network thinking,** as opposed to institutional thinking. **Be 'open, random and supportive' instead of 'closed, selective and controlling'.**

- **Look at the ecosystem in which your business operates.** How can you align yourself for maximum advantage?

- **Consider the chemistry.** Only choose alliance partners who are complementary and culturally compatible with your business.

- **Get the expectations right.** Lasting relationships are sustained when the **arrangements work for both parties.**

- **Be aware of the entirety of your supply chain**, from your suppliers' suppliers to your customers' customers. **Look for opportunities up and down the chain.**

- **Assess the qualities you seek in your suppliers.** Consider security of supply and remember that relationships should be based on more than contracts and service-level agreements.

- **Seek added benefits in relationships with bankers and professional advisors.** Consider how much they care and why they are right for your business.

└───┘

CHAPTER 15
Technology and Data Management

> **"The real problem is not whether machines think but whether men do."**
>
> — Burrhus F. Skinner

Working quicker and smarter

We live in a world that has seen computing power double every two years for the past 50. As the power increases, device size decreases. As access to data proliferates, so too does the speed at which it can be transmitted. Our world is now digital, virtual, global and mobile – all thanks to technology.

For most businesses, these advances in technology represent both an opportunity and a threat. While technology enables us to compete on a global and increasingly level playing field by giving us sophisticated tools and solutions that only larger corporations used to have, it also allows our competitors to do the same. Our competitive advantage may therefore be dependent on how well we choose, and use, technology.

On the downside, technological transformation means that there's an increasing dependency on fully functioning systems, exposing us to downtime, data loss and potential business disruption. There is also a human impact, with more and more communication taking place electronically, rather than face-to-face or on the phone. Offices are now full of people who sit in front of their screens from morning until night, often sending emails rather than speaking even to their nearest neighbour.

On the plus side, technology enables our businesses to automate, access new markets, cut operating costs, save time and improve overall performance. We are therefore more agile, embracing more flexible working models for the benefit of our staff, customers and trading partners. IT no longer impacts on individual tasks or processes but on the integrated activities at every level of an organisation.

From land lines and mobiles to VoIP; from PCs and laptops to PDAs; from instant, voice and video messaging to blogs, RSS, video conferencing and social networks – the real-time technological tools at our disposal now help us access information and people at great speed.

And what about cost? The answer is that technology has componentised and standardised, enabling businesses to start small and get products and services to market at a fraction of the cost that they would have incurred only a few years ago.

Building the foundations

In order to develop an IT infrastructure that suits your business you'll need to consider the data you wish to store, how that data will be organised and managed so that it becomes useful and accessible to your users, how your system will enable communication and collaboration, how you'll protect yourself from data loss or downtime and how you'll secure your data from third party infiltration.

In practice, the main building blocks are likely to include the following:

- a document management system to keep your documents organised and indexed

- a financial management system to deal with your accounting and cash management, whilst also keeping track of your assets and liabilities

- a human resources (HR) system to manage your staff records, document salaries and benefits and monitor performance, training and recruitment

- a project management, manufacturing or costing system to record and monitor your customer-facing costs and expenses

- a supply chain management system to deal with supply chain planning, purchasing and scheduling

- a customer relationship management (CRM) system or contact database to help with sales and marketing and customer contact and support

- VoIP, telecom, email and collaboration systems to enable fast and efficient communications, file sharing, conferencing tools and other solutions.

Together, these can form an enterprise resource planning (ERP) system that integrates all aspects of management information and reporting inside the business as well as maintaining connections with customers, suppliers and other external stakeholders.

Typically, these solutions are not offered on an 'all or nothing' basis. Different systems are available as modules so that businesses can choose the functionality they need. Most businesses, for example, will require a financial management system, while only some will wish to invest in HR, project management or supply chain management. Notwithstanding this, the more you can automate and integrate your processes, working off a single database that can support all your applications, the simpler and more coordinated your life will become. Ultimately, a hotchpotch of bespoke systems in different departments or locations is unlikely to be efficient or encourage teamwork and communication.

Always on

Technology can significantly increase our personal efficiency, helping us make the best of our time through 'always-on' systems and remote access. Until recently, staff would suffer a significant loss of productivity while they were on the road or out of their office. Nowadays, by using an internet-enabled mobile phone or wireless laptop, those who work on the move or from home can view their office systems, deal with their customers and suppliers and, in general, operate efficiently from almost any remote location.

Thanks to tablets and PDAs, orders can be processed and stock checked while products are being ordered or delivered at a customer's location. Similarly, those who commute to their offices can, if they choose, take pressure off their day by remotely accessing their emails during their journey rather than taking up valuable time plodding their way through them on arrival.

There are plenty of other benefits. Providing flexible working options such as home-working can save you the cost of housing staff in your office, reducing staff travelling time and increasing productivity by improving work-life balance. It may also open up access to a wider pool of talent – e.g. mothers wishing to work from home or individuals living much further afield.

"There's a huge wealth of knowledge out there," says Piers Daniell, MD of Fluidata. "We've recruited quite a few contractors from Facebook ads, and given students or graduates projects to help develop services for us and make us more efficient."

So, just as sending invoices by email rather than snail mail can increase efficiency, save money on postage and win accolades for forestry conservation, travel and in-house infrastructure costs can be saved by embracing real-time communication tools such as video conferencing and instant messaging to work with a broader and more distributed group of people.

System selection and implementation

If your business lacks the skills and resources to choose suitable systems, you will probably want to use the services of a specialist. All of the normal rules regarding supplier selection apply and you may also need assistance with customisation and implementation.

There are a myriad of systems and consultants to choose from, so proceed with caution on both counts. Wherever possible, try to get recommendations from people you respect and trust and, even if you have limited IT skills, take time out to consider and document the key functions that you want your system to deliver. This information can be used to approach suppliers and consultants who should be able to demonstrate their sector and software specialism as well as providing testimonials and access to relevant reference sites.

Always follow up on references and reference sites to confirm the bona fides of your consultant. It may not feel like it today, but at some stage your IT systems are likely to be mission critical. Build them on strong foundations and consider the ability to add and integrate future modules and functionality.

Where possible, use established system suppliers rather than building your own. Bespoke systems are often the brainchild and domain of their creators, leaving with you with limited support options when things go wrong.

How to harness the power of technology

Here are some pointers to help you design your IT infrastructure:

- **Begin at the end.** Spend time thinking about future business needs to develop a sustainable and expandable solution. Don't be tempted by short cuts and quick fixes – build solid foundations.

- **Define the requirements of your end users.** Consider how they can participate and collaborate without overloading them with data.

- **Consider the need for remote access.** Most businesses want to provide remote access to their staff using a virtual private network (VPN).

- Use ERP methodology to **build your systems around a single database**, enabling real time updating, avoiding duplication and providing a single view of customer, product, supplier and employee data.

- **Provide staff with interactive tools**, such as PDAs and mobile devices that can communicate with your internal systems, enabling mobile working and 24/7 access.

- **Make use of free software** and take advantage of web-based services such as Skype to increase operational efficiencies and reduce costs.

- **Use reputable consultants and financially secure suppliers** to provide support and upgrades as and when you need them.

Securing your data

Over time, businesses accumulate significant amounts of data. This will typically include details about customers and suppliers, employees, products and services, finances and a host of other mission critical information. The vast majority of this is sensitive or confidential and is now stored on computers.

Businesses need access to this information to manage their operations on a daily basis. If systems go down, sales and deliveries can grind to a halt and supply chains can be disrupted. The adverse impact on cash flows can be inconvenient, if not fatal. Similarly, the theft or manipulation of data by third parties can lead to breaches of privacy, losses, legal actions and claims, all with unfortunate reputational and/or financial consequences. Your data therefore needs to be secure as well as being protected from unauthorised access and corruption.

Apart from the threat of hackers and thieves, computers can have their own problems. Any number of components can break or fail, jeopardising your data and putting your business at risk. Backing up your data on a regular basis is therefore an essential discipline, allowing you to save and restore your critical information wherever and whenever you need it.

How often you back up your data will depend upon your situation. Some businesses will back up hourly, while others will do so on a daily or weekly basis. It just depends on what you can afford to lose and how long it will take to re-input your subsequent data.

You can back up your data online, on USB flash drives, or on internal or removable hard drives. You can also use CDs, DVDs or tapes, although these can be less convenient and reliable. Whatever you choose, you should check that your back-up functionality actually works by attempting to recover data on a regular basis.

Finally, make sure that your back ups are kept off site. The risks of fire, flooding and other catastrophes may be small, but they exist and you should never put your business at risk. In choosing your back-up location, consider the likelihood of the disaster affecting both locations. Apparently this happened on 9/11 when the primary site was in 1 World Trade Center and the back-up was in 7 World Trade Center. Both locations were destroyed in that horrendous attack.

So, apart from regular back up, how can businesses keep their data secure?

- **Install firewalls** to protect against malware and viruses. Don't forget to cater for employees who work from home or on the move.

- **Don't install untrusted software** as this may cause problems in your operating system.

- **Automate password change requests** and create policies governing PDA and memory-stick use and access to non-work related websites.

- **Use anti-virus software** and scan for vulnerability to external attack. Test for penetration by malware and viruses.

- **Keep track of who has access to what data.** Define which individuals can access, disseminate and distribute which data. Create restricted areas where appropriate.

- **Protect critical data both physically and virtually.** Lock away key data, including paper files, back-up disks, servers and laptops, and restrict access to areas in which such data is housed. Don't forget to revoke user access as soon as employees leave the organisation.

- **Consider alternative methods of data storage**, such as cloud computing, but ensure that you have strong internet connectivity and additional methods of backing up anything that is kept in the cloud.

Cloud computing

With increasing information and data to store, businesses are constantly seeking ways to increase capacity for data storage or to add capacity without the need to licence or install additional software, train more people or invest in new infrastructure.

Cloud computing is a way for these businesses to extend their storage capacity and IT capabilities, providing a lower cost, efficient and agile computing solution for growing businesses using a third-party data storage solution, on-demand virtual servers and an array of services and applications.

But there are various issues to address before jumping on the cloud...

On the plus side:

- Cloud computing offers a **leaner, less complex operating model** and a cheaper one too, with many cloud services available for free or at low cost, less software to install and less hardware to operate. You can pay a small monthly fee to rent a server in a data centre rather than buying your own. This also means that IT managers can focus their attention on core applications rather than hardware and software maintenance.

- Being available over the internet **makes your data more accessible and enables more flexible working for staff**. "We use it ourselves," says Piers Daniell, MD of Fluidata. "We virtualise a lot of our systems and services and it means that from our customers' perspective we're much more efficient because everybody can get hold of the information they need quickly, while working from home becomes more accessible."

- **Scalability is easier and barriers to entry are lower.** Capacity can be rented on-demand so organisations can smoothly scale up without having to buy multiple servers to deal with a rise in activity, data or bandwidth usage.

- **Data may be more secure and is not reliant on the hardware used to access it.** "The application/software used sits within the internet supported by data centres so the information floats between those data centres offering a much more secure environment," explains Piers Daniell. Furthermore, those servers are maintained by professionals. Plus, if your laptop dies, you won't lose all your e-mail or other data, as it is all available via a web browser from any machine.

However:

- **Data could be less secure.** Whilst data loss is rare, temporary outages do happen. The way to protect data until cloud services optimise or guarantee security and reliability is to back up all cloud-based data across multiple cloud-based services or use your own server or external hard disk to get control. The cost benefits may be reduced, but you can still take advantage of the additional benefits of cloud computing such as scalability and accessibility.

- **The potential for downtime affects everything.** Outages can temporarily cripple businesses who cannot do anything without access to their data.

- **Legal jurisdiction.** "With cloud computing you've got these three issues to consider: which country the data is uploaded from, in which country the data is stored and in which country the data is pulled off," explains Tony Fish. If these countries are different and have different laws there may be privacy or data usage issues to be considered.

- **Technological lock-in implications.** It can be problematic to move data from one cloud-based service to another due to incompatibility. It's therefore worth researching how easy it is to switch between services before committing to a particular provider.

- **Privacy implications.** Those who use free services in exchange for receiving targeted advertising will be trading an element of their privacy, as the advertisers and service providers need to know who you are and what you do online in order to effectively target their promotions.

- **Financial security.** Users need to be sure that the provider is financially stable and secure, although this can never be guaranteed.

Cloud computing is on the up. For many growing businesses, the benefits of increased scalability, productivity, efficiency and cost reduction will probably outweigh the potential threats.

Embracing change

They say that the only constant is change and technology certainly proves the rule. In one or more aspects, all industries have had to embrace continuous rather than episodic change and adopt new ways of doing things in order to keep up in a fast-moving, hyper-competitive world.

With advances in technology enabling remote teams to work together through access to file-sharing, web conferencing, real-time messaging and VoIP, now may be a good time to consider your international opportunities.

Top tips

- **Get good internal or external advice** and **build your IT infrastructure on strong foundations**.

- **Always take and follow up references** before using external IT consultants.

- **Use a single database and building blocks** that can be integrated and developed as your business grows.

- **Take advantage of the efficiencies of remote access and mobile technology** to maximise the productivity of your staff.

- **Use established system suppliers** rather than building your own bespoke systems. Ongoing support for home-grown systems may be hard to find.

- **Back up your data regularly** to avoid potential loss. Ensure that back-ups are kept offsite and **in a secure location.**

- **Use firewalls and anti-virus software** to protect your system from malware and viruses.

- **Consider the benefits and disadvantages of cloud computing** and whether this may be suitable for your business.

- **Embrace technological change** to maintain competitive advantage and **maximise your opportunities.**

CHAPTER 16
International Business

> **"Business is moving faster. Globalisation is forcing companies to do things in new ways."**
>
> — Bill Gates, founder of Microsoft

The global village and international opportunity

There was a time when businesses served their local communities, with little or no activity outside their immediate vicinity. Product sourcing and trading across borders was generally left to the very few larger enterprises, such as the Dutch East India Company or the Hudson's Bay Company, businesses founded by intrepid explorers and courageous entrepreneurs.

Thanks to these and other pioneers, times have changed. We now live in a global village, where even the smallest businesses can access international markets, buying and selling products and services all over the world. Advances in technology, communications and logistics mean that operations can now be orchestrated from almost any global location, taking advantage of lower labour and raw material costs and disintermediating traditional sales and distribution channels.

Apart from the more obvious benefits of cost savings and new markets, establishing overseas operations can enable you to attract new talent, facilitate product development and leverage different time zones to enhance operational efficiencies. These, in turn, can speed up your time to market and improve your overall performance.

In this chapter, we'll examine some of the benefits and challenges presented by this international opportunity. Despite the potential, it's not a one-way street. It can be challenging to recruit, build trust and manage the cultural differences in dispersed and diversified teams, whether those teams work directly for your business or through an outsourcer or third party supplier. And whilst the benefits may seem hugely attractive, it's vital to fully evaluate your reasons for international expansion and only invest at the right time.

As always, there are differing views. Some experts recommend that you should only expand internationally once you've maximised or outgrown your local market. James Caan, for example, believes that "[i]t's far better to focus on your domestic market first and then expand, and only then with very good reason. It's surprising that a lot of businesses expand internationally while there's still a lot of opportunity remaining in the UK. People seem to think it's easier to take their business overseas. It's absolutely not."

Conversely, others believe that you needn't wait, that due to technological advances and instantly accessible markets, worldwide expansion is less risky and less costly than ever before.

Risk is a relative term and any decision that will have such a huge impact on your business will require detailed analysis and planning. Don't forget to ask yourself some fundamental questions:

- Is the journey to becoming an international business a short step or a giant leap?
- Does your management team have the capability and capacity to manage such a challenge?
- Is your cash flow strong enough to pay for the inevitable costs of establishment, without putting undue pressure on the rest of your business?
- What happens if it doesn't work?

You have been warned! To use some hackneyed phrases, never bite off more than you can chew, fly by the seat of your pants or operate on a wing and a prayer. These courses of action generally tend to end in disaster, particularly if you are operating with new people and in an unfamiliar environment.

Notwithstanding the health warning, there is a relatively new breed of businesses that go global from the outset. They are innately international from inception. According to Neal Gandhi's book, *Born Global*, their "core competitive advantage is derived from employing, selling, sourcing supplies, purchasing or producing in more than one country".

Productivity and quality gains

In today's marketplace, growing companies are in a race to service the needs of their customers quicker and better than anyone else. Response times, productivity rates and quality levels are the new business imperatives.

By leveraging time zones you can create 24/7 operations that allow some types of service-related work to be sent, completed and returned overnight. Having such rapid turnaround capabilities will not only impress your customers. It will increase the volumes that your business can cope with and drive accelerated growth.

By harnessing the offshore opportunity, it may be possible for you to outclass your competitors by producing and delivering a product that uses better quality materials or is better made (or a product that is the same quality as the competition but which can be sold at a lower price point).

Neal Gandhi, author and founder of Quickstart Global, says: "Just because you're spending less on something, it doesn't mean you're going to get lower quality. In fact the opposite is often true. No one has a monopoly on clever people. There are hardworking, smart people across the world."

How to maximise the benefits of going global

Here are some tips on how to take your business global:

- **Plan meticulously.** Identify your objectives and the specific tasks and resources required to achieve them. Decide who will manage your offshore operations. Define timescales and key deliverables. Consider operational requirements, personnel recruitment, training and retention. Establish IT and infrastructure needs and set KPIs to measure performance and operational success. Leave no planning stone unturned – the devil is in the detail no matter where in the world you operate.

- **Get buy-in from your existing team.** Clearly define what's in it for everyone, what the precise benefits are and why change is required to positively impact the business in the future. Get everyone involved in the planning process and deal with any fears or uncertainties. Don't let your staff think they are under threat from the new overseas operations.

- **Choose the right location.** Base your decision on the availability of the specific skills you need, the cost of labour, the travelling costs and accessibility, the time zone and the cultural compatibility.

- **Assess the financial impact.** It's not only the benefit of reducing costs that should be considered, but the revenue-generating benefit of increasing your efficiency and productivity. Look at how your new location will affect your competitive advantage and bottom line.

- **Ask your accountants and tax advisors about the tax implications** of setting your business up overseas. Consider ownership structures and whether you will trade through a representative office, a branch or a separate company.

- **Take legal advice** to understand the landscape and comply with local laws and regulations.

- **Think long term.** Whilst upfront expenditure on familiarisation, infrastructure implementation and associated set-up costs may be high, this may ultimately determine the success of the venture. Cost savings and benefits may be greater later on if effective planning and a sensible level of investment has taken place at the outset.

- **Don't underestimate your costs.** Factor in some headroom and allow for the costs of communication, training and travelling to meet vendors or potential team members.

- **Make the most of technology and telephony to keep costs low.** Call employees across the world using least-cost routing; use Skype to talk; host video conferences and integrate databases into one accessible network.

- **Hire incrementally.** Hire only your core team members during a pilot or transitional period. Hire the rest of the team once the initial knowledge transfer has been completed.

- **Monitor your financial position** rigorously and constantly keep your risks under review. Trading in overseas locations requires stamina and constant awareness, particularly if they are in emerging or developing economies.

- **Build one team.** Factor in the cost of bringing your core overseas team to your head office to absorb the culture, get to know your local team and feel included. "Ideally anyone you hire should spend some time in your base office," suggests Nick Jenkins, founder of Moonpig. "They can then get to know the people and understand the culture and how things are done before taking the essence of that abroad."

The global talent pool

Setting up your business in a lower cost jurisdiction may seem like a no-brainer, but for many companies overseas growth is driven by the ability to access specialist expertise that they might be unable to source domestically. And it's not only skilled staff that businesses are employing or outsourcing work to, but board members too. In order to succeed in emerging markets, it can be worthwhile appointing foreign national and local directors to your board.

"We used to think expatriates were the best way to staff international companies," George L. Davis Jr., from executive search firm Egon Zehnder, told *Business Week*. "What the best corporations figured out was to hire local people. The same principle should apply to the board. If you're looking at local markets, get local people on your board," adds George, who estimates that fewer than 10% of the largest 500 US companies have a foreign national on their board.

Manpower CEO Jeff Joeress agrees. He sees expatriate management teams as "the most classic mistake" made by companies expanding overseas, due to their lack of the local market knowledge needed to win sales and manage staff effectively.

In practice, how far you choose to go employing local directors and managers will probably depend on the scale of your activities and your future intentions. A business that's looking to open an office purely to service or facilitate its domestic activities (e.g. research, call centre or software development activities) will have very different needs to one that is entering a new market to make sales or carry out local manufacturing. Apart from issues like substance and scale, the latter is likely to be more complex and require greater input from experienced management in the territory.

If you establish a remote facility of your own, deciding whether to send out expatriate management, hire local management or use a combination of the two is a critical decision and one that will generally need to be made early on in the process. Team leaders will be needed before other staff, so choices will have to be made. On the one hand you may want to send someone you already know and trust, a person who is already privy to the workings and offerings of your business. On the other, it may be better to hire a local manager who understands the culture, language and market, with a network of local contacts.

It will cost more to send expatriate staff due to their salary, accommodation and travel costs. Yet having an expatriate at the helm, at least initially or during a transitional period, is often seen as a lower risk option. For others, hiring a local manager, training them to embed the business culture into the offshore operation and having them liaise with an offshore manager back at head office may be preferred.

Whichever option you choose, the biggest challenge for any manager, expatriate or local, will be to provide clarity of purpose and align the different cultures to create a cohesive and effective team.

Cultural differences and alignment

"Cross-cultural competence is the top critical skill of the 21st century."

Michael Hick, author of *Global Deals*

While the world continues to shrink and customers, partners and suppliers come closer together, there are large cultural gaps in how we operate, behave, consume and communicate. These are driven not just by local custom but by religion, social class and ethnic origin. With modern communications levelling the global playing field, age also has a part to play.

"As anyone who internationalises will tell you," says Jonathan Hick, Directorbank founder, "you can't expect to roll your model out round the world exactly as it is."

"Absolutely one size does not fit all," says Alastair Lukies, CEO of Monitise. "So don't think just because something works in the UK that it's going to work in the US or in China or in India."

This will not only impact on your business model or your products and services, but will also apply to business and staff relationships, expectations and types of 'acceptable' behaviour.

India, for example, is the fourth largest economy in the world, with over six thousand companies listed on the Bombay Stock Exchange, second only to the New York Stock Exchange. It's an enormously important market with a skilled labour force and a burgeoning middle class – a potentially perfect stamping ground for a growing company.

Yet how many people know that, in India, shaking the head from side to side is a way of communicating to the speaker that you understand what they are saying and that, in many cases, you agree with them? In many other countries this gesture would indicate a definite 'no'! Who knows that, in Indian culture, saying 'no' is itself considered to be rude and unacceptable – people will go to enormous lengths to avoid saying it. This can be both charming and frustrating, but is also incredibly challenging from a business perspective. For example, if you ask whether a supplier can deliver something to a specific deadline they will say 'yes' and do their very best to deliver. However, the ensuing delay won't leave much room for rescheduling and can have a negative or even disastrous impact on your production and delivery schedules.

There are countless examples of cultural differences that can impact on your business, but if local cultural differences are known and understood, it will be possible to build harmonious teams that share a common purpose, transcending both nationality and location.

Lost in translation: business practice abroad

In **India** and **France** it is generally accepted that you must have a local person fronting your business. Joint ventures can therefore work better than establishing your own remote facilities, unless you hire local management to run your operations.

In **Korea**, business is personal. Koreans will not come to an agreement unless they feel at ease with the people involved. Negotiations are therefore likely to be long-winded and protracted, whilst the parties get to know, like and trust each other. Concessions will always be expected, so you will need to consider your proposition and how you can discount or improve it. And if you go in low without leaving room for negotiation, you are likely to cause offence.

In **China**, people do not speak with their hands, so avoid large hand movements, as these may be distracting to your host. Don't point when speaking and don't put your hand in your mouth. These acts are considered improper. Present and receive business cards with both hands and never write on anyone's business card – this is akin to defacing the person. Accept that decisions will take time. Many Chinese will want to wait for a lucky day before they make a decision.

How to create a unified cross-border culture

- **Provide cultural awareness training** to your team, making them aware of the kinds of behaviours expected when dealing with their foreign counterparts. Consider both sides of the coin – what will cause offence and what will impress in order to accelerate relationship building and trust.

- **Provide training around body language** and non-verbal communication skills.

- **Speak to people who have been there and seen it before.** Ask them what cultural differences they've experienced and how they've dealt with them.

Multinational markets – selling overseas

It's not always necessary to have your own overseas presence. You can access international markets through agents, wholesalers and distributors who may buy, licence or simply sell your products and services in their local territories. There are also export management businesses that can handle international sales. These businesses often have strong local ties and ready access to the companies you want to sell to, making it easier to penetrate new markets.

Selling to this kind of international customer base need not be as risky or complex as it seems. Businesses involved in design or manufacture or who specialise in their area of service expertise should certainly consider selling overseas rather than being limited by their domestic market.

Getting ready for international trade

- **Do your homework before entering new markets.** Assess the level of competition, the market maturity and the local needs and preferences. Consider why your product or service will be suitable to meet these needs and whether there is likely to be sufficient demand at your price point. Make enquiries through chambers of commerce, join trade missions, meet other market participants and use the internet to help you complete and interpret your research.

- **Review your organisational structure and resources.** Do you have the right staff and expertise to effectively manage your export initiatives and the logistics involved in selling offshore?

- **Consider methods of distribution.** Alternatives include selling direct from your own offshore location, via a joint venture with a local company or through a localised version of your website. Another option would be to license your product to a local supplier, taking a royalty on sales or production. Or maybe you'd be better suited to using intermediary distributors or sales agents to market and sell your products on your behalf? If you have a proven and robust business model and a strong brand, perhaps a franchise network would be the best solution? Your decisions regarding distribution will be determined by whether you want to sell directly or indirectly, how much control you wish to retain and the amount of knowledge and resources you have available.

- **Remember the cultural challenges** and consider the amount of localisation or modification that may be required to serve the needs of your new customers. Ensure that your product name, logos and marketing materials are acceptable, with no unfavourable connotations.

- **Don't underestimate the financial risks of doing business overseas.** Consider using documentary credits or other financial instruments to minimise the risk of bad debts and remember that currency fluctuations can adversely (or positively) affect your margins. Talk to your bank or your advisors about how you can protect yourself – there is a well-trodden path that you can follow.

Offshore options

If you've decided to set up overseas, there are a number of offshore business models to choose from. The one that's right for your business will depend on your strategic goals, your reasons for entering the overseas market, the location and the types of activities you intend to carry out.

Here are some of the options:

Offshore freelancing or employment

Using low-cost freelance staff to send work to can be beneficial, as can enabling your existing staff to work from wherever in the world they would prefer to be. The virtual office is now an established reality.

Businesses with diverse workforces may find that staff they employ in their primary location, and who they already know and trust, may want to return to their roots. This can often create opportunities for international expansion.

A good example of this is Moonpig, whose Australian office is staffed by the former marketing chief who wanted to go back to her homeland.

"We were very lucky because the person we employ in Australia spent three years with us in London," says Nick Jenkins. "So she was fully committed to the Moonpig culture and understands how we do things."

Offshore outsourcing

The outsourcing of IT development and support services to companies in India and other lower-cost jurisdictions is typical of this model. An external supplier is chosen and contracted to carry out a project and is given responsibility for its delivery.

These arrangements can work well, but are not entirely without potential problems.

Using a third party supplier can mean that there is less buy-in, less flexibility and less control over important issues like timing and quality. There can also be concerns about the security of valuable IP.

Outsourcing can sometimes create a 'them and us' approach, with a lack of integration and responsiveness. Being a supplier is different to being part of a team.

Other factors can also come into play. For example, priorities can frequently change during projects, and managing those changes can be problematic within a process-driven, outsourced environment. Furthermore, when you outsource projects you still need to invest in training, communication and, in many cases, travel. When the project ends the training investment can be lost as the third party provider moves on to another project.

An alternative to offshore outsourcing is onshore outsourcing where you hire a domestically-based company which has a global team and which can pass on its own cost savings through competitive pricing. While the IP, control and training issues may still apply, communications will be easier to manage.

Joint venture

Under this model, your business enters into a joint venture (JV) with an established local company in the offshore location, allowing you to share ownership and take advantage of their local knowledge and experience. By choosing your JV partner wisely, you can reduce the risks of working in an unfamiliar territory and tap in to your new partner's existing supply or sales channels.

Pooling resources can be an excellent solution, but the trick is in finding the right joint venture partner and building appropriate levels of trust. Instinct will help you here, but proceed with caution and carry out detailed due diligence. It's normally far easier to establish a relationship than to end it.

Build-operate-transfer

Similar to the joint venture model, a build-operate-transfer relationship is typically where an offshore supplier operates a dedicated centre for your business. Once it's successful and established and certain conditions have been met, you can have the option to take over ownership and run it yourself.

Offshore captive

Many companies looking to cut costs through offshore operations simply set up their own operations, known as 'captives'.

Setting up a branch or subsidiary facility on your own can require a significant investment of time and money. You'll need to consider your preferred structure and then meet with local advisors, acquire and equip your premises, build your infrastructure and interview, recruit and train your staff.

Moving from a supply-based arrangement to owning an offshore captive can often have fiscal consequences for your business. Ask your accountants about tax treaties and get their advice on esoteric but important issues like transfer pricing and thin capitalisation.

Assisted in-house

With this option, you pay a service provider to help you set up operations in suitable offshore locations. This scalable and quick solution is often appropriate for smaller, growing businesses.

The service provider can help you get to grips with the often complex aspects of working in another country, dealing with recruitment, premises, infrastructure, legal compliance, incorporation, HR and IT, and working with the local authorities. They can also help you to recruit staff.

One such provider is Quickstart Global, whose 'in-house anywhere' model helps businesses increase their profitability whilst minimising the risks associated with setting up overseas.

Acquisition/merger

For more established businesses, buying an existing company may be the preferred way to get a foothold in an overseas territory. In this case, you can acquire a ready-made infrastructure, with premises, equipment and staff, along with existing revenues and profits.

Growing your business through acquisition can lead to fast-track growth. It's a topic we'll consider further in Chapter 18.

┌───┐

— **Top tips** —

- **Don't be frightened of exploring international opportunities** to reduce costs, increase efficiencies or access new markets. **We are living in a global village.**

- **Leave no planning stone unturned.** Do detailed research and get advice from people who have been there before to understand the challenges and how you can overcome them.

- **Consider your business structure** – will you go it alone, create a joint venture or use outsourcing? Perhaps you want to acquire a business in the new jurisdiction?

- Ensure that your product name, logos and marketing materials are **acceptable in the local market**, with no unfavourable connotations.

- **Review your distribution model** and consider whether you wish to sell direct or through **third party agents or distributors.**

- **Choose your locations carefully.** Accessibility, availability of labour and raw materials or the ability to leverage different time zones may be important for your business.

- **Allow for operational and financial headroom.** Getting your new overseas business up and running may well take longer than you think.

- **Consider your management structure and who will be in charge.** Weigh up the pros and cons of using expatriate and/or local management to run your overseas business.

- **Take risk management and mitigation seriously. Set KPIs and monitor your financial position rigorously.**

- **Be aware of cultural differences** and how your behaviour will affect your business.

- **Provide training** to your team to encourage interaction and build trust.

└───┘

CHAPTER 17
Intellectual Property

"I find my greatest pleasure, and so my reward, in the work that precedes what the world calls success."

– Thomas A. Edison, inventor

Buried treasure

As consumers, we give little thought to the origins of the products and services we buy. Familiarity, design, functionality and price drive our purchasing decisions, influencing what we buy, as well as where and how we buy it.

In practice, this process is full of intervention – it doesn't happen on its own. In the beginning, the product or service has to be innovated and perfected. Then it has to be manufactured or developed. Later on, it has to be marketed, distributed and sold. The winners are the businesses – from designers, manufacturers, distributors, wholesalers and retailers – that seamlessly interact to bring us what we want, building their reputations as trusted suppliers and gaining our ongoing loyalty and support.

In order to achieve this success, businesses develop intellectual property (IP) – intangible assets that they create out of human knowledge and ideas. These may be designs, logos, words, phrases, symbols, discoveries and other inventions. They may be musical, literary or artistic creations. They use this property to create unique products and build brand association, reputation and awareness.

In essence, IP confers exclusive rights – a right to exclude others. It enables its owners to prevent others from taking unfair advantage of their painstaking time and effort, leaving them free to exploit their creativity and encouraging further innovation.

The concept of IP is not new. The earliest known patent was granted by Henry VI in 1449. In 1578, Queen Elizabeth I granted Sir Humphrey Gilbert a patent to discover and settle new English colonies "to inhabit and possess all remote and heathen lands". He was also a privateer, targeting the Spanish treasure fleet.

"IP rights are a bit like buried treasure," says Peter Finnie, a partner in Gill Jennings & Every LLP (GJE), the London based patent and trademark attorneys. "They sit beneath the surface, have enormous value and are often untapped or left unprotected by their owners."

IP is everywhere. The understanding of its relevance as a critical asset and business driver, along with its impact on valuations, is growing. According to a UK government-sponsored report, the Gowers Review of Intellectual Property (published in December 2006), a doubling of the asset values in the UK's top ten listed companies between 1984 and 2004 was matched by a tenfold increase in their values, with the difference being accounted for by intangible assets – goodwill, reputation and IP.

Types of intellectual property

Intellectual assets cover a wide spectrum. Some of these are able to be registered or are automatically protected and some are not. For example, customer contracts, supply agreements, employment contracts, trade secrets and know-how may all be considered as intellectual assets even though they cannot be protected in the same way as IP.

So what can be protected? It's a big subject, but the four main types of IP are patents, copyright, trademarks and designs. Let's consider each of these in turn:

Patents

A patent is an exclusive right granted by a government to an inventor for a limited period in exchange for public disclosure of an invention. A term of 20 years is common and the exclusive right operates to prevent others from making, using, selling, offering for sale or importing the patented invention for the term of the patent.

In order to be eligible for patent protection, an invention must be novel, involve an inventive step and be capable of industrial application. In addition, it must not be 'excluded' – certain inventions, such as discoveries, scientific theories, artistic works and business methods do not qualify.

Applying for and maintaining a patent can be an expensive business, with costs falling into four main areas, namely patent acquisition, patent monitoring, patent exploitation and patent enforcement. It's a complex process that requires specialist advice from patent attorneys who often have a background in some area of science or engineering, as well as a detailed knowledge of IP law.

For GJE, this means getting involved at the very earliest stage of entrepreneurial innovation. "Patents should be considered as part of a wider IP strategy that supports a company's business plan. There's no point in acquiring expensive patents unless they're going to make you money," says Peter Finnie.

Dyson is a great example of a company that has designed, engineered and patented its way to profitable business success. After developing more than 5,000 prototypes of its bagless vacuum cleaner and filing countless patents, Dyson products are now best sellers in a global market. If Sir James Dyson had decided not to patent his revolutionary technology, it would have been copied instantly.

As usual, there's a balance. Huge sums of money have and will continue to be wasted on filing unnecessary and unprofitable patents. For businesses like Dyson, with ground-breaking inventions and truly global potential, they are essential. On the other hand, there is often more than one way to skin a cat, so taking out expensive patents to protect something that some other clever person can find a (different) way of replicating may not always be the best solution. Simply getting your product developed and into the market may be a better option, giving you 'first mover' advantage.

If you're unsure about whether or not you should be patenting your inventions, take advice. Always consider the commerciality and be realistic about the likely benefits and costs.

Copyright

Copyright is, literally, the right to copy. It exists in relation to literary works, film, TV broadcasts, musical compositions, recordings, architectural works, choreographic works, paintings, drawings, photographs, maps, charts, engravings, sculptures and software.

The copyright owner has two sets of rights. The first is an exclusive right to copy and exploit the copyrighted work, or to license others to do so. The second is a right to prevent anyone else from doing so without consent, with the option of seeking legal remedy if they do.

In most countries, copyright is automatic and does not require official registration with any government office. It comes into effect as soon as something is created and recorded or documented in a way that it can be reproduced or communicated, for example, on paper, on tape or as an electronic record.

The length of the protection offered by copyright varies. In the majority of countries, the copyright exists for the lifetime of the creator, plus 50–70 years, but this is not universal.

The general rule is that the copyright subsists with the creator. However, there are circumstances where this does not hold true. In the US and certain other jurisdictions, for example, if a work is 'made for hire' it is the employer and not the employee who is regarded as the author. In the UK, there is something similar. 'Works produced in the course of employment', as well as the use of clauses in employment contracts, have an equivalent effect.

Trademarks

Your brands and trademarks are the outward face of your business. They are how customers distinguish your products and services from those of your competitors.

Before you begin to use a brand name, you should check that nobody else is using something identical or similar to avoid any problems later on. You can do this by getting your attorney to carry out an availability search. Remember that trademark rights are territorial and that the fact that it's available in one jurisdiction doesn't automatically mean that it's available in another. Depending on the stage of your development, the cost of getting it wrong or having to change course could be severe.

A trademark might be a word, name, number, phrase, design, logo, colour, image, shape or perhaps a combination of these. As time passes, your customers will start to recognise your name and imagery and associate that with your product or service, giving you a good (or perhaps, bad) reputation.

Trademarks can be registered or unregistered. Where they are unregistered, the rights accrue as a result of actual usage in the marketplace. Registered trademarks afford the owner the ability to bring a legal action against anyone infringing their mark, whereas unregistered trade marks rely on the application of the common law tort of 'passing off'.

Passing off happens when a third party counterfeits or imitates a trade mark or trade name, or where some other aspects of the trademark owner's business are copied. The question is whether customers are deceived and mistake the third party for the real owner. If so, and damage or losses are actually incurred, an action for passing off may be brought. Be aware, however, that it can be extremely time-consuming and potentially very expensive to enforce passing off rights as evidence may be disputed and you may well end up in court.

In terms of practicality, trademarks can be registered with the trademarks office, or trademarks registry, in a particular jurisdiction. In some jurisdictions, trademark rights can be established through registration, usage or both. In others, only registered trademarks are recognised.

"Customer loyalty to brands and trademarks should never be underestimated," says Rowena Powell, a partner at GJE, citing a 2007 survey commissioned by the UK CBI which showed that well over half of customers are willing to pay a premium for a product if they consider it to have a particularly good reputation.

It's worth remembering that it's the brand rather than the company that counts. "All that matters is that the customer can recognise the brand itself, even if not the company which actually offers that product or service," continues Rowena. "For example, how many people know, or even care, that Lucozade is made by GlaxoSmithKline?"

Designs

If you're making products that are unique because their appearance is different from anything else on the market, you may want to register your design. It's a lot quicker and easier than getting a patent and if your idea is about how something looks rather than how it works, it might be the best and cheapest option. By registering your design, you'll get exclusivity for the appearance of your product, which will supplement any copyright or unregistered design rights you may have.

The first thing to consider is where you want the protection, because registering your design in one country will not protect you in another. If you want to register a design in the UK, you can apply to the UK based Intellectual Property Office. If you want to register in the European Community, you can apply for a registered community design (RCD) through the Office for Harmonization in the Internal Market (OHIM), based in Spain. In the US, a design application is considered to be a special form of patent application, known as a design patent. If you want to apply elsewhere, you can register in most major countries by making separate applications.

A design can be registered to cover the shape of a product, the decoration applied to the product (e.g. a T-shirt) or both. The particular features may include lines, contours, colours, shape, texture and/or materials.

Design rights can typically be registered for up to 25 years. In the US, a design patent has a term of 14 years.

Managing IP risk

As the recognition of the value of intellectual assets, including intellectual property, increases, management teams are becoming more aware of the need to consider it as part of their mainstream business planning. Whilst IP and its protection will be more important to some businesses than others, no one is exempt. You will therefore need systems that enable you to capture, exploit, monitor and enforce these important rights.

Many businesses will claim that their IP portfolio is already well managed and controlled and that their key risks have been identified and addressed. In reality, this is often not the case. Unlike a physical asset, such as a car, you can't touch or feel your IP.

So have you got systems in place that identify and document your IP creation? Are you fully aware of what you actually own? Are you keeping an eye on your competitors? If not, it may be time to match what you say you are doing with what you are actually doing.

It's more than common sense. In today's knowledge economy, both buyers and investors are placing greater importance on IP portfolios and how they are administered. IP due diligence is now a key part of the investment process – they want to know how their investment will be protected and what risks the business may face.

Problems can arise in a variety of different circumstances, including:

- existing IP may be inadequately protected

- IP exists or is being created, but it is not being captured

- the IP is valueless or invalid

- the business doesn't own the IP

- the business is infringing someone else's IP

- money is being spent on irrelevant IP.

To avoid these problems, a structured approach is required. This should enable you to consider how your IP can be exploited to generate increased revenues, how you can use it to maintain competitive advantage and how it may impact on your exit value or your ability to raise finance.

Developing your IP strategy

The need for additional investment should not be used to justify the development of an IP strategy, so don't be tempted to wait. Here's a toolkit to help you start the process:

Do an initial IP audit to understand what you have

- Identify what is distinct about your business. What is it that you can and need to protect?

- Identify existing intellectual property rights (IPR) and create a central register of who owns what.

- Review the commercial impact of your existing IPR. What value is it adding to your business? Is there room for cost saving through rationalisation?

- Review existing patent, design and trademark issues. Identify the gaps and seek relevant, additional protection.

- Don't forget intellectual assets such as employee, customer and supply contracts. These may be able to be protected in other ways.

Develop an IP strategy

- Understand how your IP/IPR can help you deliver your business objectives.

- Create systems to identify and capture innovation early on.

- Develop a robust and cost-effective IP filing strategy in both local and international markets.

- Identify an IP champion or team and make key people aware of your IP strategy and its importance.

- Consider reward schemes to incentivise innovation and IP creation.

Identify IP risks and opportunities

- Examine exploitation options to build value: exclusivity, license, sell...

- Improve third party awareness about the risk of infringement.

- Deal with third party issues including IP arising through supplier contracts or joint ventures.

- Draft suitable IP clauses to include in employment contracts.

Manage and maintain your IP portfolio

- Agree and monitor an IP budget.

- Regularly review and update your IP strategy and keep a detailed IPR register.

- Assess the competitor landscape for risks and new opportunities.

- Promote your IP to investors as an integral part of your business plan and value proposition.

- Do thorough IP due diligence in advance of any transactions (trade sales, IPOs, investments etc.).

- Consider the benefits of getting expert valuations of your IP.

At the end of the day, the pursuit of IP is only relevant if it adds value to your business. By developing an IP strategy, capturing and protecting innovation and monitoring your IP assets and their exploitation, you can add to the profitability and professionalism in your business and facilitate your future growth.

To discover whether that growth should be organic or through acquisition, take a look at the next chapter.

Top tips

- **Intellectual Property (IP) gives its owner an exclusive right – the right to exclude others**. Don't underestimate its importance and value.

- The key types of IP are **Patents, Trade Marks, Copyright and Design**. Consider which of these are important to your business and why.

- **Note that certain IP rights are granted automatically**, while others require applications, registrations and fees.

- IP rules vary from country to country, so **always get protection where you need it**.

- **Don't infringe the IP rights of others.** Deliberate or inadvertent infringement is likely to involve cost, or even litigation, later on.

- **Carry out an IP audit.** Identify and record your existing rights and consider their ongoing value.

- Build your IP strategy into your business plan. **Create systems to identify and capture innovation early on.**

- **Consider IP rights ownership** in relation to IP created by employees, suppliers or through joint ventures.

- Monitor the activities of your competitors to **identify commercial risks and opportunities.**

- **Don't waste time or money** developing or protecting IP that adds little or no value to your business.

CHAPTER 18

Buy and Build

> **"It's far better to buy a wonderful company at a fair price than a fair company at a wonderful price."**
>
> — Warren Buffett

Going for growth

For successful entrepreneurs, curiosity, drive and passion fuel a constant quest for renewal and growth. They leave no stone unturned and they never, ever give up. It's inspirational and awesome to watch.

In this book, we've looked at the main ingredients required to make a successful and sustainable business. We've considered vision and strategy, management and finance. We've talked about leadership, marketing and branding. We've understood the impact of technological breakthroughs and the almost unlimited potential of the global village. If you can tick all the boxes, you're ready to run a big business.

There's always the exception that proves the rule but, for most businesses, early sales success gives way to a flatter growth curve, with many hitting a glass ceiling at some point in their development. This may be because they've saturated their local market or encouraged the emergence of competition. It may be due to a lack of focus on product development or ineffective sales and marketing. There are a host of possible reasons.

If your business is successful and profitable but bumping up against a glass ceiling, ask yourself why. If it's because of internal issues or problems, address them. If it's because of geography or competition, or the need for product or service diversification (or similar), then you might want to consider the attractions of a 'buy and build' strategy to help you achieve your goals.

The term 'buy and build' is most commonly used in the investment community. For example, a private equity firm that pursues a buy and build strategy will typically buy a company in a particular sector and use it as a platform to buy other businesses in that sector. By taking this approach, both cost and management synergies can be found (because you won't need to duplicate all the functions) and large businesses can be built in a relatively short time.

You don't need to be a private equity firm to pursue a buy and build, or acquisition, strategy. Making acquisitions may be the best and most effective way to grow your business. If you buy the right business you can instantly bolster your reach and overall capability. You can gain instant ownership of the acquired company's products, brands and services, along with their staff, facilities, technology, IP and other assets. Economies of scale may enable you to leverage your supply chain more effectively, driving down your input costs and increasing your profit margins. In addition, you may be able to save significant operational costs by removing duplication and sharing HR, finance or other back office functions.

For example, "a magazine publisher may purchase another company to expand its existing stable of titles. Car dealership groups may acquire new dealerships to broaden their geographical footprint," says Brian Livingston, head of mergers and acquisitions at Smith & Williamson. "Extra turnover and gross margin are added to the existing business without any material increase in overheads."

The combined impact of these benefits can enable businesses to accelerate their growth, whether by scaling up their activities in a chosen sector, taking more and better control of their supply chain or by diversifying into new markets, all at a far faster pace than organic expansion might allow.

"Many farmers have diversified away from core farming activities to expand into land management or leisure," explains Brian. "Other businesses choose to diversify into complementary activities – so a business providing catering and security may choose to add cleaning services."

The possibilities are endless, but it's not a one-way street. If you're going to pursue an acquisition strategy, you need to understand the risks. First, you'll need to finance your acquisitions. This may mean taking in new equity or debt, putting you and your business at the mercy of third parties, particularly if things go wrong.

Then there's the planning, due diligence, completion, post-deal integration and cultural alignment, putting pressure on management time to successfully bed down the acquisition and smooth some inevitable ruffled feathers.

There will be multiple issues to address but, if you've done your due diligence on the business and are happy with what you've found, the most challenging aspect will be the people. An acquisition will normally mean a realignment of people on both sides, with some changing their roles and some departing. The unexpected, as well as the expected, will almost certainly happen.

It's quite normal, for example, for key people in the acquired company to want to go and do something else. They may have made money from the sale and feel that their time has come. In the home team, you may find that your own people feel that they have been passed over or usurped as part of the process, causing tension and unscheduled departures.

"In my experience, people tend to work for people rather than for companies," says entrepreneur Seb Bishop. "If you sell a business and some of the senior team go, it's inevitable that some people who were at the organisation specifically because of those senior individuals will leave too. And that's a very expensive problem to solve. Having good people disappear out of a business is a huge cost, because you've got to recruit, retrain and reinspire and that can be very difficult."

Buy-in from both businesses can be a problem as staff from the acquired and the acquirer jostle for position with different expectations and working methods. Cultures frequently clash and it's not easy to integrate the two into a unified team that shares and works towards the same vision.

"The reason why a number of mergers don't work is that the people side of it is not taken seriously enough," says Bobby Hashemi, a partner at private equity firm Risk Capital Partners.

And when should you acquire? Is there a good or bad time? Some advisors suggest that the best time to acquire is during upturns and periods of economic growth. Certainly these periods tend to see increased M&A activity.

On the other hand, recessions can be a great time to find worthwhile and affordable businesses. If profits are down and funding is tight, prices are lower and owners may be uncertain about their ability to weather the storm. "Research shows that buying for growth in a downturn can often add significant value, but don't take that for granted," says Brian Livingston.

How to grow through acquisition

It may be exciting, but it's generally accepted that badly targeted or poorly managed acquisitions destroy value far faster than they create it. Don't be one of the many losers. To get it right you'll need patience, a cool head and a process to keep you on track:

- **Identify the key reasons for making an acquisition.** Acquisitions carry risk, so examine all of the available alternatives before going down this route. If you want to enter new markets, consider appointing agents or distributors. If you need to strengthen you sales force, look at recruiting key staff from your competitors. Making an acquisition may look like your best option, but it's almost certainly not your only option.

- **Clarify your strategic aims and objectives.** "Long-term strategy is imperative," says Seb Bishop. How an acquisition is likely to help you achieve your long-term goals will dictate which businesses to consider and why.

- **Be specific about the type of target you are seeking.** Prepare a detailed acquisition mandate. Set out the key features you need from your target, e.g. IP, market access, management, production, supply, location etc. "Size is one of the main criteria for the buying business," comments Brian Livingston. "Too small and the acquisition is unlikely to be worth the cost and management time. Too big and it will unbalance the existing business."

- **Be proactive, not passive.** Research the market and actively seek out targets that match your mandate. Circulate your acquisition criteria and work with corporate finance advisors to identify potential targets. Consider the merits of using your advisors to approach your targets. "A financial advisor provides a useful buffer between the target and the buyer," says Brian Livingston. "Sometimes the fact that the advisor approaches the target is sufficient to elicit curiosity from the target and encourage them to take the call. The advisor is familiar with this world; acquirers are often not."

- **Buy businesses you understand.** However tempting it may sound, it can be dangerous to enter unfamiliar territory. "Mergers within the same industry tend to work much better than mergers across different industries," says Bobby Hashemi. "The conglomerate model has been seen not to have worked in the past, partly because people are buying businesses they don't understand."

- **Buy success.** If a business is doing badly, find the cause. Buying a good business with poor management is everyone's dream – a real money-making opportunity. In other cases, there may be good reasons why the business is underperforming. "When a management with a reputation for brilliance tackles a business with a reputation for bad economics, it is the reputation of the business that remains intact," says Warren Buffett.

- **Look for synergies.** Cost-savings or revenue enhancements are the main drivers in most acquisitions. Consider the back office or other costs that can be saved by bringing the two businesses together. Look at how the combined customer base can be used to drive your sales. Remember that diversification rarely presents opportunities for synergistic savings.

- **Assess your capability.** Acquisitions need time, management and money. Consider whether your management team can handle the additional load without damaging your existing business or taking its eye off the ball. Identify your cash requirements and how you will fund the acquisition and growth. Be realistic about the costs of lawyers and financial advisors.

- **Don't forget the culture.** After the deal, the businesses will be part of one family, but the course of true love never did run smooth. So before you sign on the dotted line, consider the potential for clashes and have your integration plan written and ready to go. "If there's too wide a gap around values or culture, I would be looking very hard as to whether I had the overall competency to effect a quick culture change," advises Sir Eric Peacock.

Negotiating the deal

Identifying and approaching your target is the first step. If the discussions progress, you'll need to think about terms, structure and price.

There's a potential dichotomy here. On the one hand, the seller will want to know what you are offering and how you will pay. He won't want to waste his time unless he knows you are serious and that his price expectations can be met. On the other hand, unless the seller is running a formal sales process and distributing detailed information about his business, you are unlikely to have had much access to his business and the details needed to assess it.

Notwithstanding the difficulties, there is a reasonably well-trodden path. In practice, unless you are either very brave or very foolish, you are likely to be guided by experienced advisors who live and breathe the process.

Establishing the price

There's no such thing as a 'right' price for a business. Pricing is subjective and dependent on the willingness of a buyer and seller to reach an agreement. Typically, this will end up being above the price that the buyer wants to pay and below the price the seller wants to achieve. It's called negotiation!

Pricing in the real world will depend upon a variety of factors – the economy, access to funding, scarcity, demand, anticipated growth and a host of other issues. However, there are a number of ways to put a theoretical value on a business and these can be calculated independently to develop a range of values to guide the purchaser. These include valuing a business on an 'assets' basis (i.e. by reference to the value of its net assets) or on an 'earnings' basis (by reference to its profits and cash flows).

An 'assets' basis of valuation will typically be most appropriate for businesses holding property or other assets, where the assets produce a regular and predictable income stream for the business, while an earnings basis of valuation is more regularly used for trading businesses. In the latter case, the value will be based on a multiple of the earnings (probably EBITDA or EBIT – see Chapter 5). The multiple used will differ from sector to sector and from business to business. Unsurprisingly, businesses that are growing will attract a higher multiple than those that are contracting. Similarly, businesses that can demonstrate sustainable profits will generally be more valuable than businesses that suffer from profit setbacks or volatility.

One technique that is often used is to compare a business to its publicly quoted peers, assuming these exist. Businesses that are quoted on a stock exchange have market values that can be ascertained from their share price. These are generally based on a multiple of profits and this ratio can be applied to privately owned businesses, usually with a discount (i.e. a reduction in the multiple) to reflect differences in size (smaller companies are generally less robust and carry higher risk) and marketability (there is no ready market for shares in a private business).

Given these general parameters, together with a strong recommendation that you seek guidance from experienced advisors, here are some tips on how to pay the right price:

- **Use a variety of valuation methods.** Consider price/earnings ratios, EBITDA multiples, net asset values and turnover multiples. If the business is capital intensive you may want to replace EBITDA with EBIT, giving a lower price and reflecting the need for investment in plant or other assets. "The key value is what the business is worth to the buyer rather than what the seller wants to sell it for," says Brian Livingston.

- **Don't overpay for the future.** Sellers of businesses often want to be paid for the hope value in their company – what it may be worth in two or three years' time. Take account of future prospects and, if appropriate, make your offer at the higher end of your price range, but *don't* get carried away by a mirage of optimism.

- **Don't pay for the benefits that you bring.** If 2+2=5, then buying a business should enable you to increase your profits above and beyond those you're acquiring with your target. This may be because of cost savings or other synergies and may reinforce your reasons for doing the deal, but you shouldn't have to pay for them.

- **Consider 'value' as well as 'price'.** If you've found the perfect business, this will probably be just as evident to the seller as it is to you. You may have to push the boat out further than you'd like in order to win it. "An acquisition should not be made simply because it is cheap, but because it makes sense," suggests Brian Livingston.

- **Consider alternative values.** It may be simpler and cheaper to acquire the target business than set up on your own. Assess the likely cost, and don't forget to include expensive management time.

- **Set a clear ceiling.** Decide on your maximum price and stick to it. Don't stretch yourself or pay more than you think it's worth – it will probably come back to haunt you. There are (normally) plenty of fish in the sea, so always be prepared to walk away.

- **Maintain integrity and transparency.** Make your offer and any conditions you are attaching to it clear and transparent from the outset. Be clear about 'dealbreakers' and issues that would cause you to reduce your price. Don't be a 'chipper'. "It's a small world out there and one thing that shouldn't be done is to be a chipper, to go to the last minute and then start chipping the price down, that's not good for one's reputation," comments Bobby Hashemi.

- **Don't pay more than you can afford.** Ensure that you have sufficient financial resources to complete the deal and fund your ongoing expansion. Consider ways of minimising your cash outflows by obtaining vendor finance (a loan from the seller), deferring part of the purchase consideration and paying it later on, or issuing new shares.

Settling the terms

Once you've agreed the price, the best way to document the deal is to put together some 'heads of terms' (sometimes called 'heads of agreement' or simply 'heads'). Heads of terms are used to record the 'in principle' agreement between the parties before they begin to incur significant costs progressing the transaction and entering into definitive, contractual documentation.

Heads of terms are largely non-binding. This is because the buyer needs an opportunity to look at the business in detail, a process known as due diligence (DD). This may expose issues that impact on the purchase price, the terms of payment or the form and content of the sale and purchase agreement (SPA).

Certain elements of the heads of terms are, however, likely to be binding. For example, the purchaser may seek an exclusivity period during which he can carry out his DD and get his legal advisors to draw up the SPA. There may be provisions relating to the treatment of confidential information or perhaps a 'break fee' if either party pulls out.

Here's a summary of the main issues to be dealt with in your heads of terms:

- **The parties and the description of the transaction.** Details of the parties and the nature and timing of the transaction, together with any other background information.

- **Purchase price.** Details of the purchase price (also known as 'consideration') offered by the buyer to the seller as well as how and when it will be paid. Purchase consideration will typically be satisfied in cash, shares or loan notes, or even a combination of all three. Elements of the consideration may be deferred and paid on the achievement of certain milestones (e.g. future profits) or on the happening of a particular event (e.g. the winning of a new contract).

- **Exclusivity.** The heads may include an exclusivity clause to stop the seller from negotiating or soliciting offers from other parties for a period. This is designed to give the purchaser a clear run at assessing and completing the transaction.

- **Confidentiality.** The treatment of confidential information is likely to be covered in the heads. The vendor will wish to set out how such information can be used and what should happen to it if the deal falls through.

- **Conditions.** The heads will set out details of any conditions. These may include:

  o   the satisfactory completion of due diligence by the purchaser

  o   availability of finance to satisfy the purchase price or to give access to working capital

  o   the existence of certain minimum net assets or profits at completion

  o   regulatory approvals (e.g. competition) and consents from third parties (e.g. lease assignments)

  o   board approval

  o   break fees; details of the circumstances under which a break fee might become payable by the buyer to the seller, or vice versa

  o   governing law and jurisdiction; the law applicable to the heads and any disputes that may arise.

Know your target: due diligence

Unfortunately, you can never be entirely sure about what you've bought until it's too late. The proof of the pudding is always in the eating, but that doesn't mean you shouldn't do your level best to find out everything you need to know during the acquisition process. This is where due diligence comes in.

DD is a process of discovery designed to tell you everything you need to know about the target business. If you're buying a company, rather than a bundle of trading assets (e.g. premises, goodwill, stock), this can be particularly important. Companies come with all of their past history intact. When you buy a company, you acquire it 'warts and all' with all of its assets, as well as all of its liabilities, including contingent and past liabilities. So it's important to establish what they are!

There are three main types of due diligence: commercial, financial and legal. Most of the activities carried out by a business can be pigeonholed in one of these areas, although it's worth checking that nothing falls through the cracks. Other things like IT systems and processes, environmental and health and safety issues, should not be lightly passed over.

Commercial due diligence, also known as market due diligence, is the review of a company's business plan and capabilities in the light of its industry, its markets, its competition and the general economic environment. This is a fundamental review of the commercial viability of the target business and is often carried out by the acquirer. Specialist firms also exist to provide this service.

Financial due diligence is the review of all the financial aspects of a business. It tends to be historic in focus and looks at financial performance, as well as the assets and liabilities of the target. Due to its specialist nature, this kind of due diligence is generally carried out by accountants and tax advisors.

Legal due diligence consists of the review of the target company's legal affairs including reporting on title, contracts, employment law, IP, data protection, disputes and any other matters of a legal nature. This kind of DD is usually carried out by a mixture of commercial, IP and property lawyers.

The idea of DD is to confirm the buyer's underlying understanding of the business and to confirm its past performance and future prospects. Whilst past performance may not be a definitive guide to the future, it often is. So look out for missed forecasts, over exuberant budgeting, et al.

"Having sector specific skill to ask the right questions and being able to anticipate where the skeletons are buried is key to avoiding those skeletons appearing once you've acquired a company," says Bobby Hashemi.

Here's a way to approach your DD process:

- **Assemble your DD team.** Decide on what you'll do internally and what you'll outsource to your advisors. Put someone in charge of the process. Provide clear terms of reference to external advisors in order to keep costs down and complete investigations within an acceptable time frame. Adopt a 'horses for courses' approach to get the right outcome – don't use a conveyancing lawyer to draft the SPA and don't use a bookkeeper to review the tax.

- **Carry out commercial due diligence.** Assess the commercial standing of your target and consider how it fits into its market. Evaluate the market size, your target's current market share and the overall economics of the sector. Try to get a 360 degree view of the business and consider its growth potential. Consider commercial threats including competitors, their size, what they do and don't offer, and how they may respond to your acquisition. Speak to key customers. Assess the likelihood of technological change. Do your research on the background and reputation of the management team. Identify any holes in the team and assess its ability to deliver on its business plans.

- **Consider culture and values.** "The first step in evaluating a merger, and what people often neglect, are the cultural issues: making sure that there's a cultural fit between the businesses is key," says Bobby Hashemi. "Long-term strategies of both organisations have to be aligned," concurs Seb Bishop, who thinks that "culturally the businesses have to be very similar" in order for an acquisition to work. For example, if one business has an authoritarian, controlling culture and the other has a collegiate, supportive culture, fall out is likely to occur.

- **Focus on financials.** Carry out your detailed financial due diligence. Look at historical financial information, budgets and forecasts to see how the business has performed against the expectations set by management. Consider future projections and the assumptions that lie behind them. Look at liquidity and working capital requirements and how these are managed. Attempt to identify all of the assets and liabilities of the business, whether actual or contingent and whether or not they are shown in the target's balance sheet. Check the suitability of accounting policies, particularly in relation to revenue recognition, intangible assets and work in progress. Review the tax status of the business and its compliance with financial and fiscal laws and regulations.

- **Brief your legal team.** Identify and investigate title to the tangible (e.g. property, machinery, equipment) and intangible (e.g. intellectual property) assets. Examine leases, commercial contracts and supply agreements. Consider banking agreements, employment contracts, pensions, incentive arrangements, insurance and regulatory requirements. Look at environmental issues and health and safety. Review the status of actual and pending legal actions by or against the business.

- **Evaluate critical operational issues** including production, supply chain, delivery and fulfilment. Review IT systems, document flows, quality management standards, marketing and customer relationship management.

- **Discuss material findings.** Hold regular meetings and discussions with your internal team and external advisors to discuss their findings and any challenges these present. Address these with the target. If the issues are sensitive or difficult, consider how you can maintain good relations by tasking your external advisors.

- **Don't use DD as a weapon.** The DD process is often stressful and emotional – don't make it any harder than it needs to be. Remember that it's you that wants to buy the target, so try to maintain good relations. If you find problems during the process, the acquisition price or terms may be affected. However, this is not the purpose of your DD.

- **Post-deal planning.** Use the DD process to help you plan your future. What you do immediately after the deal is likely to have a profound impact on the success or failure of your deal. Start preparing your 90-day post-integration plan.

Completion

Everyone's got a story to tell about completion. Typically these lawyer-centric affairs are scheduled to take place in the middle of the day, with an army of advisors, bankers and lawyers from both sides turning up to approve and sign the final documents and hand over the money. In practice, they tend to go on for hours and, for some unknown reason, generally finish in the middle of the night. During the course of a 12 to 15-hour meeting, it's not unusual for participants to gorge themselves on crisps, takeaway pizzas and other dubious delights, before (eventually) catching a taxi or even the milk train home!

It's only at completion that you realise the sheer number of people involved in your transaction, the incredible amount of paperwork that's been generated and the impact of months of negotiations. The documentation includes the sale and purchase agreement, together with suitable warranties (things that the vendor has given assurance on to the purchaser – e.g. collectability of debts) and indemnities (things that the vendor has indemnified the purchaser against – e.g. unexpected tax or other liabilities.) There will also be a raft of other documents, including banking documents, share transfers and comfort letters.

My most memorable completion took place many years ago. As the advisor to the purchaser of a small business from a large corporate, I was unhappy with a particular aspect of the deal. My worry was that a particular liability had not been fully reflected in the target's accounts. After many hours of haggling, the vendor eventually agreed to indemnify my purchaser for any shortfall. When the dust settled, we discovered that we were right. Having paid about £2m for the company, we got over £1m back.

Turnaround opportunities

Some purchasers like to buy businesses in distress. These are generally accessed through insolvency and restructuring practitioners (IPs) and can sometimes be great bargains. However, there may be challenges and pitfalls to face along the way.

In the first place, a lack of time and information means that due diligence is likely to be limited, so it may be difficult to assess what you're buying. Secondly, continuity of trade can be challenging if contracts have been terminated or suppliers or customers have been alienated. And finally, any purchase from an IP is likely to come without warranties or indemnities, leaving your purchase unprotected.

If you're buying a distressed business, it's important to find out what happened. In some cases, there may be good reasons why a business failed and why it may recover in the future. Perhaps it was overleveraged by bank debt following an earlier transaction, or perhaps it was the subject of a fraud.

If you're buying a salvageable business from an IP consider the different ways of acquiring it. "These may include different deal structures, e.g. purchasing assets versus shares and arranging short-term bridge funding to see the business through," advises Anthony Spicer, head of restructuring and recovery at Smith & Williamson.

"Your offer will be benchmarked against 'going concern' and 'liquidation' values," explains Anthony. "IPs generally don't like deferred payments so you'll probably need funds available immediately."

Be clear about what you are purchasing and take advice on the potential risks. Be aware of the IP's timetable and be prepared to move quickly.

Post-deal integration

It may have taken huge amounts of time, effort and money, but you've succeeded in completing your deal. So what's next?

"People are generally tired when they've been through a due diligence process, as part of a merger or acquisition. So what most people do when it's over is go back to their day job. But there's a better way" says Brian Livingston.

It may be tempting to have a rest, but now's the time to implement the 90-day action plan you put together during the due diligence and acquisition process. You have a unique window of opportunity to integrate your businesses and get your (combined) staff on side.

┌─ **Top tips** ─

- If you're bumping up against a glass ceiling in your business, ask yourself why. **Address internal issues before beginning to look outside.**

- **Organic growth can be accelerated by making acquisitions.** Consider the merits of a buy and build strategy to help you spur your growth.

- **Be specific about the type of target you are seeking.** Prepare a detailed acquisition mandate that sets out what you want.

- **Only buy businesses that you understand.** The grass may always look greener on the other side, but **it's dangerous to enter unfamiliar territory.**

- **Use established valuation techniques** to help you fix your price. Set a clear ceiling and don't offer more than you can afford.

- **Carry out detailed commercial, financial and legal due diligence** on your target. Take every possible step to get to know the business inside and out before you sign on the dotted line.

- **Don't use the due diligence process as a weapon.** It's stressful and emotional, so don't make it any harder than it needs to be.

- **Maintain good relations with your target and be open and transparent** in your dealings. **Don't become known as a 'chipper'** – a person who reduces the offer price at the last minute for little or no good reason.

- **Implement your post-deal integration plan immediately** following completion. This unique window of opportunity will not recur.

- Remember that **badly targeted or poorly managed acquisitions destroy value** far faster than they create it.

CHAPTER 19
Business Succession and Sale

"Every exit is an entrance somewhere else."

— Tom Stoppard, British playwright

Planning for succession

It's hard to build a successful business, so the idea of leaving or handing over the reins is likely to engender a mixture of fear, grief and other conflicting emotions. But nothing lasts forever, so, whether you're selling your business, passing it on to the next generation or simply retiring, you'll need to plan for your succession.

As we discovered in Chapter 8, great businesses are generally run by leaders who spend the majority of their time working *on* their business, as opposed to *in* their business. By definition, businesses run by these types of leaders can survive, and even thrive, without them. Apart from their valuable strategic input, their management roles will be capable of being filled through normal recruitment channels, meaning that their businesses are not owner-dependent.

If you've achieved this enviable status, your succession will be far easier than for peers who are still up to their necks in the day-to-day muck and bullets. If not, then there's still some work to do.

Owner-dependency has many negative connotations, the most important of which are that the business cannot be successfully run without the owner's involvement and that the business is unlikely to have any meaningful value.

If you accept this prognosis, it's important to start your succession planning early. Leaving it too late is a common mistake. In addition, succession should not only be considered when you're selling your business or planning for your retirement. After all, what would happen to your business if you were hit by that proverbial bus?

Your succession plan will depend on whether you are selling, retiring or considering other 'what if' scenarios. You might simply be trying to free yourself up to carry out a more strategic role, or it might just be part of your plan to ensure that your business can survive and succeed without you.

Unless you are selling the business and departing, succession will be focused on two key aspects – the appointment and development of the right successor and the change in your own role.

Appointing and developing your successor

Barring wholesale changes of management, perhaps as a result of a sale or an MBI, most businesses favour the appointment of internal rather than external candidates to succeed their outgoing CEOs. Methods of recruitment may vary, depending on whether there's an obvious internal candidate, the potential for both internal or external candidates, or just an external candidate.

Views on this can vary. I was once a director of a company that wanted to consider both internal and external candidates for the CEO role. In that instance, the outgoing CEO chose to run two processes – one to get the views (in fact, votes) of the staff to elect the best internal candidate, and one to identify external candidates. The process was run by an external headhunting firm, who interviewed the resulting shortlist and presented back to the board. Eventually, an internal candidate was chosen.

It was an interesting, if not unusual, approach. What it definitely succeeded in doing was to create uncertainty and take everyone's eye off the ball, as the process took some months to complete.

At the end of the day, it will probably depend on your culture. If there's an obvious internal candidate in a smallish business, I would probably just go ahead with the appointment. In a bigger business, more formality may be required. "Even if you end up recruiting somebody internally you should still have gone through a robust recruitment process where you get the best professional help that you can afford," says David Molian.

Another approach may be to create development plans for one or more 'candidates in waiting'. Nick Jenkins, the chairman of Moonpig, took this approach by appointing a commercial director and then handing over more and more of the daily work to him until he was happy that he could take the CEO role on. "You really need to understand whether they can do it," says Nick. "So I brought Iain in and didn't tell him that I wanted him to take over my job, because if I'd realised he was the wrong person for the job I'd have needed to bring in somebody else above him."

Whatever you decide to do, you should define the scope of the role and the qualities required to fill it. You should also discuss it openly with your senior team. In addition, if you know that one or more team members have designs on the role but that you would not consider their appointment, take time out to meet them. Help them understand why the role wouldn't suit them and why they're important to you where they are.

Once the candidate has been selected, decisions will have to be made on timing and implementation. Will the new role take effect immediately or, as with Moonpig's commercial director, will there be a staged transfer of responsibilities? This may differ between internal and external appointments.

Don't let go of the reins until you're ready. Some friends of mine, who had years of experience in their industry, ran a brilliant business making £2–£3m per annum of profit. Notwithstanding this, they managed to convince themselves that a 'professional' CEO could do a much better job. Through their headhunters, they found a high profile candidate from a much larger company who appeared to have all the right attributes for the role. They made the appointment and handed over the reins. Within months, they were loss making and had to take in substantial extra investment just to enable them to survive. Needless to say, the new CEO was dismissed, but not until after the damage had been done.

Changing your role

If you turn the same handle, you get the same result, so think about how your role should change to help both you and your successor. Remember that you don't need to disappear overnight!

Here are some options to think about:

- **Consider promoting yourself from CEO to Chairman.** This can be an executive role, at least initially, with a view to becoming non-executive at some time in the future. By liberating the title of CEO, you've made a significant step.

- **Shift your remit from running the company to running the board.** Become more of a strategist. Aim to spend more of your time thinking about the future of your business rather than working in it.

- **Become a mentor and coach.** After running your business for many years you'll have developed a sixth sense about what is and isn't important. Spend time with your successor and let osmosis take its course.

- **Gain experience on another board.** Think about taking a non-executive role in someone else's business. "Prior to making the change, serve on somebody else's board as a non-exec and observe the dynamics of how a board runs," suggests David Molian. "That way you can take a view on what you'd like to see (and not see) on your own board."

- **Don't interfere or undermine.** Once a new CEO is on board it's important to give them space and let them do things in their own way. Don't meddle unless you can see (rather than imagine) the holes in the road ahead.

Planning for your future

With succession taken care of, you'll have opened up your options. If you haven't already decided on your future, now may be the time for reflection. With a successful business and a strong management team, there are a number of opportunities to consider.

Here are the most likely alternatives:

Stay as you are

This may not seem like the most exciting option, but it certainly worth considering. There are a few things to think about here:

- It is generally accepted that many entrepreneurs sell their businesses too early, giving much of their potential future value to their purchasers. At least a part of this can be put down to first timers (the majority) who want to see tangible rewards for their efforts. With previously unaffordable homes and the prospect of attractive 'toys' appearing on the horizon, it's not a surprising call. If there's a next time, however, they may well be slower to sell.

- You may love your job and your involvement in the business that you've created. By selling it, you'll lose control and probably end up leaving in the short to medium term – it can be difficult for an entrepreneur to work for someone else. If that happened, or if you agree to leave following your sale, what will you do with your time? Most successful entrepreneurs dream about sunshine, holidays and yachts, but this attraction quickly wanes. You're either driven by the cut and thrust of business or you're not.

So if you're profitable, growing and have a great management team, why sell the best business you'll ever own? Where better to invest your money than in your own business?!

You may think you can be a serial entrepreneur and go round again. People do and maybe you can, but there are many who are never able to repeat their initial success.

Keep it in the family

If you've got a family and they work in or are interested in the business, you may want to help them to take it over. If you're financially secure, you might be happy to continue as the owner of all or part of the business, perhaps continuing in a non-executive role. Alternatively, you could improve your financial security by engineering a family buy-out. A successful business should be able to raise some external debt for this purpose, and you could top it up by making loans that the business repays over time.

Part sell the business

A part-sale of the business might offer the best of both worlds. In this situation, you could cash in some, but not all of your chips, whilst remaining in role and participating in future growth. A part-sale might typically be to a private equity house, who would take a meaningful stake in the business, giving some of the cash to you and putting some into the business for expansion.

Float the business

If you want to raise cash for acquisitions and if you're happy to be in the public eye, floating (or IPOing) your business on a stock exchange like AIM may be a real and interesting option. As a public company, with third party shareholders, you would need to be comfortable with the increased regulation and formality this brings. On the flipside, having a stock market quote can facilitate acquisitions, with sellers sometimes accepting shares in your business, instead of (or in addition to) cash. Your visibility will also increase, although this can sometimes be a double-edged sword. Bad news travels fast in the public markets.

Sell the business

If you don't like the other options, there may only be one left. The rest of this chapter is therefore dedicated to this interesting and challenging topic.

Selling your business

Selling your business is likely to be the most important financial transaction of your life, so it's important to get it right. Given the Herculean effort that most people put into building their businesses, it's amazing how many of them fail to plan their exit. Serendipity often rules, with many accepting apparently flattering or friendly offers without even bothering to market their businesses.

It's worth a story to illustrate this point. Some time ago, an ex-colleague of mine was approached and asked if he could help a management team with their sale. In this case, there was a group of shareholders rather than a single owner. They told him that they knew who was going to buy their business (a competitor), and for how much (£3 million). They asked if he would represent them and, rather than charging his normal fee (a retainer and a success fee), whether he would accept a reduced fee, given that they had already done all the hard work!

Given these circumstances, my colleague agreed that he would represent them, but that he would only do so if they allowed him to market the business more widely. If the business was sold to the competitor for the anticipated price, then a reduced fee would be charged. However, if another buyer was found and the sellers accepted this alternative offer, normal fees would apply.

The business was duly marketed and a cash-rich company (it had sold its previous business) expressed its interest. It wanted to buy the seller's business and use it as a cornerstone to build a much bigger business in the sector. Following negotiation, the business was sold for around £9 million.

To show what a difficult life an M&A advisor can have, the sellers then proceeded to dispute the fee. They argued that my colleague must have known how much the business was worth and that he had obviously taken advantage of them. In reality, nothing could have been further than the truth. By marketing the business widely and following a structured sale process, my colleague had unearthed a non-obvious buyer (a 'NOB') and achieved a stellar price.

How to achieve a successful sale

Your exit will be your final chance to be rewarded for all your efforts, so let's look at the steps you need to take:

- **Preparing for sale.** What to do to get your business ready.
- **Maximising capital value.** Remember that price is what people pay and value is what they get.
- **Market timing.** Identifying the right time to sell.
- **Doing the deal.** Finding the right buyer and selling for the right price.

Preparing for sale

The best way to prepare your business for sale is to consider what buyers and their advisors will be looking for when they come knocking on your door. If it's not available they'll lose confidence. If they lose confidence, the deal will either collapse or you'll end up on the back foot, compromising on your terms or accepting a lower price.

People buy businesses for all sorts of reasons, so it's important to think about who might buy yours and what's likely to be important to them. It might be that you've got some unique IP, a great sales team, or some valuable contracts. Imagine, then, what will happen when your buyer discovers that your IP is largely or even completely unprotected, or that your sales team is actually outsourced, or that your valuable contracts are about to expire. With the benefit of forethought, much could have been done to resolve these value-busting, or even deal-breaking, issues.

I was once involved in a business that had an excellent customer base and good levels of turnover. In this particular case the business was not dependent on its owner, but on its supplier, who had been fortunate in securing a long-term contract with them on extremely favourable terms. The value of the business was, in effect, embedded in a supply contract that was fundamental to the successful servicing and retention of the customers. Whilst the business was capable of growing, the principal benefits of that growth always ended up with the supplier. By entering into a long-term contract and by promoting the excellence of the supplier as the key reason for customers to use the business, management had effectively given away its value. At the end of the day, the supplier bought the business for a song.

What things looks like on the outside may not be well represented on the inside. The challenge is to get them both aligned.

"We're now in an environment where due diligence is more onerous than it's ever been," says Brian Livingston, head of M&A at Smith & Williamson. "During the DD process people look for reasons not to do a deal rather than reasons to do it. And if you are difficult or you're not ready or you won't supply data, you raise your chances of not doing a deal."

Having established and sold many businesses of his own and now being involved in the private equity market, Jonathan Hick believes that being prepared for exit is just good business practice. "I've learned that you should always plan for exit even if you don't want to exit tomorrow, or even if you don't intend to sell up at all," says Jonathan.

Here are some thoughts to help you prepare for exit:

- **Plan well in advance of the sale.** "Typically business owners don't allow long enough," says David Molian. "My view is that if you're going to sell a business you should expect at least two years between the decision to sell and the actual sale taking place. Many owner-managers are unrealistically optimistic about how quickly it can happen."

- **Identify your potential acquirers.** Non-obvious buyers are rare, so think about who might want to acquire your business and why. "Know who you intend to sell to and their strategy going forward," suggests entrepreneur and investor James Caan, who also recommends considering this "two years before you actually intend to sell the business." "Identify immediately who your suitors are," Seb Bishop suggests. "Then evaluate those suitors and their potential reasons for buying you. Is revenue important to them? Is profit important to them? Is geographical footprint important to them? Read up on what public information you can find on them. Look at where they're struggling because that's what's going to make you most attractive to them," adds Seb.

- **Give yourself time.** As a minimum, selling your business will be a part-time job. Given its importance, David Molian takes it further: "Recognise that selling a business successfully is a full-time job," advises David. "That's why having a two-year exit plan makes sense, because there's time to put in place the necessary processes for the business to carry on."

- **Focus on your trading.** Consider how the business will be run during the sale process to demonstrate its strength. "You often see a real dip in a company's trading performance at a time when its owners are trying to sell it, which of course is the worst time for a dip in trading to take place," says David, "because that signals to the sellers that the business is in decline, whereas actually the business may be fine but the owner/manager has taken his/her eye off the ball."

- **Organise your data.** "Have systems in place that provide transparency to the buyer," recommends Bobby Hashemi. "If you don't, it'll make the buyer's job much more difficult." Pull together the leases, asset registers, insurances, staff and customer contracts, accounts and business plans etc. Consider setting up an online (AKA 'virtual') data room to store and update this information so you can make it available as and when required. "Many companies we've dealt with thought they were ready to sell, yet we've discovered it would take us weeks to get the data right. Because they're not used to selling a company, they don't have all the bits and pieces they need," explains Brian Livingston. "And what you must never, ever do is give data to the buyer that turns out to be incorrect, because that doesn't help your position."

- **Normalise costs and investments.** Make it easy for the buyer to understand your trading performance. Where possible, your accounts should be the guide, but these are often clouded by one-off, exceptional or even quasi-personal expenditure. It can get messy trying to pick out costs that won't recur and if you're selling your business on an earnings basis, remember that any unnecessary costs will reduce your price by a multiple of their value.

Maximising capital value

In simple terms, the acquisition of a business gives a buyer the right to its future profits and cash flows. These may be generated by the target itself (from your point of view, the better and more valuable scenario) or through synergistic savings or efficiencies. The buyer will therefore be thinking about the prospects for realising these profits and cash flows, as well as sustaining them in the future.

It's difficult to generalise, but most trading businesses are sold on an earnings basis. This means that their value is calculated as a multiple of their profits (or EBITDA/EBIT). The clue is in the word 'multiple'.

If you've got a business making £2m p.a., and the multiple used for the purchase is 5, your business will be sold for £10m. However, if the business is making £1m but the multiple used for the purchase is 10, the sale value will still be £10m.

Too many entrepreneurs focus on profits, paying little attention to the impact they can have on their multiple. It's a big mistake. To maximise your value, you need to focus on both. "The way to achieve a big multiple is to have a well-organised, growing business," says Brian Livingston, adding that "if your business is ex-growth, your profitability is volatile or there are questions about your management or your systems, the multiple is likely to suffer."

Here are some pointers on how to maximise your capital value:

- **A strong management team.** There's no getting away from this one. It's highly likely that any purchaser will place fundamental importance on the ability and retention of your key management.

- **Profitability and stability.** In an ideal world, your business will be able to demonstrate steady turnover and profits growth, along with low volatility and efficient systems and processes.

- **A stable workforce.** A well-motivated and incentivised staff is less likely to jump ship on a change of ownership.

- **A scalable business model.** Scalability creates value. If a buyer can identify realistic opportunities for exponential growth, he will value your business far more highly. As an example, consider the software/games model, where an existing product can be sold to an almost unlimited number of users at little extra cost.

- **A growing sector.** Keep up with the times. A business that positions itself to access an emerging or growth sector will be more attractive than one which operates in a saturated or declining market. "You need to have some tangible blue sky that's achievable in the next few years," comments Brad Rosser.

- **A strong brand.** Consider opportunities to raise awareness of your brand and become more prominent in your sector. Write articles, make videos, become a thought leader, attend and speak at industry events. Businesses that get noticed get bought.

- **Gather case studies and testimonials.** Ask your customers to attest to the benefits of working with your business. Publish their comments in marketing materials and blogs.

- **Back office.** Don't skimp on HR, finance and administration, but don't create unnecessary bureaucracy. Streamline processes and avoid the build-up of annoying and unnecessary rules.

- **Get good advisors.** Choose advisors who have been there and done it before. Ask about their track record and experience. Assess their suitability for your sector and, if appropriate, their international capability. Above all, seek rapport and get them on board early. Give them both the opportunity and the time to help you maximise your value.

Market timing

As if there wasn't enough to think about, timing your sale is critical to maximising your value and achieving a successful outcome. Trying to sell your business in the depths of a recession, when prices are low and finance is hard to come by, is not the best idea.

"Think not only about when you're ready to sell, but when the marketplace is ready to buy," advises Brian Livingston. Market dynamics and activity can ramp up a company's perceived value and present a window of opportunity which can be seized before the buoyancy in the sector declines.

Economies and the markets within them always move in cycles. Selling towards the peak of the cycle in your particular sector should ensure a string of interested buyers and an opportunity to create competitive tension.

"Assess whether you can make it through to the next peak of the next cycle," advises Julie Meyer. "Or whether your business could deteriorate in value in a downturn, making it very difficult and essentially meaning you'll have to build value all over again."

The best time to sell your business is when you don't need to. So, if you are being approached and the marketplace is creating an opportunity, you should sit up and take note. On the other hand, business owners sometimes have no choice in the matter. There may be financial, health or family reasons which precipitate a sale. "If personal circumstances are forcing a sale and that segment of the market is suffering a cyclical decline, that's a really unfortunate place to be," comments David Molian.

Doing the deal

If the timing feels right and you've got your advisors on board, it's time to prepare your information memorandum (IM). The IM is the primary source of information for potential buyers, describing the business, its products and services, its markets, its management and its financials, plus any other relevant information. Both you and your advisors must be happy that the IM is correct and credible in all respects and contains sufficient detail to enable prospective buyers to put forward their proposals.

With the IM in hand, it's just a matter of finding the right buyer and convincing him to pay the right price!

Finding the right buyer

Buyers can fall into different camps. The four that are most common are trade buyers, strategic buyers, financial buyers and management teams. Sometimes these can come together, for example when a financial buyer (e.g. a private equity house) provides funding to enable an MBO, or perhaps an MBI.

A sale to an incumbent management team is a well-trodden path for many retiring owners and is often the simplest form of deal. The management is already familiar with the business and, in certain circumstances, the deal may require less due diligence. The SPA may also contain fewer warranties and indemnities, an advantage from a vendor's point of view. However, a sale to management can create conflict, as the parties are on opposing sides. If the deal fails to complete, future relationships may be challenged.

Larger companies often divest their non-core subsidiaries and a particular experience I once had highlighted the potential for management to be 'the enemy within'. In this case, I was engaged by a business that interrupted an MBO, making a better offer and ultimately succeeding in making the acquisition. Following completion, we discovered that the MBO team had significantly undervalued their stock. Our acquirer unwittingly benefited, making the deal very attractive indeed. Having said that, an owner-manager is likely to be much closer to his business than a corporate owner, but the potential for conflict is clear.

Trade buyers and strategic buyers share similar characteristics. They are either in the same industry (trade buyer) or in a similar line of business that can benefit from the acquisition of the target (strategic buyer). A strategic buyer, for example, might simply want access to the target's customer base, as opposed to its products and services. Trade and strategic buyers can often benefit from synergies or economies of scale and are normally long-term investors, with no intention to sell the acquired business in the future.

Financial buyers may be investment groups, private equity houses or even established or emerging entrepreneurs who want to own their own business. Financial buyers are constrained (and may therefore offer less) because they are buying in isolation and can't benefit from synergies or economies accessible by businesses in the same or a similar trade. Their focus is more on structuring the deal, buying low and selling high. Ownership periods of three to seven years are common for this type of buyer.

It's worth noting that financial buyers can also become trade or strategic buyers. As mentioned in Chapter 18, a 'buy and build' strategy may involve the purchase of a cornerstone business, to which other businesses are then added in the future.

Brian Livingston points out that the most likely and best potential buyer may not always be someone you want to talk to. "If someone is going to have huge synergistic gain because your company can really add value to theirs, they must know your industry, understand what you do and probably compete with you regularly. You don't necessarily want to talk to them. And if you do, you need to think through how to release detailed data to somebody who competes with you or is your biggest customer!"

Nevertheless, the company with good reason to buy your business is most likely to be well-known to you and operating within your sector. "If you've got a chain of chemists, it's quite likely that Boots or someone similar would buy the company," adds Brian.

How to market your business for sale

- **Prepare a detailed information memorandum.** Set out the facts and figures so that prospective buyers can evaluate your business and make an offer.

- **Think international.** In a global village, don't ignore the possibility of selling your business to an overseas buyer. Pick an advisor who has access to and is active in this important market.

- **Be discreet.** Shouting from the rooftops that you're selling your business may not be a wise course of action. Think about the potential impact on staff, customers and suppliers.

- **Research your buyers.** Talk to your advisors to discuss the different types of buyer and their likely appetite for your business. Prepare a short teaser or story board to send to your agreed targets.

- **Follow up.** Get your advisors to follow up and note any expressions of interest.

- **Ask for non-disclosure.** Get interested parties to sign a non-disclosure agreement (NDA) to protect your sensitive data.

- **Give initial data.** Consider the benefits of a face-to-face presentation versus the delivery of an IM. Provide access to your data room at the relevant time.

- **Be active, not passive.** You may have an advisor, but that doesn't mean you can't add value. "You know more about your business than anyone else," says Brad Rosser. "It's not a case of ringing up someone who deals in the sale of businesses and leaving it completely to them, because they won't know the business as well as you." So stay involved, attend meetings and work with your advisor to generate interest in your business.

Selling for the right price

Getting the right offer for your business will require excellent negotiating skills and a good dose of psychology. The price you eventually receive will be affected by scarcity, demand, emotion, vision and competitive tension. This is a potent mixture and the sell side objective must be to get the buyer to the point where it would be an unmitigated disaster if he lost the opportunity to someone else.

According to Brian Livingston, the process is likely to involve the creation of a storyboard. "A storyboard will lay out, in four or five simple slides, how the business is positioned and where it's going," says Brian. "That storyboard is then adopted by the buyer, who is quite busy, so he/she presents your truth as his/her truth."

By giving the buyer your vision, they'll start to champion your sale, making it easier for you to achieve your price.

It's important to get any bad news on the table at the outset. So if you've got a particular problem in your business, don't hide it. Get it out in the open along with your thoughts as to how the issue can be addressed. You will not only impress your prospective buyer with your honesty, but also avoid potentially damaging and price cutting disclosures later on.

"Don't tell everybody all the good news immediately. Tell them as much of the bad news as you can," recommends Brian. "For example, if your factory is ugly, and the buyer only sees it after he's made his offer, you're liable to lose the price. However, if you've told everybody the bad news up front, say by sending a video clip of it round as part of the information pack, then they can't reduce the price for something they already know. You can combine that with the fact that actually you've won quite a nice contract. So when the offer first comes in, you wait a little while and then you tell them something like 'we've just won a new contract (which gives us permission to increase the price)'.

This is not to say you hide anything, just that you reveal a key strength as a tactic to negotiate the price up rather than giving the buyer ammunition to drive the price down (as is often the case) by trying to sweep the weaknesses under the carpet.

"It's always better to reveal your flaws," says James Caan. "Because they'll come out during the due diligence process anyway and if they uncover them before you explain them, they'll think you were trying to hide them. It also allows you to have the conversation about the negative things on your terms."

Revealing your weaknesses needn't be negative. In many ways it can focus the buyer on the (positive) things that he can do to improve the business, creating an even bigger opportunity to add value.

"If you are so good at absolutely everything, how can the buyer improve the business?" asks Brian Livingston. "You've got to leave something on the table for somebody else."

Here are some ways to maximise your selling price:

- **Build empathy with the buyer.** Tell them your vision and how they, rather than you, can achieve it. Change the focus so they become the champions of the deal, rather than you.

- **Be open and transparent.** Tell them the bad news and how it can be fixed. Don't let them make price-adjusting discoveries later on.

- **Set your minimum price.** Discuss your minimum price with your advisors, but make sure you both agree. There's no point in wasting everyone's time if price expectations are unlikely to be met.

- **Wait for the buyer's offer.** Don't disclose your price. Ask the buyer to make an offer. "In any negotiation, it's always beneficial to have the other party reveal their hand before you do," advises James Caan. "If you can get your buyer to put a stake in the ground early, you know where they stand and it then allows you to react accordingly." Brian Livingston agrees. "Never tell the party the number because, if you do, they'll think it's a ceiling, not a floor. For example, a client of ours wanted £20m, but I advised him not to say a word. The first offer was £37m and we settled at £42m."

- **Make sure your price allows for a win-win.** "The most important thing for both sides to understand is that there has to be something in it for the other party," advises Jonathan. "You've got to push it as far as you can and as far as it's worth, but don't be greedy. Deals fall down because people are greedy."

- **Focus on future value as well as existing value.** "The buyer will say I believe it's worth this today," says Jonathan. "So persuade them to pay you some of tomorrow's value too. You've got to see what you can negotiate."

- **Create competitive tension.** If there's interest from more than one party, the value will often be driven up. "If you can run a controlled auction and have competition, either real or perceived, you tend to maximise the value," says Brian.

- **Maintain good relations.** Don't fall out with the purchaser. When difficult issues come up, use your advisor as your gladiator. You will probably have to work with your buyer, at least for a while.

- **Be flexible.** Make life easy for the buyer and help him achieve his goals.

After the sale

You're financially secure and free to pursue your dreams. Perhaps you'll retire to enjoy the well-earned fruits of your labour or, then again, perhaps you'll be back!

Whatever you decide, be sure to share your wisdom and lend a helping hand to the next generation.

Top tips

- **Deal with owner dependency** to create value in your businesses.

- **Choose your successor with care.** If there's a suitable candidate, promote from within rather than going outside.

- **Change your role to help your successor. Become a mentor and coach and let osmosis take its course.**

- **Don't ignore the option of keeping, rather than selling, your business** – why sell the best business you'll ever own?

- **If you decide to sell, appoint experienced advisors early.** Work with the experts and **take their advice.**

- **Remember that buyers do detailed due diligence.** Take time to prepare and **make sure your business stands up.**

- **Listen to the market and avoid being a forced seller.** Only sell when the marketplace is ready to buy.

- **Get your buyer on side.** Make them believe your vision and how they, rather than you, can achieve it.

- **Share bad news early.** It will be difficult for a buyer to chip your price if you've already disclosed your problems.

- **Wait for the buyer's offer and never disclose your price.**

INDEX

E

F

Get the eBook version of
From Vision to Exit
for free

As a buyer of the printed version of *From Vision to Exit*, you can download the electronic version free of charge.

To get hold of your copy of the eBook, simply point your smart phone camera at the following (or go to **ebooks.harriman-house.com/fvte**):

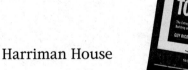

Hh Harriman House

The free *From Vision to Exit* eBook is an ePub file, the industry standard developed by the International Digital Publishing Forum. It is compatible with the widest range of eReaders, including Apple iPad, Sony eReader, and Adobe Digital Editions on PC and Mac.